This is an important book on a [barcode: MW00334819]
Preaching that does not land in peo⌐
wants to sanctify us by the truth, so biblical preaching should result in
transformation.

Not all people who are especially gifted by God are able to teach
others what they do when they use their gifts. Murray Capill is an exception to this general rule! He is a gifted preacher with a special gift in
effective application. In this book he explains what he does, and how he
does it, in a way that makes it helpful and profitable for all who preach.

I have benefited deeply from Murray's sermons and from his teaching on application. I am sure that other preachers will benefit as well
when they read this book.

It is always worth investing in improving the quality of our preaching. This book will help beginners and experienced preachers alike.

—**Peter Adam,** itinerant preacher; author; former principal of
Ridley Melbourne Mission and Ministry College

Preaching the Word of God is more than an explanation of a portion of
Scripture. It necessarily includes application, for by it God still speaks
to his people. Capill shows so clearly and cogently how exegesis of all
the data of the text in its canonical context, coupled with eisegesis of
the human heart in the light of Christian truth, dissolves the pressure
to be "relevant" that so often bedevils preachers' minds and cripples an
authoritative "Thus says the Lord."

—**Hywel Jones,** professor of practical theology, Westminster Seminary California

With biblical balance and pastoral wisdom, Dr. Murray Capill's *The
Heart Is the Target* addresses the preacher's vital task of serving the
heart-transforming purposes for which God has given his Word. Experienced preachers are well aware of the pitfalls that pervade the terrain of
application in preaching: moralism that imposes duty and guilt without
grounding Christian living in the grace of the gospel; in reaction to such
moralism, avoiding any application that calls listeners to repent and resist

sin; fixation on behavioral change instead of piercing into the heart's motives and affections; and speaking in vague generalities that float above our listeners' concrete spiritual struggle rather than following Scripture's lead in bringing specific, realistic, and diverse exhortations. *The Heart Is the Target* not only provides biblical and theological correctives to such errors and imbalances, but also offers practical guidance in the preparation processes for yielding sermons that serve the transformative purposes for which God has given the Bible.

> —**Dennis E. Johnson,** professor of practical theology, director of field education, Westminster Seminary California

Well written, well researched, and comes across with real conviction. Extremely well informed on its chosen theme, and the argument is persuasively supported at all points. Murray Capill has obviously thought deeply and long about sermon application and clearly has a passion for it—one that is highly appealing to the reader. He also shows a sensitive awareness of the situation of the "average preacher" and throws out helpful "ropes" to him where he is likely to feel overwhelmed by the sheer demand of effective application. I wish I had had this text in my hands when I began preaching over fifty years ago.

> —**Bruce Milne,** traveling preacher and teacher of pastoral leaders; former pastor of First Baptist Church, Vancouver

The
HEART
Is the
TARGET

The HEART Is the TARGET

PREACHING PRACTICAL APPLICATION FROM EVERY TEXT

MURRAY CAPILL

P&R PUBLISHING

P.O. BOX 817 • PHILLIPSBURG • NEW JERSEY 08865-0817

Unless otherwise indicated, all Scripture quotations are from the HOLY BIBLE, NEW INTERNATIONAL VERSION®. NIV®. Copyright © 1973, 1978, 1984 by International Bible Society. Used by permission of Zondervan Publishing House. All rights reserved.

Scripture quotations marked (NASB) are from the NEW AMERICAN STANDARD BIBLE®. Copyright © 1960, 1962, 1963, 1968, 1971, 1972, 1973, 1975, 1977, 1995 by The Lockman Foundation. Used by permission.

Italics within Scripture quotations indicate emphasis added.

ISBN: 978-1-59638-841-3 (pbk)
ISBN: 978-1-59638-842-0 (ePub)
ISBN: 978-1-59638-843-7 (Mobi)

Printed in the United States of America

Library of Congress Control Number: 2013919179

In memory of my father,

Don Capill (1930–2013),

who passionately taught me and many others
that biblical truth must be applied to the whole of life.

CONTENTS

ACKNOWLEDGMENTS

IN THE SECOND HALF OF 2010, I enjoyed a semester of study leave. I had various notions of how the time might be spent, but writing this book was not one of them. However, during that time I presented some seminars at the Ridley Preaching Conference in Melbourne, Australia, where I received warm encouragement to write up the material. So I decided to invest much of my remaining leave doing just that. A year later, I returned to speak at that conference and was again encouraged to complete the work that had been commenced. So I am indebted to friends at Ridley for persuading me to write.

It was there that I met Andrew Malone who offered to proofread anything I wrote on the topic. He did so, and not only picked up a thousand small mistakes, but also prompted a major rethinking of the overall model and how best to present it. This work has been greatly improved by Andrew's kind, generous, and discerning input.

Study leave was kindly granted to me by the Board of the Reformed Theological College in Geelong, Australia, and made possible by my colleagues covering for me while I was away. It has been my privilege to work there for the last twelve years with excellent staff and many capable students. Many of the ideas in this book have grown in the context of teaching preaching at the RTC. Special thanks to Alastair McEwen, with whom I have had so many stimulating conversations and who read the first draft of the manuscript, giving valuable feedback. I am also indebted to Karl Deenick, a student from a few years back, whose interaction in class and subsequent feedback on what I have written has been a great help.

I'd like to thank the excellent team at P&R Publishing, who have been wonderful to work with and have greatly enhanced the readability of this book.

While much of the manuscript was written in 2010 and some tweaking took place in 2011, I returned to finish it only in late 2012. It has been a long-term project. Throughout that time, and for many years before, my wife, Wendy, has been my most faithful friend and constant companion. Her selfless love has allowed me to travel, preach, speak, and write, for which I am most thankful. But surpassing that, her keen love of God's Word and of applied preaching, along with her deep commitment to prayer and godliness, is a constant inspiration, a great encouragement, and sometimes a timely rebuke.

I am indebted to many others, too, some of whom I've never met. Preachers from earlier centuries, like the Puritan Richard Baxter, and many excellent contemporary preachers who will be quoted in the pages to follow, have helped shape my thinking. We are blessed to live in a day when there is something of a revival of applied expository preaching and enormous access to the best of preaching via the Internet. I thank God for these fine people and for the stimulation they are to ordinary preachers like me.

Finally, then, I acknowledge my indebtedness to God. I have experienced in so many ways his unrelenting faithfulness and limitless grace. I write not as a noted preacher, but as an ordinary sinner who has been shown great mercy and who has been given the privilege of heralding God's Word and training others to do the same. I hope that what I have written will encourage preachers to proclaim his Word in life-changing ways, to his glory alone.

INTRODUCTION:
WHAT'S PREACHING
ALL ABOUT?

THROUGH THE LONG HISTORY of the church, nothing has won as many souls, changed as many lives, built up as many saints, and strengthened as many churches as the faithful preaching of God's Word. Although there are many other ways to communicate the gospel and edify God's people, in his wisdom God has given preeminence to the preaching of his Word. His Word is powerful and, when it is proclaimed clearly and its message is applied pertinently to those who listen, it has massive, Spirit-laden potential to change lives, either suddenly and dramatically or quietly and incrementally.

This reality is fueling a renewed interest in expository preaching. Seemingly against the odds, expository preaching is experiencing something of a revival. Seminaries are training students to be expository preachers, an increasing number of churches want to hear Bible exposition, and many pastors have become convinced that consecutive expository preaching is the best way to feed their church a healthy spiritual diet. Some of the great preachers of our day are providing inspiring models of the effectiveness of an expository ministry. Tim Keller, John Piper, and many others, for all their differences in style and approach, are demonstrating the effectiveness of applied biblical preaching. Their messages grip and stick. They are biblically substantial and strike home to the heart.

But we must recognize that not all expository preaching is having this kind of impact. Too often, congregations are left largely unmoved and unchanged by biblical preaching. If preachers are concerned solely with biblical faithfulness, they can end up with preaching that is little more than an information dump. They unload on their longsuffering congregations vast exegetical and doctrinal deposits, heaping truth upon truth and dispensing God's Word undiluted.

Can such biblically sound sermons ever really be regarded as ineffective sermons? That depends on what preachers are aiming at and what the purpose of preaching really is. If the main game is biblical faithfulness, then an exegetically sound sermon always hits the mark. If the goal is solid Bible teaching, then a sermon full of the truth always comes up trumps. But if the goal of expository preaching is that God's Word changes lives—converting sinners and sanctifying saints—then, all of a sudden, the stakes are much higher and the number of goals kicked may be fewer. If the point of preaching is that people, through the Word of God proclaimed by the preacher, hear the very voice of Christ in a life-impacting way, then far more is called for than biblical faithfulness alone. Application is required.

It is always possible, however, to overcorrect by sacrificing substantial preaching of the Word on the altar of relevance. Some preachers are so concerned to be practical and applicatory that they skim very lightly over God's Word. They spend little time opening up the biblical text, opting, instead, to focus primarily on people's concerns, hurts, needs, and aspirations. One might expect this to be tremendously helpful and lead to great spiritual growth in people's lives. Often, however, it does the very opposite. It easily breeds spiritual immaturity because what stands at the center of the preaching agenda is not God's timeless, powerful Word, but people's ever-changing desires.

Effective expository preaching takes place when biblical faithfulness and insightful application are inextricably bound together. One is neither substituted for, nor overshadowed by, the other. The two work together in an inseparable and powerful combination as the Holy Spirit breathes out his Word again today through the voice of the preacher, speaking presently into the lives of those who hear the Word. Understanding just how these two dimensions of preaching work together, and how in the actual art and craft of sermon preparation they feed into and from each other, is fundamental to effective preaching. Stunning, well-balanced application doesn't just happen. We must put in the hard yards of study, thought, reading, and prayer that alone form a wellspring from which powerful application flows.

To begin understanding the dynamics of these two great tasks of the preacher, we need to ensure that our theology and methodology of preaching are driven not by what works, or by what we most like, or by what we have always done, but by what God intends preaching to be. What is the God-intended purpose of preaching the Word?

THE GOAL OF PREACHING

The apostle Paul clearly seems to expect preaching to do more, not less, than provide faithful teaching. In 1 Thessalonians, he commends the church for having received the preaching of God's Word "not as the word of men, but as it actually is, the word of God, which is at work in you" (1 Thess. 2:13). That Word had come to them "not simply with words, but also with power, with the Holy Spirit and with deep conviction" (1:5) and they had "welcomed the message with the joy given by the Holy Spirit" (1:6). This seems to speak of more than a Bible exposition that they appreciated as true, but of a living Word from God that impacted their hearts because the Holy Spirit was powerfully at work in them through the preached Word.

In Romans 10, Paul quotes the prophet Joel: "Whoever will call on the name of the LORD will be saved" (v. 13 NASB). But then he asks, "How then will they call on Him in whom they have not believed?" (v. 14 NASB). It is a logical point. People must first believe in Jesus if they are ever to call upon him and be saved. But that prompts the next question: "How will they believe in Him whom they have not heard?" (v. 14 NASB). This question is particularly significant and loaded. Paul does not ask merely, "How can they believe in the one *of* whom they have not heard?" but, "How can they believe in Him *whom* they have not heard?"[1] They need to actually hear Christ if they are to really know him and come to faith in him. Paul then drives home the stunning implication with his next question: "And how will they hear without a preacher?" (v. 14 NASB). In preaching, Paul expects people to hear the voice of Christ. He expects that this is the way people will encounter Christ himself, and so come to believe in him and call on him for salvation. Finally, then, "How will they preach unless they are sent?" (v. 15 NASB). Preachers are sent, ultimately by God himself, to be his heralds proclaiming the very word of Christ.

Paul's high view of preaching is again evident. It is speaking the very words of Christ to people today. For Paul, preaching was not just about giving the meaning of a biblical text. It was about speaking so that people might hear Christ and be changed by him.[2] In the words of Colossians 1:28, where Paul summarizes the thrust of his own ministry, "We proclaim him [Christ], admonishing and teaching everyone with all wisdom, so that we may present everyone perfect in Christ."

Clearly, preaching that aims simply to teach the Bible aims at too little. Preachers should never aim at less, but the real goal is far greater. In expository preaching, the message of the biblical text is spoken

1. The NASB here differs from most English translations, but it provides the best translation of *pōs de pisteusōsin hou ouk ēkousin*, taking *hou* as the genitive of the person heard speaking. See R. C. H. Lenski, *The Interpretation of St. Paul's Espistle to the Romans* (Columbus: Wartburg, 1945), 662. Dunn, whom John Stott follows, comments, "In accordance with normal grammatical usage the *hou* must mean the speaker rather than the message" so that the correct translation is "the one whom" rather than "the one of whom." See James D. G. Dunn, *Romans*, Word Biblical Commentary (Dallas: Word, 1988), 620; John R. W. Stott, *Romans: God's Good News for the World*, The Bible Speaks Today (Downers Grove: IVP, 1994), 286. The same approach is taken by John Murray, who says, "A striking feature of this clause is that Christ is represented as being heard in the gospel when proclaimed by the sent messengers. The implication is that Christ speaks in the gospel proclamation." John Murray, *The Epistle to the Romans: the English Text with Introduction, Exposition and Notes*, The New International Commentary on the New Testament (Grand Rapids: Eerdmans, 1968), 58.

2. Historically this high view of preaching was voiced most clearly in Reformed theology in the Second Helvetic Confession, 1566, written by Henry Bullinger, the successor to Zwingli. It states, "The preaching of the Word of God is the Word of God. Wherefore when this Word of God is now preached in the church by preachers lawfully called, we believe that the *very Word of God* is proclaimed and received by the faithful." Quoted in K. Runia, *The Sermon Under Attack*, The Moore College Lectures (Exeter: Paternoster, 1983), 33.

afresh to God's people today by the preacher in such a way that those who hear the message sense that God himself is speaking to them and is dealing with their lives. From beginning to end, the congregation hears a message that is both from him and for them. The message is rooted and grounded in a particular text, which is treated with great attention to its original context and authorial intent. But the sermon is not a lecture or exegetical commentary on the text with, perhaps, a few applicatory thoughts attached. It is, rather, a proclamation today of the meaning of the text for God's people here and now. The primary aim is not to achieve increased biblical understanding along with a few practical ideas for applying it to life. Rather, the aim is that as the biblical text is proclaimed, people will encounter God himself in a life-shaping way today. His Word will be pressed close to their lives. It will impact their hearts. It will make a difference to the way they live. Some people will be saved; others will be sanctified. Of course, they will also, through such preaching, come to an increased Bible knowledge. But that is not the chief goal. The main aim is that they hear God speak in a life-shaping way.[3]

THE WEAKEST LINK

Such a view of preaching is suggestive of what application in preaching really is. But before we explore that further, we must first examine the fact that application is a struggle for many expository preachers. I have spoken to dozens of preachers committed to expository preaching who freely acknowledge that this is the weakest link in their preaching chain. They are diligent in their study of the biblical text, careful in forming well-structured sermons, and earnest in delivery, but they struggle to apply God's Word effectively.

3. Commenting on Col. 1:24–2:7, Dennis Johnson says, "The purpose of preaching is not only to inform or even to elicit assent to its truths. Preaching God's Word produces change in those who hear it, and the change is not merely intellectual or academic. . . . Through preaching Christ, Paul seeks to recreate people into the image of God, so they enjoy God's presence in unashamed purity, serve his will in unreserved love, express God's justice and mercy in relationships with others." Dennis E. Johnson, *Him We Proclaim: Preaching Christ from All the Scriptures* (Phillipsburg, NJ: P&R, 2007), 65–66.

This is of concern not only to many preachers but also to their congregations. Generally speaking, those who listen to expository preaching week by week want to hear a Word that impacts their lives. Believe it or not, most people in church on a Sunday morning are not there just dying to know more about ancient Near-Eastern treaties or the geography of Asia Minor! That's not because they are all blatant pragmatists who simply want to be given the keys to a successful life. If they were, they could easily find a church where they would get what they were looking for. Many preaching ministries hover lightly over God's Word but major on very practical suggestions for better living. The people I am thinking of are different. They want to sit under an expository ministry and they have come to church to be fed spiritually. They understand that when they hear the Bible, they should hear God speak and his voice should make a difference in their lives. They want to be doers as well as hearers of the Word. They are not looking for slick quick fixes for life, but genuinely desire biblical preaching that will help them live well and die well.

Biblically sound preaching that remains largely unapplied to life leaves such people in a difficult place. They have heard biblical truth, but they have not been as greatly helped by it as they might have been. It hasn't strengthened their faith, warmed their hearts, or drawn them as close to God as it might have. Sound preaching that fails to stir us may do some good, but it falls far short of the good God's Word is intended to do us. People will be loath to criticize a sermon that is full of truth, yet the reality may be that the message makes little difference to the way they live. Much of what is said is quickly forgotten, and frequently the whole experience is somewhat disappointing, if not downright boring. Preachers may not receive this kind of feedback very often because their dutiful flocks don't want to discourage them; neither do they want to sit over the Word but, rather, under it. But dissatisfaction and disappointment may be the reality more often than we might like to think.[4]

4. In *Why Johnny Can't Preach*, David Gordon bemoans the state of contemporary expository preaching, arguing that preachers are generally not subject to any formal review and are, therefore, often oblivious to the widespread negative response to their preaching. See T. David

18

Why is this? Why do preachers struggle to apply the Scriptures? I suspect it is primarily because too many preachers have a fundamentally flawed view of what application really is. Application is understood as something we add to the message after we have explained the text. Application is the way we finish the message off, after the main part of the sermon, which is essentially a textual commentary. Application is the practical bit at the end, or along the way if you're lucky. It is the few suggestions, the practical thoughts, the final ideas on how this lump of theoretical teaching relates to life.

This defective view of application stems from a deficient view of preaching. It is not adequate to view preaching as explanation plus some application. Explication and application are the two fundamental tasks of preaching, but the relationship of the two is vital. Application must not be a subsequent addition to exposition but the end goal of the exposition. Biblical exposition itself must be applicatory in thrust.

While a defective view of the place of application in preaching is the base line reason for poor application, there are other reasons, too.[5] One is that good application is *exceptionally hard work*. It's hard enough to draw correct lines from the past to the present. Once they are drawn, it's hard to be fresh and varied, incisive and perceptive, specific and direct. It's hard, in the language of earlier generations of preachers, to both wound and heal, sing and sting, disturb the comfortable and comfort the disturbed. It's hard to speak to the many different people represented in a church on any given Sunday.

Lacking the skills to develop such application, but keenly sensing that they should have at least *something* practical to say, many preachers find themselves opting for "bolt-on" applications. Bolt-on applications are predictable, vague, weary applications that are just tacked on to a commentary on the text. Most commonly these are the "more" applications: love more, give more, serve more, pray more, read your Bible

Gordon, *Why Johnny Can't Preach: The Media Have Shaped the Messengers* (Phillipsburg, NJ: P&R, 2009), 22, 33–34.

5. For a similar but different list of reasons, see David Veerman, "Apply Within," in Haddon W. Robinson and Craig Brian Larson, eds., *The Art and Craft of Biblical Preaching: A Comprehensive Resource for Today's Communicators* (Grand Rapids: Zondervan, 2005), 283.

more, trust more, come to church more, and so on.[6] But the problem with "more" applications, quite apart from their bolt-on nature, is two-fold. First, they fail to do justice to the great richness of God's Word that confronts us with far more than a list of basic evangelical duties to enact. Second, they fail to adequately reflect the glorious grace of the gospel. "More" applications very easily turn gospel preaching into mere moralism, leaving people with the feeling that, while they are saved by grace, they are sanctified by their own diligence in praying more, loving more, serving more, trusting more, and so on. Such preaching is, as Chapell says, sub-Christian.[7]

Another reason good application is all too rare is that, in their ministry training, most preachers are given *few, if any, methods for developing effective application.* In most seminaries, students for the ministry will be given many tools and resources for thorough exegesis. They will even learn entire languages to aid their study of the biblical text, and they will be drilled in the skills of examining the grammar, syntax, history, and context of the text, with a view to correct interpretation. Alongside this they will also receive training in the fundamentals of effective communication. But most will receive few tools or resources for developing rich, varied, penetrating application of the central meaning of the text.[8] In 2001, in the second edition of

6. Chapell speaks of "The Deadly Be's" such as be like, be good, and be disciplined. Bryan Chapell, *Christ-Centered Preaching: Redeeming the Expository Sermon* (Grand Rapids: Baker, 1994), 281–84.

7. Ibid., 268.

8. One of few books that address application in preaching in any detail is Daniel M. Doriani, *Putting the Truth to Work: The Theory and Practice of Biblical Application* (Phillipsburg, NJ: P&R, 2001). Doriani notes that scholars barely addressed the issue of application from 1950 to 1970, that specialized works on biblical genres in the 1980s still passed over the question of application and, more recently, books on interpretation and homiletics typically include a chapter on application but "publications on the subject remain rare" (viii). The exception, Doriani notes, is the publication of a few popular works, such as Jay Adams, *Truth Applied: Application in Preaching* (Grand Rapids: Ministry Resources Library, 1990); Jack Kuhatschek, *Taking the Guesswork out of Applying the Bible* (Downers Grove: IVP, 1990); and David Veerman, *How to Apply the Bible*, Life Application Books (Wheaton: Tyndale, 1993). There are few recent additions to the literature, though some valuable contributions are John Carrick, *The Imperative of Preaching: A Theology of Sacred Rhetoric* (Carlisle: Banner of Truth, 2002); Michael Fabarez, *Preaching That Changes Lives* (Nashville: Nelson, 2002); Johnson, *Him*

his landmark book that has become the standard text for homiletics, Haddon Robinson noted that "Homiliticians have not given accurate application the attention it deserves. To my knowledge, no book has been published that is devoted exclusively, or even primarily, to the knotty problems raised by application."[9]

Ministry students, therefore, find that in their training, exegesis and application are often in two separate boxes, one with lots of tools included, and the other with few. So, in their preaching, the two remain in separate boxes and one is much lighter than the other. Application is left largely to the preacher's intuition. Consequently, many expository preachers don't spend a lot of time on application because they don't know how to spend much time on it. If good applications come to mind, great! If not, such is life. They simply don't have the categories or tools with which to think deeply and broadly about how the Word applies today. Besides, the exegetical work takes so long there is little time left for applicatory work.

To this reason we may add another: some preachers are *wary of putting too much emphasis on application.* They know that application is easily abused.[10] In an understandable reaction against preaching that is largely anthropocentric in the focus it gives to people's felt needs, many expository preachers are fearful that an emphasis on application makes us pander to what people want to hear. They recognize the danger of an obsession with relevance that leads us to filter God's Word through the grid of what people want.[11] By contrast, these preachers strongly believe that they are called to explain the biblical text, believing that there is such power in the Word of God that when people come to understand what the Word means, they will, with the aid of the Holy Spirit, inevitably be changed by it. Application in this view is not the work of the

We Proclaim; and Daniel Overdorf, *Applying the Sermon: How to Balance Biblical Integrity and Cultural Relevance* (Grand Rapids: Kregel, 2009). A further problem for the preacher is that many exegetical commentaries make little attempt to address the matter of application.

9. Haddon W. Robinson, *Biblical Preaching: The Development and Delivery of Expository Messages* (Grand Rapids: Baker, 2001), 86.

10. See Haddon Robinson, "The Heresy of Application," in Robinson and Larson, eds., *The Art and Craft of Biblical Preaching*, 306–11.

11. See Christopher Ash, *The Priority of Preaching* (Fearn: Christian Focus, 2009), 112–13.

preacher, but of the Word and of the Spirit alone.[12] Explain the Word and it will apply itself.

It is a noble but flawed view. The avoidance of pandering to people and using God's Word for our own ends is laudable. Belief in the power of God's Word when applied to the heart directly by the Holy Spirit is absolutely right. However, settling for explanation of the Word but not application of it to life fails to do justice to the fact that the Spirit uses means, and his means include the preacher's proclamation of the Word to his people in his day. Our survey of biblical preaching in chapter 1 will demonstrate that clearly.

Others may avoid application simply because it seems *too culturally or politically inappropriate*. Our relativistic, pluralistic culture of tolerance makes directive application from the pulpit seem not only anachronistic but offensive. How dare we tell others what do? In sensitivity to this, preachers may opt for being suggestive rather than overt in their applications. Narrative forms of preaching have become popular as a way of connecting to people's lives in a culturally appropriate way. Story can leave ambiguity. It can raise issues that are left to the hearer to consider and resolve. It is a powerful applicatory method that Jesus himself used. But preachers need to remember this was not his only approach. He was also prepared to be specific, pointed, and confrontational if required. It is one thing to be appropriately subversive in preaching, as Jesus often was; it is another to be merely politically correct.

A final reason for some expository preachers being weak in application is that *they have over-intellectualized the faith*. It is not that they object to application. They may well prize it. But their entire experience

---

12. John Stott addressed this issue as long ago as 1982, criticizing conservative preaching for its failure to connect the Bible to the modern world. "And if we are called to account for our practice of exposition without application," he says, "we piously reply that our trust is in the Holy Spirit to apply his Word to the realities of human life." John R. W. Stott, *Between Two Worlds: The Art of Preaching in the Twentieth Century* (Grand Rapids: Eerdmans, 1982), 140. He proposed, in place of this, his bridge-building model, which is helpfully critiqued and replaced with a fuller "360-degree" model in Michael J. Quicke, *360-Degree Preaching: Hearing, Speaking, and Living the Word* (Grand Rapids: Baker; Carlisle, UK: Paternoster, 2003), 45–52.

of the Christian faith is predominantly intellectual.[13] The main thing for them is knowing the truth. When they apply, they apply abstractly. They are more naturally theorists than practitioners. They love the truth and firmly believe that all Scripture is not only God breathed but also useful for teaching, rebuking, correcting, and training in righteousness. It's just that their teaching, rebuking, correcting, and training is not that well earthed in real life. Their illustrations feel remote, often being drawn from church history and the lives of preachers; their sermons address theological controversies that may live in the academy but are distant from the lives of many of their hearers; they address principles of application but not practice; and so while their messages may be suggestive of how the truth is to be applied, they are seldom drilled down into life.

PREACHING VERSUS LECTURING

Whatever the reason for weakness in a particular preacher's ministry, the reality is that when preachers are committed to biblical and doctrinal preaching but lack the skills or convictions to apply God's Word well, the result will almost invariably be lecturing rather than preaching.[14] Lecturing is about passing on information; preaching is about transformation. One is about getting people to understand biblical truth; the other is about pressing biblical truth on their lives. One is about explanation; the other is about proclamation.[15]

13. For a useful description of an intellectualized approach to the faith, see Dennis Hollinger, "Preaching to the Head, Heart and Hands: A Holistic Paradigm for Proclaiming and Hearing the Word," *Journal of the Evangelical Homiletics Society* 7, no. 1 (2007): 18–24.

14. I am not here referring to the distinction between teaching (*didachē*) and preaching (*kērygma*) made famous by C. H. Dodd, *The Apostolic Preaching and Its Developments* (London: Hodder & Stoughton, 1944). That distinction has long been shown to be unsustainable biblically. The biblical categories of teaching and preaching have considerable overlap, so that preaching includes teaching. See, for example, the useful definitions given in Stuart Olyott, *Preaching—Pure and Simple* (Bridgend: Bryntirion, 2005), 12–16. By lecturing, I mean a discourse aimed at the transfer of information.

15. Tim Keller comments, "All the old Puritans (especially Edwards) knew better the difference between a lecture and a sermon. The sermon was more 'edifying'—more oriented to the affections and less oriented to detailed cognitive arguments." Email quoted in Johnson, *Him We Proclaim*, 61n74.

Actually, in any field the best teaching is really more like preaching. In a great lecture there is infectious passion and fire on the part of the lecturer so that the students are inspired and challenged, not merely informed. They are not just given some facts to regurgitate in the end-of-semester examination, but are enthused and motivated to study further. Years ago I came to love history, in large measure, because of my history teacher in high school. She brought history alive. She conveyed her own love of it and motivated me to read and write, not because I loved doing so (actually at sixteen I hated reading and writing) but because she had sparked an interest in history.

If the best teaching and lecturing is really a kind of preaching, surely the best preaching ought to be preaching! It is not merely giving a talk about the Bible.[16] It is not simply explaining a passage of Scripture. It is proclaiming the truth of the biblical text in such a way that it comes alive in the lives of the hearers today. It is a demonstration that God's Word still speaks. It shows the difference that the truth of the text makes to life, so that people leave not merely with a few intellectual truths or moral encouragements, but with a fresh vision of the kingdom and an agenda for change. Michael Fabarez states the issue well.

> We must not settle for a style of preaching that replicates the schoolroom experience. Preaching should be loftier than that. It should be designed to do much more than fill or even tantalize the mind. We must not simply set our sights on conquering the intellects of our congregants, essential as that may be. Preaching is designed by God to make an impact on their entire lives.[17]

HOLISTIC APPLICATION

What is needed, instead of bolt-on applications or mere lecturing, is a holistic approach to application. When something is addressed holistically, there is a concern to deal with the whole and not just with the parts. A holistic approach to health addresses not only an immediate

16. See Ash, *The Priority of Preaching*, 48, 61–62.
17. Fabarez, *Preaching That Changes Lives*, 21.

health problem, but a person's diet, social life, psychological well-being, and overall physical condition. The patient walks away not only with a script for medication, but with a plan for eating, resting, exercising, building positive relationships, thinking healthily, and so on. A holistic approach to education is concerned not only with jumping through academic hoops, but with the intellectual, emotional, social, physical, and spiritual development of students. Similarly, a holistic approach to application is concerned with bringing the message as a whole, to the person as a whole, for life as a whole.[18]

Holistic application is concerned first with ensuring that the entire message is applicatory in thrust. The applicatory task is too large and important to be confined to a few minutes at the end or a few asides along the way. The entire sermon must be shaped as a message for God's people today. All the explanation of the text, of which there may be a considerable amount, is done with a view to this. The structure will be chosen to serve this end. The illustrations and examples are to aid this. The level and depth of instruction is determined by this. The entire message is shaped with a view to people coming away from the preaching event sensing that God has dealt with them in a profound way: he has addressed, challenged, convicted, comforted, and changed them. They leave feeling that God has done business with them. The goal is not only that they understand the text better, or that they have picked up a few tips for living, or that they have merely enjoyed a great message. The goal is that people sense that they have met with the almighty, holy, glorious, gracious God and that they have heard from his timeless Word a timely word. That is the overall impression of the sermon.

Second, holistic application is concerned with addressing the whole message to the whole person. Too often application is addressed only to the will. We think that application is the bit that tells us what to do. But a holistic view of application recognizes that God's Word also impacts how we think and feel. It addresses not only our actions but our heart attitudes. It speaks not only to our relationship to God but also to our relationship to ourselves, to others, and to the world around us. It deals

18. See Hollinger, "Preaching to the Head, Heart and Hands," 34.

not only with how things should be, but also with how things actually are. It addresses life as it really is in all its dimensions, bringing the truth of the text to bear on people's spiritual, intellectual, emotional, and social well-being.[19] It persuades the mind, convicts the conscience, and stirs the passions. It presses truth against life so that people are enabled to know it not just in their heads but by experience.

Such holistic application recognizes that we are incredibly integrated beings. How we relate to God profoundly affects how we relate to others, to our work, and to ourselves. What we think affects what we do, and what we love affects what we think. Our social life impacts our spiritual life, and vice versa. It is our life as a whole that must be yielded to God—and he will not tolerate compartmentalization.

Third, holistic application that brings the message as a whole to the person as a whole does so for life as a whole. Holistic application refuses to acknowledge any separation of the sacred and the secular. All of life is to be lived for God, so whether we eat, drink, or whatever we do, all is for his glory. Every area of life—work, leisure, recreation, family life, finances, the arts, entertainment, commerce—is of interest to the preacher. The preacher wants to help people build a biblical worldview in which all the parts of life fit into the great goal of "glorifying God and enjoying him forever." This is done not only when we are engaged in gospel or church work, but as we engage in all facets of life as servants of Christ and citizens of his kingdom. Holistic application brings the realities of God's kingdom to bear on the many facets of life and culture.

TAKING UP THE CHALLENGE

Broadening application to this extent may sound utterly daunting. "It was hard enough before," you say. "Now it sounds virtually impossible!" It is true that holistic application raises the bar, but it is not an impossible

19. This kind of application has been known in the history of preaching as *experimental* or *experiential* application. See Joel Beeke, "Experiential Preaching," in R. Albert Mohler and Don Kistler, *Feed My Sheep: A Passionate Plea for Preaching* (Morgan: Soli Deo Gloria, 2002), 94–128. See also Murray A. Capill, *Preaching with Spiritual Vigour: Including Lessons from the Life and Practice of Richard Baxter* (Fearn: Christian Focus, 2003), 15–18.

hurdle. Far from it, because this is exactly what preaching is intended to do. It is for this that the Spirit's power is given to the preacher. If you are a preacher, this is why you were sent (Rom. 10:15). As well as enormous Spirit dependence, however, two other things are also needed. One is a mindset that enables the preacher to think in terms of holistic application from the beginning of the sermon preparation process to the end. The other is a set of tools for knowing how to drill truth down into people's lives. With the right mindset, some practical tools, and the enabling of the Spirit, powerful application is possible. This kind of preaching ought not be left to a few rare homiletical giants. There have been great exponents of this kind of preaching over the centuries, including Martin Luther and John Calvin, the Puritans, George Whitefield, Jonathan Edwards, Charles Haddon Spurgeon, Martyn Lloyd-Jones, and, today, men like Tim Keller and John Piper. But it is also possible for those of us who are ordinary, week-by-week preachers in smallish churches, sensing keenly our limited time and capacities, to develop holistic application.

This book is a guide for ordinary expository preachers who want to do just that. In chapter 1, we begin to get our bearings with a beginner's guide to application. Then, in part 1, we look at the living application preaching process—the process of moving from the living Word of God, via the life of the preacher, to the lives of the hearers. Each stage of this process must shape and inform application, and when it does, the preacher's application cup runneth over! Chapters 2–6, therefore, give preachers tools for exploring the applicatory potential of a text as they work carefully through each stage of the living application preaching process. These chapters provide a model for approaching application systematically rather than just relying on our hunches and intuition.

In part 2, we will apply the living application approach to some of the specific challenges of preaching, keeping our eye on the importance of holistic application. Chapter 7 deals with the way application grows when we preach from a kingdom perspective; chapter 8 provides help with the challenging task of applying redemptive-historical narratives; chapter 9 examines what is called for when we bump into the "ives"—indicatives, imperatives, and subjunctives; and chapter 10 pulls everything together by looking at how preachers can engage in the entire preaching process from the perspective of living application.

Of course, simply reading this guide to expository application won't make a preacher good at applying the Bible. Everything depends on what happens after reading it. A couple of years ago, on a visit to London, I thoroughly enjoyed a tour of the Tower of London. The entertaining Beefeater who led us around couldn't make us experts on the Tower's rich history in the sixty minutes we had with him. But with engaging and often gruesome stories, with facts and a little fiction, he was able to inform us, orient us, and intrigue us, whetting our appetite to explore the Tower more fully ourselves afterwards. This book is much the same, though it is conspicuously lacking in gory stories and historical fiction. Hopefully it will inform, orient, and intrigue preachers to look into the rich world of expository application more fully afterwards. If preachers will chew on the ideas presented here, and slowly, with prayerfulness and dependence upon God, explore them and implement the ones that seem useful, they should see growth in their ability to apply the Bible effectively. That will honor God and be good for his people.

DISCUSSION QUESTIONS

The questions at the end of each chapter can be used for individual reflection, but they will be of particular value when used by a small group of preachers who discuss these issues together. Participation in a preachers' group with several other pastors or trainee preachers can be a great aid to honing one's preaching skills.

1. Why is it inadequate to regard the goal of preaching as simply the faithful teaching of the Bible?
2. What is the difference between a preacher who preaches and a preacher who just lectures?
3. Can you identify any "bolt-on" applications you have used recently? Why did you resort to "bolt-ons"?
4. In what ways do you struggle with application in preaching? What are your application weaknesses?

28

| 1 |

A BEGINNER'S GUIDE
TO APPLICATION

OUR FRIENDLY BEEFEATER knew his stuff. History oozed out of him. He was obviously telling us only a fraction of what he knew and, as we strolled from site to site, questions would extract more information. So he didn't tell us everything, and what he did tell us he mixed with humor, friendly asides, riveting stories, and constant threats to the children about their possible execution if they misbehaved. History came alive.

The preacher's task is not dissimilar. We must seek to bring truth alive. That won't usually happen if the sermon is a massive information dump. We need to speak selectively and engagingly so as to help people grasp what God has said and is saying. This takes great skill. In the chapters that follow, we will look at the skills required for developing engaging and varied application of God's Word. But before we come to that, it is helpful to lay a foundation on which to build. Preachers need a working theology of biblical application. They need a sense of what application is, a picture of how the biblical preachers applied God's Word, convictions concerning the work of the Holy Spirit in application, and a clear grasp of the preacher's task in developing applicatory messages. These things will be the focus of this chapter—a kind of beginner's guide to biblical application.

The word *apply* has many shades of meaning. We speak of applying pressure to get what we want, of suddenly applying the brakes in a car, of applying a coat of varnish to the door, or of applying a principle in a certain situation. We also speak of applying for a job or applying ourselves to our work.[1] The root idea behind these uses of the word is that of putting one thing on or against another or of bringing things close together.[2] Pressure is put on a person, brakes are put on the wheels, varnish is put on the door. The word also carries the meaning of making use of something or putting it into action. The car brakes are put into action; use is made of a principle in a certain situation. In the words of Jay Adams, "To 'apply' is to bring one thing into contact with another in such a way that the two adhere, so that what is applied *to* something affects that to which it is applied."[3]

These shades of meaning make it a valuable term for Bible interpreters and preachers to employ as long as it is understood holistically.[4] Preachers take biblical truth and press it against or put it on the lives of people. But they don't just tell them how to put the truth into action; they actually put it into action in the act of preaching. They must preach so that people experience and appropriate the truth, feeling its sting or tasting its sweetness during the preaching. They need to bring it up close to their hearers so that they are impacted by it. Truth is not handled as something detached and largely irrelevant to those who are listening. It is real and people must sense its import as the preacher consciously presses it against their lives.

BIBLICAL MODELS

A brief survey of biblical preaching quickly establishes that this pressing of truth against people's lives is a hallmark of true preaching. We

---

1. These examples are taken from "apply," *Merriam-Webster*, accessed September 27, 2010, http://www.merriam-webster.com/dictionary/apply.

2. "Apply" comes from the Latin *applicare*, "to attach to, to devote oneself to," from *ad-* "to" + *plicare* "fold". The etymological sense is "to bring things in contact with one another." See "apply (v.)," *Online Etymology Dictionary*, accessed September 27, 2010, http://www .etymonline.com/index.php?term=apply.

3. Jay Adams, *Truth Applied: Application in Preaching* (Grand Rapids: Ministry Resources Library, 1990), 15.

4. Other terms that have been used by earlier generations have been "improving" and "using" the text.

begin with Moses, who took the law delivered at Sinai and preached it to the people of Israel on the plains of Moab as they were about to enter the Promised Land. He didn't simply repeat the laws verbatim; neither did he merely explain them. He applied them to the lives of those before him. Even though none of them (bar two) had been present forty years earlier when the law was given, he said to them,

> The LORD our God made a covenant with us at Horeb. It was not with our fathers that the LORD made this covenant, but with us, with all of us who are alive here today. (Deut. 5:2–3)

That is a remarkable statement because, on the face of it, it isn't true. The Lord made a covenant with their forefathers, not with them. But as far as Moses was concerned, what God said then he says now, and the covenant he made with their forefathers he made with them, as if they had been there. So on that basis Moses pleads with them, warning and encouraging them. He sets the law in the context of their recent history, recounting their rebellion, their desert wanderings, their victories, and now their new opportunity to enter the Promised Land. He urges them to listen and to obey.

> Hear now, O Israel, the decrees and laws I am about to teach you. Follow them so that you may live and may go in and take possession of the land that the LORD, the God of your fathers, is giving you. Do not add to what I command you and do not subtract from it, but keep the commands of the LORD your God that I give you. (Deut. 4:1–2)

In the great conclusion to his address, he exhorts them to "choose life" and he warns them of the dire consequences that will come on them if they don't.[5]

Moses was a passionate, urgent preacher of the Word of God, applying the law powerfully to the situation of his people. And he was not alone in that. All the prophets who followed him did the same.

---

5. For a helpful treatment of Moses' preaching in Deuteronomy and its import for preachers today, see Christopher Ash, *The Priority of Preaching* (Fearn: Christian Focus, 2009).

Old Testament prophetic preaching was marked by its robust, fearless, compelling appeal to God's people. It never presented abstract truth but always applied truth to the lives of God's people—often God's erring people, but sometimes, as for example in Haggai, God's discouraged people; or, in Habakkuk, God's perplexed people; or, in the latter part of Isaiah, God's distressed people. Whatever the situation, the prophets spoke powerfully to the present life situation of their hearers.

Zephaniah affords a compelling example of this. Prophesying to the southern kingdom of Israel during the reign of King Josiah, about a hundred years after the northern kingdom was exiled, he warned Judah and Jerusalem that they now faced the same fate. They stood on the precipice of the day of the Lord (1:7, 14), which is the theme tune of Zephaniah's prophecy. He doesn't begin his sermon with a heartwarming illustration but launches straight into a pulpit-thumping warning of universal judgment (1:2–2:3). God will sweep away everything—man and beast, birds and fish. Why? Because of their great sin. Zephaniah exposes the evils of seventh-century Judah: their idolatry, syncretism, and spiritual complacency. He declares that the Lord is angry and is preparing to make war against his people, so it is urgent that they repent. Perhaps they will find mercy (2:3).

In the second section of his message (2:4–3:8) he broadens the scope of the Lord's judgment. He looks west to Philistia, east to Ammon and Moab, south to Egypt and Ethiopia, and north to Assyria and especially Nineveh. To us, they sound like faraway lands. But they weren't for Israel. They were near neighbors. It was like an Australian hearing a message concerning New Zealand and Indonesia, or an American hearing threats made against Mexico and Canada, or perhaps an Englishman hearing of God's judgment coming upon Scotland and Wales or Spain and France. But then, in the same breath, Zephaniah points the finger again at Jerusalem because her sins were no different from those of the surrounding nations. They were all the same—proud and arrogant, mocking God and acting as if they owned the world.

Yet although Zephaniah's words were filled with the most terrible warnings of impending doom, like nearly all the prophets he also brought a word of hope (3:9–20). There would be a remnant who would be puri-fied by God and would bring to him true worship. So the day of the Lord would be not only a day of judgment but also a day of salvation.

Zephaniah's preaching is undeniably applied preaching. It is direct, pointed, and specific. The "day of the Lord" was not an academic, theological principle that needed to be understood, but a terrible, immi-nent reality that demanded response. With red-hot zeal, God's prophet warned, pleaded, and comforted.

Turning to the first pages of the New Testament, we find exactly the same kind of preaching. John the Baptist's indictment of sin was specific, his call to repentance was powerful, and his foretelling of One to come was humbly winsome. He spoke to the people of his day, addressing the great needs of the moment, albeit in a somewhat bizarre way. We need not take his dress code, diet, or location as a model for contemporary preaching. Camel-skin suits, locust salads, and desert pulpits have never really been my thing. But we do need to note that his preaching was in line with the tenor of all biblical preaching. It was forcefully applied to the lives of those who listened.

No one demonstrates this more clearly than Jesus himself. The master preacher is the master of living application. Whether you think of the stinging attacks he made on the Pharisees (e.g., Matt. 23), or the brilliant twist in the tail of some of his parables (e.g., Luke 15), or the immensely practical counsel about true righteousness given in the Ser-mon on the Mount (Matt. 6), or the strong warnings given to would-be followers (e.g., Luke 14:26–35), or the gracious comfort ministered to his grieving disciples (John 13–17), the fact is that his preaching always spoke directly and personally to the people to whom he was speaking. It was the scribes and Pharisees who specialized in dull discourses that revolved around quoting dead rabbis and dissecting the minute details of the tradition of the elders. Jesus specialized in cutting to the heart of an issue and speaking to the hearts of his hearers. Little wonder that "the crowds were amazed at his teaching, because he taught as one who had authority, and not as their teachers of the law" (Matt. 7:28–29). As Michael Quicke has observed, "Jesus Christ seemed to leave no room for neutrality or boredom whenever he preached. From explosive beginnings in Nazareth, he created impact every time."[6]

It is not surprising that the apostles, having been trained by Jesus, followed suit. The book of Acts describes the relentless advance of the gospel from Jerusalem to Rome. Despite persecution from without, and times of both division and corruption within, the early church grew and expanded with the public preaching of the gospel driving the mission forward. Luke records speeches to both Jews and Gentiles, in settings as diverse as the temple courts, the courts of the Sanhedrin, synagogues, rural towns, and the Areopagus. Not all would qualify as sermons in the way we currently use the term, but all were a kind of preaching in the sense of being public, verbal proclamations of gospel truth.

As with the preaching of Jesus and the prophets, the sermons and speeches of Acts are always directly and pertinently applied to the audience at hand. They are all *occasional* sermons. The Pentecost sermon, for example, specifically addressed the protest of skeptics who thought that the effect of what was, in reality, the outpouring of the Holy Spirit was nothing other than drunken and disorderly behavior. Peter explained that it was not drunkenness but Spirit-fullness as foretold by the prophet Joel. But it was not enough that they understood this as the fulfillment of prophecy. They needed to understand the potentially devastating implications. It meant Jesus, whom they had crucified, was alive. The one they had tried to dispose of was, in fact, reigning as Lord and Christ and had poured out his Spirit as he had promised. There is no doubt that Peter was driving at exactly the Spirit-enabled response that came: "When the people heard this, they were cut to the heart and said to Peter and the other apostles, 'Brothers, what shall we do?'" (Acts 2:37).

In his address to the Sanhedrin, Stephen similarly drove at heart conviction. Although much of the speech recounted Israel's history, it did so with an agenda. Stephen was making a case throughout that built to the climax: "You stiff-necked people, with uncircumcised hearts and

6. Michael J. Quicke, *360-Degree Preaching: Hearing, Speaking, and Living the Word* (Grand Rapids: Baker; Carlisle, UK: Paternoster, 2003), 23.

ears! You are just like your fathers: You always resist the Holy Spirit!" (Acts 7:51). That's probably not the best way to win friends and influence people when you're on trial, but it was the best way to bring God's Word to bear on an apostate generation facing the imminent wrath of God. They needed to hear that truth stacked up against them and hear that they were guilty before the God of heaven. As far as God was concerned, it was not Stephen who was in the dock, but the Jewish nation.

Paul's speeches in the synagogue at Pisidian Antioch, in Lystra, and in the Areopagus also provide fascinating cameos of audience-targeted preaching. Each message was directed to particular people in a particular place with particular spiritual needs. The Jews in Pisidian Antioch needed to be convinced that Jesus was the promised Old Testament Messiah in whom there is forgiveness of sins. Paul directly challenged them to believe in Christ and not to reject what God had done. The pagan crowd in Lystra needed to be persuaded of something very different: that the apostles were not gods. They needed to realize the difference between the Creator and creatures. They needed to turn from worthless idols and acknowledge the living God who had blessed them with crops and food. The educated philosophers of Athens really needed the same message, but they needed it in a very different way. It was essential that they also turn from idolatry, but Paul found a way into their mindset by declaring to them who the "unknown god" was to whom they had erected an altar. With sensitivity to their culture and appreciation of their learning, he appealed to them to repent and acknowledge Christ as judge. Each speech was quite distinct because the audiences were very different. While the gospel remains the same, the messages differ because the intent was never a detached presentation of truth but an application of gospel truth to the lives of those being addressed.

The narrative of Acts highlights that such preaching always provokes a response, which Luke is careful to record.[7] Typically, some

---

7. Of the thirteen main speeches in Acts (2:15–39; 3:12–26; 4:8–12; 5:29–32; 7:1–53; 10:34–43; 13:16–41; 14:15–17; 17:22–31; 20:18–35; 22:1–21; 24:10–22; and 26:2–29), Luke records responses for eleven. Only the speeches in Acts 3 and 24 record no immediate response.

are converted, some are incensed, and some are keen to talk further.[8] These responses are not incidental to the narrative but are at the heart of it. Luke is at pains to show that preaching, by its very nature, is designed to elicit a response—very often a dramatic one. The gospel is surging forward and it makes an impact on people's lives. To some it is the fragrance of life and to others the stench of death. It is never merely academic information leaving people untouched.

GRACE-FILLED APPLICATION

It would be easy to expand this brief survey of biblical preaching, but the same picture is seen wherever we turn. Biblical preaching is always truth applied. More precisely, it is always gospel truth applied to the heart. That leads us to two essential dimensions of holistic, living application: first, it must always reflect the grace of the gospel because biblical preaching is gospel preaching, and second, it must always be heart-oriented because the gospel demands a heart response to God.

First, biblical preaching must be grace-filled as it applies the gospel to people's lives. The preacher is a herald of good news. Isaiah spoke of the "beautiful . . . feet" of messengers who "bring good news, who proclaim peace, who bring good tidings, who proclaim salvation, who say to Zion, 'Your God reigns!' " (Isa. 52:7). Initially referring to the joyful news that Israel was to be brought back from her captivity, Paul quotes this verse for the wider and more glorious work of the gospel preacher who proclaims salvation in Christ (cf. Rom. 10:14–15).

Preaching must, in the first place, help people marvel at the astoundingly good news that we are embraced in God's plan of redemption by grace alone. We do not have to earn our way into his kingdom or merit the forgiveness of our sins by somehow trying to outweigh our bad deeds with good ones. We need only look to Jesus, who has won the prize for us. We simply trust in him and, on the basis of faith alone, we are justified by God.

8. For faith responses, see Acts 2:37, 41; 10:44; 13:48–49; 17:34; 20:37. For further inquiry responses, see 13:42–44; 17:32. For direct opposition, see 4:13, 18, 21; 5:33, 40; 7:54, 57–58; 13:45, 50; 17:32; 22:22–23; 26:24.

Next, preaching must herald the wonderfully good news that we are not only saved by grace but sanctified by grace. Christ now lives in us, empowering and enabling us to obey him and to do the good works that he has prepared in advance for us to do. It is not just that our efforts are a response to God's grace. They are the fruit of Christ now dwelling in us by his Spirit. We do all through Christ who strengthens us. His sap flows through the branches, his power is worked in us, his grace sustains us, his love comforts us, and his glory awaits us. We do not simply look to Christ's example; we depend, day by day, on his inward presence and enabling. That is why Paul prayed that the Ephesian believers would "know the hope to which he has called you, the riches of his glorious inheritance in the saints, and his incomparably great power for us who believe" (Eph. 1:18–19).

This good news, however, is not limited to God's blessing in our lives as individuals. The proclamation of the gospel preacher is, "Your God reigns," and he reigns over all people and all nations. Christ has come into our world as God's appointed king. With divine power, he has defeated the forces of evil and triumphed over sin and death. The kingdom of darkness is being progressively pushed back as the kingdom of God increasingly invades this world, righting what is wrong and establishing justice and righteousness. Christ is redeeming not only a people, but this whole physical world, for himself. Creation itself will be restored and liberated when the work of redemption is brought to its consummation.

Both personal salvation and creation restoration are works of glorious grace—unsought and undeserved. God is the initiator, and the preacher is the herald of what he is doing. The preacher trumpets his gracious, powerful works so that all may hear and respond. The onus is on the preacher to ensure that the heralding really does exalt God and his grace. Sermons ought to be full of the merits of Christ. They ought to major on what he has done. They ought to declare loudly the victory he has had and the power and authority he presently wields. They ought to send people away with hope and with a vision of the majesty of Christ and the triumph of his kingdom.

Such preaching will enthuse rather than berate; it will excite and not discourage; it will make people look far more to Christ and what he is doing than to themselves and what they are doing; it will build up, not tear down. The gospel does not send people away trying to improve themselves or trying to keep a string of rules. Nor does it leave them feeling burdened and hopeless. It was the message of the Pharisees that heaped heavy burdens on people. The message of Christ is that of rest and hope for the weary.

Of course, preaching the good news demands that we also preach the bad news. We must expose the wickedness of rebellion against God's appointed King. We must speak plainly of the rule of Satan, the power of sin, the destructiveness of evil, the depravity of human nature, the hardness of fallen hearts, and the utter lostness of all people outside of Christ. But these truths are never the bottom line. The bottom line is that Christ has triumphed.

If you go to a jewelry shop to buy a ring, the jeweler may spread out on the counter a black satin cloth on which to display each ring. Against the black, the ring sparkles. But it would be a depressing spectacle if the jeweler laid out black cloth after black cloth without ever producing a ring for you to admire. Sadly, some preaching is like that. It is so intent on making sure the bad news is clear that the good news is scarcely heard. People leave having seen a lot of black but not many sparkling diamonds. Gospel preaching should not be like that. The black cloth will be laid out, but the main focus will be on the beauty of the gospel ring.

HEART-ORIENTED APPLICATION

If the great task of preaching is proclaiming tremendously good news, we must never forget that this news is not to wash over people but to penetrate their hearts. Night after night we may watch the evening news on TV, and we easily become immune to the impact of the mostly bad news we see and hear. We may groan a little in the face of terrible violence, devastating natural disasters, or devious politicians, but then we get up to wash the dishes, largely unaffected by what we've just witnessed. That is never meant to be the case after hearing the good news of salvation. Preachers must seek to present the gospel in a heart-penetrating way.

In the Sermon on the Mount, Jesus was unrelenting in his "heart attack." Beginning with the character of those to whom God's kingdom is revealed (the poor in spirit, those hungering and thirsting after righteousness, the pure in heart, and so on), he went on to target the application of the law at the level of heart motives. Adultery is not just the outward act of the flesh but the inner lust of the heart; murder is not just the external act of killing someone but the inward attitude of hating someone. Jesus has not just come to improve people's behavior; he has come to change their lives from the inside out. The essence of the new covenant is a new heart (cf. Jer. 31:31–34).

It is useful, therefore, to make a distinction between practical application, of which there is plenty in the Sermon on the Mount, and heart application. Practical application addresses how to live for God: how to witness, how to serve, how to lead, how to love, how to pray, and so on. Such application is important and helpful. We ought to be as practical as possible in our preaching. But application to the heart goes deeper. It deals with our underlying attitudes, mind-set, motivations, aspirations, character, and goals. It aims not just at getting us to do the right thing but at acquiring wisdom for life.[9] It tells us not only what to do but who we are, who we should be, and what by God's grace we can be. It wades more deeply into the soul and is more searching. It may well leave us feeling exposed. But if heart application is filled with grace, then it does not leave us feeling hopeless. We may feel unclean and undone, as Isaiah did (cf. Isa. 6:1–8), but we know, as he also came to know, that cleansing comes from the altar and commissioning from God.

TWO ESSENTIAL ALLIES

Grace-filled, heart-oriented gospel preaching should lead people to a deep awareness of their need of God and of God's readiness to meet them

9. Doriani argues for four aspects of application: duty, character, goals, and discernment. The "duty" category matches practical application while the other three are more heart-oriented. See Daniel M. Doriani, *Putting the Truth to Work: The Theory and Practice of Biblical Application* (Phillipsburg, NJ: P&R, 2001), esp. 97–157.

in their need. But it is not only those who hear such preaching who are in great need of God's aid. So is the preacher in the actual act of preaching. It is impossible for any of us to preach effective, grace-filled, heart-oriented sermons in our own strength. Left to ourselves, we cannot make the slightest impact on the human heart, no matter how skillful we might be. In fact, even God's all-powerful Word itself falls on deaf ears and hard hearts if God himself is not actively involved in opening ears and softening hearts.

The preacher, then, can never work alone. He needs help and his help is received from two main sources. First and foremost, his help comes from the Holy Spirit, who empowers and enables preaching and transforms the hearts of the hearers. Secondly, his help comes from the believing church community that provides the God-ordained context for gospel preaching. The story of the early church suggests that these are the two essential partners of biblical preaching. We have seen in Luke's account of the relentless advance of the gospel that preaching leads the way. But the advance is the result not of preaching alone, but of preaching in connection with the presence and power of the Holy Spirit and with vibrant spiritual community.

The story of Acts begins with the disciples waiting in expectation for the outpouring of the Holy Spirit. Without the presence of the Spirit, they dare not begin to preach. Only with the Spirit's power will a man like Peter, who had previously felt such pressure from an unnamed slave girl that he denied his Lord three times, be enabled to speak boldly and courageously to thousands and be useful to God in the salvation of many souls. On the day of Pentecost, it is preaching that brings in the first gospel harvest, but it is Spirit-empowered preaching. The same fruit would have been quite inconceivable just one day earlier.

From that point onward, the Holy Spirit constantly features in the narrative. Although Peter and the believing community have been filled with the Spirit at Pentecost, we are told a little later that they are again filled with the Spirit (4:8, 31). The Spirit gives them special enabling and boldness to speak his Word.[10] The first inward crisis comes to the

10. Luke speaks of the fullness of the Spirit in two senses. One sense is that of an ongoing condition of the Spirit controlling and influencing a person, as seen in Acts 6:3, 5; 11:24;

church when two of its members lie to the Holy Spirit (Acts 5:3, 9). When the seven are appointed to help with the daily distribution of food, men known to be full of the Holy Spirit are chosen. It is said of Stephen that his opponents "could not stand up against his wisdom or the Spirit by whom he spoke" (6:10). After his speech, it is expressly noted that he was "full of the Holy Spirit" as he looked into heaven and saw the ascended Christ. The gift of the Spirit was so amazing that Simon the Sorcerer thought that the ability to impart the Spirit would be a great trick to buy (8:18–19). When Paul was converted, the Holy Spirit came on him, as also on the people at Cornelius's house when he—Cornelius—was converted. It was the Holy Spirit who spoke to the church in Antioch, telling them to set aside Paul and Barnabas for mission work (13:2). Frequently, in the narrative, the Holy Spirit prompts and directs proceedings, sending people here or there, opening or closing doors, and always strengthening and encouraging the churches (see 8:29, 39; 9:31; 10:19; 11:12; 13:4; 15:28; 16:6, 7; 20:22, 23).

There are many other references to the Holy Spirit in Acts, but the point is clear. The Spirit is never far from the action. Or more correctly, the action of Acts is the action of the ascended Christ by the power of the Holy Spirit working in and through his people.[11] Just as the advance of the gospel in Acts cannot be understood apart from the central place of preaching, neither can preaching be understood apart from the central role of the Spirit.

This theme stands alongside another prominent emphasis in the narrative. Luke repeatedly stresses the spiritual vibrancy of the early church community. The church is empowered by the Holy Spirit and lives in dependence upon the Spirit. This is seen clearly by the emphasis Luke places on prayer. At the beginning of the story, as they are waiting

---

13:52 (cf. Eph. 5:18). The other sense is that of a special equipping for particular tasks. This kind of "filling" leads to boldness, courage, and power. See also Martyn Lloyd-Jones, *Life in the Spirit in Marriage, Home & Work: An Exposition of Ephesians 5:18–6:9* (Edinburgh: Banner of Truth, 1974), 40–54.

11. John Stott's preferred title for Acts is "The Continuing Words and Deeds of Jesus by his Spirit through his Apostles." John R. W. Stott, *The Message of Acts: To the Ends of the Earth* (Leicester: IVP, 1990), 34.

in Jerusalem for the outpouring of the Spirit, they "all joined together constantly in prayer" (1:14). Following the coming of the Spirit, one of the hallmarks of the new church community was its devotion to regular prayer (2:42). In the face of opposition, the people joined together in special prayer (4:24; 12:5), receiving some astounding answers that surpassed their own expectations. The apostles themselves made prayer, along with the ministry of the Word, their foremost priority (6:4) that could not be set aside even by a significant church crisis.

The believing community was also marked by radical love as the believers surrendered their personal property to assist one another. The community spent much time together, publicly and privately, formally and informally. They were devoted to the breaking of bread together, to fellowship with one another, and to the apostles' teaching. It was a Word-shaped, Word-hungry community, as highlighted by the commendation of the Bereans who received the Word eagerly and readily searched the Scriptures to check the accuracy of Paul's preaching (17:11).

It was also a community that was forced to take holiness seriously. The dramatic exposure of the sin of Ananias and Sapphira, and the swift judgment brought on them for their deception, served as a sobering warning to the community that they were to be holy before the Lord who sees all. The context of growing persecution also ensured that early Christianity was not for those who wanted a halfhearted allegiance to Christ. The cost was high enough to make one serious about commitment.

Finally, it was a community actively engaged in evangelism. The persecution that drove the believers out of Jerusalem following Stephen's death saw a multiplication of witness among ordinary believers, as those who were scattered spread the gospel wherever they went. The vast impact of such gospel witness is seen in the story of the church in Antioch, which in time proved to be one of the strongest missionary-sending churches of the era. It was established not by the apostles or some planned church-planting program initiated by the church in Jerusalem, but by the spontaneous witness of individuals who then received the support of Barnabas and Paul.

The early church was, then, a spiritually dynamic, prayerful, gospel-hearted community that was both a base from which mission was launched and a loving family into which new converts could be enfolded.

These aspects of the story of the early church are significant for our study of application in preaching. They make clear that a holistic view of application demands a holistic view of preaching, and that, in turn, demands that we are firmly persuaded that preaching can never stand alone. There are circumstances in which preaching flourishes and circumstances in which it withers. Acts describes the former, showing us that preaching is the foremost activity of the church's gospel work, but that ordinarily it is powerfully effective only when it is rooted in and grows out of a loving, holy, evangelistic, prayerful, Spirit-filled community. The Holy Spirit and a healthy church are the indispensable allies of effective preaching. That means that no pastor can afford to major on preaching to the exclusion of all else. Healthy preaching grows out of a healthy church life. Peter Adam rightly says, "Our ministry may be pulpit-centered, but it should not be pulpit-restricted, for such a ministry of the Word will suffer severe limitations."[12]

RESPONDING TO PENTECOST

There are three ways we can respond to the central themes of the narrative in Acts, and especially to its focus on the Holy Spirit. One way is to continually seek repetitions of the day of Pentecost. Charismatics and Pentecostals treat the events of that day as normative, and so they look for spectacular signs as manifestations of the Spirit's presence today and for the baptism of the Spirit as an experience subsequent to conversion. However, this view flattens out the peaks and troughs of redemptive history, failing to take note of what is unique about the day of Pentecost in the unfolding story of salvation. It marked not so much an event to be repeated as it did the beginning of a new era.

A second response, therefore, is to see Pentecost as unrepeatable but having initiated the last days between Christ's first and second comings. In these last days, the Spirit is always present with his church. The spectacular

12. Peter Adam, *Speaking God's Words: A Practical Theology of Preaching* (Leicester: IVP, 1996), 75.

markers of his arrival have disappeared but the Spirit is still present. All believers possess the Spirit and the church community is the temple of the Holy Spirit. Such a view encourages confidence that God is with us now through his Spirit, so when we preach, witness, or lead in the church we may be sure that the Sprit is present. But while this view accurately reflects the unique redemptive-historical significance of the day of Pentecost, it easily leads to too little expectation of what the Spirit is able to do. The presence of the Spirit is taken as a given, and we now just get on with the work of preaching, knowing that he is with us. The Holy Spirit's presence is assumed, with the result that he often features little in the life or vocabulary of the church.

A third position is possible and desirable. Pentecost can be viewed as a unique and unrepeatable event that ushered in a new era in salvation history. But the era it ushered in is one in which the Holy Spirit, who now dwells in and with his people, is able to bring to individuals, churches, and even nations seasons—long or short—of immense spiritual blessing. Just as Peter, who had been filled with the Holy Spirit on the day of Pentecost, was filled again when he spoke before the Sanhedrin (4:8), and just as the entire community that had received the Spirit on the day of Pentecost received further power and boldness after fervent prayer in the face of persecution (Acts 4:31), and just as the Spirit's power was extended powerfully beyond Jerusalem to the Samaritans and the Gentiles (8:14–16; 10:44–46), so we may reasonably expect today that the Spirit is able to come on us with fresh and even overwhelming power. This is not looking for a "second blessing" experience for individuals, accompanied by speaking in tongues. It is looking for a second, third, fourth, tenth, or hundredth blessing for the church community, as the Spirit works with great gospel power, converting sinners and sanctifying the church.

Sometimes this will be evidenced in a time of revival or spiritual awakening, but it need not take only that form. The Spirit may bring times of refreshing, of power, or of special grace that fall short of what we would call revival and yet do not in any way fall short in generating gospel effectiveness. We should not just wait for the big earthquake. We should respond to all the smaller tremors as well. Preachers and their churches need to be fervent in prayer, asking that God would pour out his Spirit in great measure on each message and on the church as a whole. We need to be expectant of what God in his power can do. We should be eager to see many conversions. We should have high hopes for what the church can be. We should pray without ceasing and call on God for great spiritual power.[13] Without this, any techniques for holistic application are essentially hollow and vain. The greatest need of the day is Spirit-anointed preaching. Only with the Spirit's power will applications strike home powerfully into people's lives.

THE PREACHER'S TASK

We can now summarize and clarify the expository preacher's task when it comes to application. The following key points have been made:

- In expository preaching the message of the biblical text is spoken afresh to God's people today by the preacher in such a way that those who hear the message sense that God himself is speaking to them and is dealing with their lives.
- Biblical preaching is, therefore, directly addressed to the hearers today; it is not a lecture or verbalized commentary on the text but a proclamation of the truth of the text applied holistically to the lives of those who hear it.
- Holistic application is concerned with bringing the message as a whole, to the person as a whole, for life as a whole.
- As gospel truth is applied in this way, it must always be preached in a grace-filled, heart-oriented way.
- Such holistic, applicatory preaching never stands alone but is dependent on the presence and power of the Holy Spirit, the fervent prayers of God's people, and the support and reinforcement of a spiritually dynamic church community.
- The Spirit's power in the church and in preaching is not to be assumed but is to be earnestly sought and expected because the Spirit has been given to the church by the ascended Christ to empower gospel witness.

13. See Arturo G. Azurdia, *Spirit Empowered Preaching: The Vitality of the Holy Spirit in Preaching* (Fearn: Christian Focus, 1998).

Armed with such convictions, a preacher sits down to start preparing next Sunday's message. What needs to happen? How is he going to approach the task? If he's right-headed and soft-hearted, he'll begin with prayer, asking God for the message he would have him preach, and seeking insight into his Word and into the lives of the people to whom he will be preaching. He will plead that God will give him a word for his people.

Then, in a prayerful spirit, he will begin to chip away at a threefold task, as depicted in diagram 1.[14] The preacher moves from the "there and then" world of the Bible to the "here and now" lives of his people, discerning en route what the timeless truths are that need to be proclaimed afresh today. The first task is to exegete the text. The Bible text is "there and then," set at least 2,000 years ago, written to different people, at a different time, in a different culture from that of the people who will be listening on Sunday. So a key part of the preacher's task is to spend ample time in the "there and then" world of the text, endeavoring to understand it and enter into it.

Diagram 1: From Then to Now

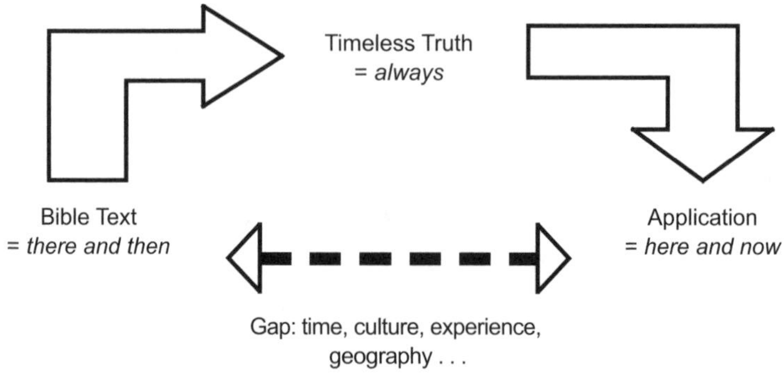

Timeless Truth
= *always*

Bible Text
= *there and then*

Application
= *here and now*

Gap: time, culture, experience, geography . . .

The next task is to consider what truth in the text remains true for hearers of the Word today. What are the timeless truths of the passage?

14. A similar process is described more fully in J. Scott Duvall and J. Daniel Hays, *Grasping God's Word: A Hands-on Approach to Reading, Interpreting, and Applying the Bible* (Grand Rapids: Zondervan, 2001), 21–25, 203–13.

Timeless truths are the "always" truths of the text. They are the abiding truths that are of enduring relevance. "There and then" truths may sometimes be "always" truths. "You shall not murder" is a command as relevant today as it was in Moses' day. It is timeless in a way that the command not to "cut the hair at the sides of your head or clip off the edges of your beard" is not (Lev. 19:27). For texts like this, identifying the timeless truth necessitates moving up one or two levels of abstraction.[15] If you go right up to the highest level of abstraction with each text, then every sermon will be about the glory of God. Ultimately, that's what the whole of the Bible is about. But while that is a great theme, it ought not be the main theme of every sermon. It's too broad. We want to go up only the number of levels of abstraction necessary to derive a timeless "always" truth.

Timeless, however, does not mean static. Timeless truths revealed in the past actually come to us with greater force and power because of subsequent redemptive history. Truths that God revealed to Abraham, Moses, or David, for example, come to us via Jesus Christ and the full realization of the gospel in his redeeming work. In handling "always" truths, therefore, we must not leapfrog from the past to the present, ignoring the progress of redemptive history and the climactic work of the Messiah. Rather, we must examine and apply truths revealed at earlier times in the history of God's people in the light of the finished work of Jesus, our current place in salvation history, and the future that is yet to be fully revealed. They have relevance *always*, but their relevance to us is shaped by the work of Christ.[16]

Suppose I am preparing to preach from Haggai 1. I see the "there and then" details of the text: the time of Darius, the governor Zerubbabel, the high priest Joshua, the nation of Israel, the neglect of the rebuilding of the temple, the building of paneled houses, timber up in the mountains, failed crops and poor returns, and, eventually, renewed zeal

15. Haddon Robinson explains the idea of abstraction in "The Heresy of Application," in Haddon W. Robinson and Craig Brian Larson, eds., *The Art and Craft of Biblical Preaching: A Comprehensive Resource for Today's Communicators* (Grand Rapids: Zondervan, 2005), 308.

16. Chapter 8 explores more fully the importance of a redemptive-historical, christocentric application of biblical truth.

in working on the house of the Lord. I need to explore and understand each detail and come to a sense of what the chapter as a whole is about. In "there and then" terms, it seems that the people of Israel need to stop and think about what is happening to them, and see that they are not being blessed physically by the Lord because they have not prioritized the building of his house, for his glory, as they ought to have.

That theme, however, like the details of the text, is distant from the lives of people in the twenty-first century. So now I need to think about how that message might have a bearing on people today. What is the message of Haggai that people today need to hear? What, out of the specifics of that situation, are "always" truths of enduring importance? And how do those timeless truths come to us in the light of the work of Christ? That is not so easy to answer. Does this apply to the church or to nations today? Is the equivalent of building the temple today building up church ministry, or evangelism, or more generally doing whatever the Lord has called us to do? Does God still discipline us through failed crops, drought, famine, financial crises, and other physical difficulties? Can we expect that when we do what is right before God, material blessing will follow? Is it wrong to put home construction ahead of gospel ministry?

As I reflect on such questions, I become wary of making tight equations: Israel equals the church, temple building equals church ministry, crops equal income, difficulty equals punishment, drought equals God's displeasure. Surveying a wider biblical theology, I see there are too many variables to make simple one-to-one equivalents. Haggai had an advantage. He was giving an inspired interpretation of events that I cannot claim to be able to do. So, instead, I opt to zoom in on the command to "give careful thought to your ways," found twice in the text (1:5, 7). There may be no tight, clear-cut equations possible, but it is always right and necessary for us to stop, think, and see if perhaps God is speaking to us about our priorities having gone awry. It is a timeless truth that God calls his people to consider their circumstances and to be sure that they are prioritizing the honor of God. More particularly, followers of Christ and churches of the Lord Jesus need to consider whether they are prioritizing the honor of Christ and the work of the gospel as they ought.

That truth sets me on an applicatory track, but it will need to become much more specific and nuanced if it is to be drilled down into people's lives in the *here and now*. I need to find compelling ways of preaching, *here and now*, the main message of the text—namely, *God challenges our priorities because Christ's glory is at stake*. In this way, biblical truth is made as specific as possible for present-day hearers of God's Word. They are left not with something of only historical interest (the "there and then" theme of the text), nor with something general (the timeless "always" truth), but with something pressed against their lives today (the "here and now" message from God).

But even when we have shaped a one-liner that sets the direction for our message, we still have much work to do to develop excellent application. As Haddon Robinson has said, "In application we attempt to take what we believe is the truth of the eternal God, given in a particular time, place, and situation, and apply it to people in the modern world, who live in another time, another place, and a very different situation. That is harder than it appears."[17]

The three distinct and essential tasks the preacher undertakes are not entirely sequential. A conversation needs to be set up between the three, and particularly between the text and today's hearers—between *there and then* and *here and now*. Klaas Runia put it this way:

> The secret of relevant preaching is that the message of the gospel and the situation of the listeners are related to each other in such a way that the listeners discover that its message really concerns their life as it is. *Relevance occurs at the intersection* of the *unique message of the Bible* . . . and the *unique situation of the people* in the pew.[18]

17. Robinson and Larson, eds., *The Art and Craft of Biblical Preaching*, 307. Daniel Overdorf says, "Effective preaching includes application that, first, allows the Word of God to speak (which requires biblical integrity) and, second, allows the Word of God to speak as explicitly and concretely today as it did originally (which requires contemporary relevance)." Daniel Overdorf, *Applying the Sermon: How to Balance Biblical Integrity and Cultural Relevance* (Grand Rapids: Kregel, 2009), 15.

18. K. Runia, *The Sermon Under Attack*, The Moore College Lectures (Exeter: Paternoster, 1983), 75 (italics in original).

Runia, however, does not suggest that this happens by way of one-way traffic, from either text to audience or audience to text. He advocates, instead, a dialogue between the text and the audience. First, since the text has primacy, we start with reading it carefully, getting the "feel" of it and formulating in a preliminary way its basic message. Second, "As soon as we think we have succeeded in this, we reverse the poles and try to look at the text *through the eyes of our listeners.*"[19] We try to see this text as they will see it. How will they react to it? Will they understand it, accept it, resist it, or embrace it? Third, we return to the text for the hard labor of exegesis. We now dig into the text in detail, seeking out its true meaning but doing so with our hearers and their questions in mind. We are mining the text for a message for them. Fourth, we relate the message of the text, once it is fully laid bare, to the reactions of our listeners. The preacher here has a "double task of being representative for both his text and his people."[20] Fifth, we are in a position, Runia says, to determine the aim of the sermon. The aim is the message of the text in motion, moving toward and into the situation of the hearers. Finally, we are ready to prepare the outline of the sermon.

While taking six distinct steps may not be necessary, the process he describes is instructive. A dialogue is set up between the text and the present-day audience so that in forming the message from the biblical text, the hearers are never forgotten and application is no mere afterthought or add-on. When we exegete, we are digging into God's Word to discover what God would say to his people today. Our exegetical work is done with a view to discovering a message for today, and the "there and then" truth of the text is explored and understood in terms of what it says to us *here and now.*

Such a dialogue will help us develop holistic application rather than bolt-on applications. But to engage in this dialogue, we need to learn how to ask applicatory as well as exegetical questions of the text, we need to find ways of interfacing the truths of the text with life as it actually is, and we need to have some real understanding of the hearts

19. Ibid., 91.
20. Ibid., 92.

PART 1

The Living Application Preaching Process

What makes a sermon a "good sermon"? When you leave after hearing someone preach and you say, "That was a great sermon," what was it that made it great? When you find yourself rolling your eyes during the sermon and wondering when it will be over, what is it that makes it so bad?

There is never a single answer to these questions. Good preaching is the result of several things coming together under the enabling of the Spirit. Recently, homileticians have emphasized the relevance to preaching of Aristotle's three marks of great oratory: *logos, ethos,* and *pathos.*[1] All three are necessary for an effective speech, and in preaching, all three have a distinctively biblical shape and spiritual focus. Tim Keller has posited three different but related aspects of effective preaching: the biblical, the personal, and the situational.[2] The *biblical* embraces the text and the world of the Bible; the message must be exegetically sound and clear. The *personal* concerns the person of the preacher; the message must come from someone

1. See, for example, Bryan Chapell, *Christ-Centered Preaching: Redeeming the Expository Sermon* (Grand Rapids: Baker, 1994), 25–26. See also Jeffrey D. Arthurs, *Preaching with Variety: How to Re-create the Dynamics of Biblical Genres* (Grand Rapids: Kregel, 2007), 93.

2. Timothy Keller, "A Model for Preaching (Part One)," *Journal of Biblical Counseling* 12, no. 3 (1994): 36.

who speaks with fire from the Holy Spirit so that the message is warm and forceful. The *situational* addresses the importance of the message being adapted to the needs and capacities of the hearers; it needs to be insightful, vivid, and practical.

Keller emphasizes that these three aspects of preaching belong together and are closely interrelated. "In a sense, these three elements are not really 'parts' of preaching. They cannot be separated. In fact, each element really includes the others."[3] Together, these three aspects are the raw materials of what we are likely to call a "good sermon."

While the three aspects belong inseparably together, in the actual process of preaching there is a logical sequence to how they work together. Expository sermons move from the biblical text to the life situation of the hearers via the person of the preacher. Couched in the language of communication theory, a sermon moves from the source (the text), via the medium (the preacher), to the recipients (the congregation). But each part of the process is living and active, not static. So it is most compelling to think of the process as a movement from the living Word of God, via the life of the preacher, to the lives of the hearers (see diagram 2). This is living application.

Living application grows out of sermon preparation that works intentionally with each of these three stages of the preaching process. Preachers first need to think about the applicatory thrust of each text. Every portion of Scripture is loaded with applicatory significance. The expositor must exegete not only the original meaning but the abiding significance of the text; not just the "there and then" but the "always" meaning of it. We will explore this stage of the process in chapter 2.

Next, the preacher must bring the truth of the text to bear on his own life and bring to the text the questions and realities of living the truth today. The preacher's life is the laboratory in which biblical truth is tested. Preachers must live the application before they can make it live in the lives of others. If the preacher has a narrow or superficial experience of biblical truth, his messages are

3. Ibid.

likely to be narrow and superficial in their application. But, if his experience of the truth is rich and varied, he will be able to develop far more insightful and penetrating applications for *here and now*. In chapter 3 we will look at how the preacher's life interfaces with the truths of the text.

Diagram 2: The Preaching Process

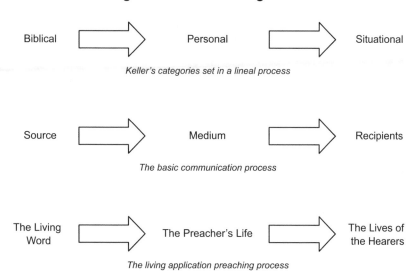

Keller's categories set in a lineal process

The basic communication process

The living application preaching process

Third, preachers must wrestle with the text and its meaning for life in terms of the realities of their hearers' lives. They need to be shaping messages for real people in real-life situations. They need to be mindful of the heart conditions and spiritual realities experienced by their hearers, both individually and corporately. This third part of the process will be our focus in chapters 4 and 5.

Finally, the application developed from these three stages of the preaching process needs to be brought home to people's lives in a way that stings and sings, wounds and heals, convicts and compels. Preachers must not only develop the right applications, but find ways of making those applications live. We will look at the main ways of doing this in chapter 6.

The whole process can be depicted as follows:

Diagram 3: The Living Application Preaching Process

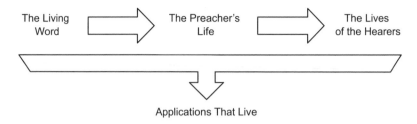

Applications That Live

These four things together provide the preacher with a model for developing living application. First, the applicatory potential of the text is explored; then the applications of the text are interfaced with the preacher's life experience; once owned by the preacher, they are shaped for the realities of the hearers' lives; and finally, ways are found to bring those applications to life in the actual act of preaching. Depicting this as a process helps us think logically and sequentially about developing living application, but we need to remember Runia's observation about a dialogue between the text and the hearers. We will find ourselves moving backward and forward as we wrestle with a text.

We will also find that, in time, much of this can happen quite intuitively and spontaneously. But in the early stages of learning to apply God's Word, this model will be of great help. It will, in fact, usually enable a preacher to see many more avenues for application than can be used in a single sermon. But that is much better than scratching around, desperately trying to find some kind of application to tack on at the end.

| 2 |

THE LIVING WORD:
IT HAS WORK TO DO

MOST COMPLEX PROCESSES require getting the starting point right. Whether you are beginning a jigsaw puzzle, baking a cake, writing an essay, undertaking a home renovation, or starting a business, it pays to stop and think about where to begin. Where do I start? What's the best first step? In most projects, large or small, the order in which we do things matters. And that's true in preaching as well. When an expository preacher sits down to start working on a sermon, what should happen first? Exegesis? Word studies? Reading commentaries? Prayer, perhaps? Meditation on the text? Where is the beginning of the preaching process? No doubt preachers have their own patterns, but we must realize that the order matters. If we begin technically, we will most likely end technically; if we start mechanically, we will probably finish ploddingly. Preaching is a spiritual work and from the beginning it must be undertaken as a spiritual task.

Fundamental to approaching the biblical text spiritually is the realization that the process we are embarking on is not so much about us working on the text as about the text working on us. Yes, we have work to do, but more importantly God's Word has work to do. It has work to do on us and, when we preach, on our hearers. It has God-given work to do. God inspired his Word with the intention that it would

57

make a difference in people's lives. So, when we come to the Bible, we must examine the text in the light of its intended, life-shaping purposes.

THE PURPOSES OF GOD'S WORD

The Bible's applicatory intent is spelled out clearly in a number of key verses:

All Scripture is God-breathed and is useful for teaching, rebuking, correcting and training in righteousness. (2 Tim. 3:16)

Preach the Word; be prepared in season and out of season; correct, rebuke and encourage—with great patience and careful instruction. (2 Tim. 4:2)

But everyone who prophesies speaks to men for their strengthening, encouragement and comfort. (1 Cor. 14:3)

For everything that was written in the past was written to teach us, so that through endurance and the encouragement of the Scriptures we might have hope. (Rom. 15:4)

What shall we say, then? Is the law sin? Certainly not! Indeed I would not have known what sin was except through the law. For I would not have known what coveting really was if the law had not said, "Do not covet." (Rom. 7:7)

For the word of God is living and active. Sharper than any double-edged sword, it penetrates even to dividing soul and spirit, joints and marrow; it judges the thoughts and attitudes of the heart. Nothing in all creation is hidden from God's sight. Everything is uncovered and laid bare before the eyes of him to whom we must give account. (Heb. 4:12–13)

I write these things to you who believe in the name of the Son of God so that you may know that you have eternal life. (1 John 5:13)

Every discussion of biblical application recognizes that 2 Timothy 3:16 is a foundational text.[1] In the previous verse, Paul has reminded Timothy that the Holy Scriptures, on which he has been reared from childhood, are able to make him wise to salvation. That is, the whole Bible reveals the way of salvation. But the value of Scripture is not exhausted when we have been brought to faith. The God-breathed Scriptures have further "usefulness" or "profitableness."[2] The four values of God's Word that follow are in a chiastic structure: it is able to teach right doctrine and rebuke false teaching, and it is able to correct false conduct and train in righteous living. It has value, then, for both doctrine and life, and it has both a negative and a positive function. It teaches and trains, and it rebukes and corrects.

Scripture as a whole is profitable for these things. That doesn't mean that each and every text we choose will give rise to all four, but it does mean that the Bible as a whole is intended to have this kind of usefulness in our lives.[3] As interpreters of God's Word, we should be interested in its value and usefulness for life, not just its original meaning. Scripture is, in particular, profitable for these things in the life of "the man of God" (2 Tim. 3:17). The immediate referent is no doubt Timothy. He is the man of God, taught, rebuked, corrected, and trained by God's Word, and so, by it, thoroughly equipped for every good work. But such profit is not for him as a pastor alone. Scripture will be his chief tool in teaching, rebuking, correcting, and training others. Just a few verses later, Timothy is charged with using Scripture in the same way in ministry. He is always to be ready to preach the Word, correcting, rebuking, and encouraging others with careful instruction.[4]

1. See William Perkins, *The Art of Prophesying and The Calling of the Ministry* (1606; repr., Edinburgh: Banner of Truth, 1996). Perkins takes 2 Timothy 3:16 to indicate two kinds of application: mental application, which concerns the mind and involves doctrine or reproof, and practical application, which has to do with lifestyle and behavior and involves instruction and correction (64–68). See also the discussion in Daniel M. Doriani, *Putting the Truth to Work: The Theory and Practice of Biblical Application* (Phillipsburg, NJ: P&R, 2001), 41, 55–58.

2. The Greek adjective is *ōphelimos*, used only in the pastoral epistles: here, twice in 1 Timothy 4:8, and once in Titus 3:8. It speaks of that which is beneficial, helpful, valuable, or useful.

3. See Doriani, *Putting the Truth to Work*, 55.

4. Both verses refer to "teaching," using the related nouns *didaskalia* in 3:16 and 4:3 and *didachē* in 4:2; "rebuking" in 3:16 is *elegmos* and in 4:2 the related verb *elenchō*; "correcting" in 3:16 is *epanorthōsis*, which has no direct parallel in 4:2 but has a counterpart in *epitimaō*,

In describing the ministry of prophets in 1 Corinthians 14:3, Paul uses terms similar to those in 2 Timothy. The prophets speak for people's strengthening, encouragement, and comfort.[5] While the preacher is not a prophet, the similarity of the tasks of preacher and prophet has often been recognized, in terms of not a revelatory but a proclamatory gifting.[6] The function of the preacher is similar to that of the prophet as one designated to proclaim authoritatively a word from God.

Similar value in God's Word is again highlighted by Paul in Romans 15. He states that encouragement leading to hope is given through the teaching of Scripture.[7] In Romans 7, however, a different purpose of the Word is supplied. God's law has the particular role of highlighting our sin and convicting us of how far short of God's standards we have fallen. The law doesn't show us so much how bad we are as how good we are not. It sets the benchmark and reveals that we have come up well short. In fact, in the entire Old Testament era, the law functioned as a tutor or guardian, teaching God's people their need of a savior (Gal. 3:24).[8]

This aspect of God's Word received great attention from earlier generations of preachers. They believed strongly in preaching the law to bring people under conviction of sin and then applying the grace of the gospel as a balm to their souls. In the earliest English homiletical

---

"warning"; "training" in 3:16 is *paideia*, which refers to the broad educational task of raising a child and finds a counterpart in the verb *parakaleō* in 4:2, which includes shades of exhorting, comforting, encouraging, and counseling.

5. The words are *oikodomē*, *paraklēsis*, and *paramuthia*. We have already encountered *paraklēsis* in 2 Timothy 4:2. "Strengthening" (*oikodomē*) could also be translated "edification" or "upbuilding." "Comfort" (*paramuthia*) in classical Greek could refer to any dimension of speech: persuading and stimulating or comforting and consoling. This is the only NT usage, but it is generally thought to refer to comfort or consolation.

6. Perkins's early homiletical text was entitled *The Art of Prophesying*; more recently Christopher Ash has argued that the preacher continues the work of ruling God's people by the Word as the OT prophets did. See Christopher Ash, *The Priority of Preaching* (Fearn: Christian Focus, 2009), 24–37.

7. Romans 15:4 uses the two nouns *didaskalia* and *paraklēsis*.

8. The Greek noun in Galatians 3:24 is *paidagōgos*, referring to the stereotypically strict guardian of wealthy young boys, who was charged with forming their life and morals before the age of maturity.

textbook, William Perkins began his treatment of application at exactly this point:

> The basic principle in application is to know whether the passage is a statement of the law or of the gospel. For when the Word is preached, the law and the gospel operate differently. The law exposes the disease of sin, and as a side-effect stimulates and stirs it up. But it provides no remedy for it. However the gospel not only teaches us what is to be done, it also has the power of the Holy Spirit joined to it. . . . The law is, therefore, first in the order of teaching; then comes the gospel.[9]

In this way the Word of God tests our hearts. It searches and exposes us, judging our heart thoughts and attitudes, as Hebrews 4:12 says. It is the means by which the all-seeing eye of God searches us out and his Spirit convicts us of sin. In fact, in 2 Timothy 3:16 and 4:2, the words translated as "rebuking" and "rebuke" could well be translated "convict." Jay Adams explains: "The Holy Spirit does not merely make charges; He fully substantiates them. The term *elengcho* comes from the law courts. It means not only to prefer charges, but also to so pursue the case against the one who is charged that he is *convicted* of the crime of which he is accused."[10]

The testing function of God's Word, however, is not confined to exposing and convicting us of sin. It also tests and proves genuine faith. This is the emphasis of 1 John, in which the purpose of the letter as a whole was to help believers, unsettled and attacked by false teachers, to discern whether they truly belonged to God.[11] If they loved the brethren, walked in obedience to God, and believed that Jesus Christ was the Son of God in the flesh, they could be assured that they belonged to God.

9. Perkins, *The Art of Prophesying and The Calling of the Ministry*, 54.

10. Jay Adams, *Preaching to the Heart: A Heart-to-Heart Discussion with Preachers of the Word* (Phillipsburg, NJ: P&R, 1983), 27.

11. See 1 John 5:13. John Stott helpfully analyzes this letter in terms of three tests: the moral, social, and doctrinal tests of true faith. The tests deliberately counteract the false teaching of the early Gnostics. John R. W. Stott, *The Letters of John: An Introduction and Commentary*, Tyndale New Testament Commentaries (Leicester: IVP, 1988).

Again, in the history of preaching, this emphasis on the value of God's Word as a test of our lives and of our faith has been prominent. In the *Westminster Directory of Public Worship*, for example, the following statement clarifies the value of preachers establishing such tests for their congregations:

> It is also sometimes requisite to give some notes of trial, (which is very profitable, especially when performed by able and experienced ministers, with circumspection and prudence, and the signs clearly grounded on the holy scripture,) whereby the hearers may be able to examine themselves whether they have attained those graces, and performed those duties, to which he exhorteth, or be guilty of the sin reprehended, and in danger of the judgments threatened, or are such to whom the consolations propounded do belong; that accordingly they may be quickened and excited to duty, humbled for their wants and sins, affected with their danger, and strengthened with comfort, as their condition, upon examination, shall require.[12]

Four Main Purposes

Taking this selection of verses as a whole, we can discern four core purposes of God's Word (see diagram 4). These are not the four functions of 2 Timothy 3:16 but a broader classification. The four main purposes of the Word are:

- teaching the truth and rebuking false doctrine;
- training believers in godly living and correcting wrong patterns of behavior;
- testing the state of people's hearts and bringing conviction of sin;
- encouraging and exhorting people according to their particular needs.

12. "The Directory for the Publick Worship of God," in *The Confession of Faith* (Inverness: Free Presbyterian Publications, 1981), 380.

Diagram 4: Stage One—The Living Word

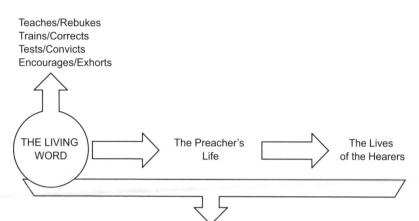

Teaches/Rebukes
Trains/Corrects
Tests/Convicts
Encourages/Exhorts

THE LIVING WORD → The Preacher's Life → The Lives of the Hearers

Applications That Live

Preachers can examine the biblical text in terms of these common purposes of the Word. It is essential to note that all four are applicatory functions. If we are to have a holistic view of application, we must avoid the tendency to reduce application to telling people what to do. In that case, the second and fourth purposes would be regarded as application but not the first and third. Rightly understood, all four are strongly applicatory.

Teaching/rebuking. The teaching/rebuking purpose of the Word focuses on doctrine or truth. Teaching should not be regarded as non-applicatory or merely pre-applicatory. While teaching can be purely academic, it need not be. Teaching does not just provide truths that can then be applied. It may itself be the application needed. In addressing the grief of the Thessalonians, for example, Paul judged that they needed a better doctrinal understanding. He did not want them to be ignorant of what would happen at death or at the return of Christ, so he provides teaching (1 Thess. 4:13–17) and then says, "Encourage each other with these words" (v. 18).[13] That is, encourage each other with this doctrine.

13. The Greek verb is *parakaleō.*

The division of a number of Paul's letters into doctrine first and then practice later can be somewhat misleading. It may lead us to think that doctrine and application are quite separate and distinct. But Paul's doctrine is never given just for the sake of correct theology, and his applications are always deeply rooted in the gospel. He never states truth without pastoral intent. Even in Romans, arguably the most doctrinal of his letters and the most clearly demarcated into doctrine (chapters 1–11) and practice (chapters 12–15), there is a strong pastoral purpose that drives all the teaching. Paul shapes the entire letter around his passion and ambition for the gospel. The letter has gospel bookends (1:1–17 and 15:14–33). He wants the believers in Rome to join him in his gospel venture, and so he opens to them the fullness of his gospel so that they are, as it were, on the same page as he is. More than that, he wants to enthuse them and warm their hearts with this glorious gospel, and he wants it to do its work among them. So the doctrinal teaching is loaded. It is not spoken into a vacuum or without intent. It has pastoral purpose.

This is how most teaching ought to be in a preaching ministry. Our teaching of truth ought to be loaded. We teach the Bible not only so that people have their theology right. We teach it so that they will live right theology. Without right doctrine, right living is impossible. In the Pastoral Epistles, Paul speaks often of "sound" doctrine. The word means "healthy," and only when the teaching is healthy can the life of faith be healthy.

That is also why rebuke is necessary. False doctrine leads to wrong behavior and unhealthy living. The false teachers lurking in the background of 1 John, for example, are damaging the faith and assurance of God's people. The truth must be asserted so that the gospel can be lived and enjoyed. Effective applicatory teaching, therefore, opposes what is wrong. It addresses the flip side of the truth. This is extremely countercultural today. Our culture teaches us to be positive not negative, accepting not condemning. But the Bible calls for the negative as well as the positive.[14] We must be prepared to speak against things that are wrong, be they Western consumerism at the expense of those working in sweatshops,

14. See Phillip D. Jensen and Paul Grimmond, *The Archer and the Arrow: Preaching the Very Words of God* (Kingsford, New South Wales: Matthias Media, 2010), 135–43.

or neglect of the poor in our own cities, or extreme feminism, or moral evils like abortion, or theological aberrations such as antinomianism or the prosperity gospel, or a thousand other spoilers of the true gospel. Not that we should ever take cheap potshots at such things. We must show why they fall short of God's better purposes and design.

If teaching in and of itself can be immensely relevant and practical, we do well to ask, *when* is it so? When is teaching, pure and simple, truly applicatory? When we answer this, it is important that we do not become so utilitarian in our view of truth that we fail to see the importance of laying theological foundations. All truth is practical and correct knowledge is intrinsically useful, but it is not necessarily immediately useful. A young child learning times tables at school does not sense the immediate usefulness of this knowledge, but it is a foundation on which many later practical skills can be built. Similarly, preachers need to preach sermons that lay theological foundations without always being assessed in terms of how immediately useful they are. There might be no immediate life-changing impact, but these are truths we need to know.

Beyond that, however, there is applicatory punch to truth when the doctrine under consideration has direct and obvious relevance to life today. If you wade into a river in the Northern Territory of Australia and someone calls out, "There are crocodiles in the river," that piece of factual information is relevant because of where you are and what you are doing. The fact doesn't need application; it is directly applicable as it stands. If I go to my doctor with a heart problem and she draws a diagram explaining how the chambers and arteries of the heart work, that information is relevant to me because of my condition. Similarly, imagine a preacher speaking to a congregation that has recently been broken by division and is grieving due to the departure of several core members. He says, "When Jesus comes again, every division will be healed, every barrier broken down, every conflict resolved. He came into this world to reconcile us to God and to one another and, when he comes again, that reconciliation will be fully realized." The statement of truth is so loaded in that context that it has immediate relevance. The truth itself comforts, encourages, stirs hope, and puts things in perspective.

Preachers, therefore, need to speak pertinent truths into the real-life situations of their hearers. We should never doubt the applicatory value of relevant truth stated clearly and plainly.

Training/correcting. The training/correcting purpose of God's Word is different. In recent years, many churches have rediscovered the importance of training ministries. It has been recognized that it is one thing to teach people faithfully; it is another to equip and train them. Preaching about prayer doesn't necessarily train people to pray. Teaching about the importance of evangelism is very different from equipping people to be competent in sharing their faith. Rebuking false views of headship is different from correcting poor or wrong patterns among fathers. Many churches, now recognizing this difference and acknowledging that they have often trained people poorly, have begun intentional training ministries, frequently by way of mentoring, discipleship, and coaching relationships as well as through seminars and training courses.

It is easy, however, to overlook preaching as a training tool. At the most basic level, expository preaching trains people how to read the Bible. It models responsible use of the Scriptures and trains people to think about context, authorial intent, original meaning, and so on. This may be done quite intentionally by exposing some of our "workings" during the course of a sermon. We don't only serve up the meal, but take people into the kitchen and show them what we have done.

But preaching can train in many other ways as well. This generally happens through "how to" applications. We speak of not only what people should do but how they might do it and how they should not do it. Jay Adams has pointed out how much Jesus does this in the Sermon on the Mount.[15] For each command, he gives instruction on how to live it out. In speaking about prayer, for example, Jesus says how not to pray (not so as to be seen, nor in vain repetitions) and how to pray (in your room, privately, along these lines—and he gives them the Lord's Prayer as a model). Jesus is training his disciples to pray.

15. Jay Adams, *Preaching with Purpose: A Comprehensive Textbook on Biblical Preaching* (Phillipsburg, NJ: P&R, 1982), 127–29.

Following Jesus' example, preachers should do plenty of training from the pulpit. As well as exhorting husbands to love their wives, help them know how to do so. Give some practical suggestions. As well as urging people to prioritize giving to God's work, train them how to do that. Talk about budgeting, about planned giving, about specific ways of giving, about frequency of giving and privacy and whatever else will help people know how to do what you are calling for. Paul himself makes this kind of practical application in 2 Corinthians 8 and 9 as he addresses the matter of giving. If this is the only kind of application a preacher gives, the preaching may be too shallow. But if preachers never do this, the preaching will not be practical enough.

Testing/convicting. The third purpose of the Word is perhaps the most neglected of the four in contemporary preaching, though it has been a hallmark of great preaching in the past. The use of "tests" is of immense value in helping people examine their own hearts. It is not uncommon for preachers to ask questions like, "How is your prayer life? Is it growing? Is it healthy?" Or, "Are you in danger of falling from grace? Have you begun already on the slippery, backsliding slope?" Such questions are fine, but they will gain far greater traction if they are backed up by tests. The preacher may give some marks of a healthy prayer life by which people can test themselves, or give some indicators of the early stages of backsliding so people can examine their own experience more carefully.

Tests may be provided for almost any area of spiritual life. The most fundamental and critical area of testing is to provide marks of genuine conversion. We can address the question, "How do I know if I'm saved?" But tests may also be provided for such things as a servant heart, a genuine work of the Holy Spirit,[16] being a doer and not just a hearer of the Word, or true humility. Taking the last of these as an example, a preacher may say something like this:

16. This test is developed most rigorously in Jonathan Edwards's landmark work, *Distinguishing Marks of a Work of the Spirit of God.* See Jonathan Edwards, *The Works of Jonathan Edwards, vol. 2* (Edinburgh: Banner of Truth, 1974), 257–69.

We know that we are called to Christlike humility. But the problem is, we so easily deceive ourselves. Even pride can take the guise of humility and we become proud of how humble we are! So we need to check our hearts rather carefully. Let me suggest four marks of genuine Christian humility. Check yourself against these.

The first mark is that you find in your relationship with God that you readily confess sin and you constantly seek his grace. You sense keenly your need of God and you readily cry out to him for help.

Second, you have a constant sense of unworthiness before God. You feel unworthy of his blessings, of the gifts he's given you, of the opportunities you have, of the salvation you've received. But this unworthiness hasn't led you to despair. It's led you to being deeply thankful to God. You're often amazed at his grace. You stand in awe of how good God has been to you, knowing you do not deserve it.

Third, in everyday situations you are prepared to serve others without thanks. You don't mind doing small, menial things that others might think are beneath your dignity. You don't mind if they're not noticed or appreciated. You are pleased to be able to help others out. Status and reputation are not big on your agenda. You know Christ was a servant and you want to be one too.

Finally, a fourth mark of genuine Christian humility is this: you listen to others. You listen to their problems. You listen to their advice. You listen to their opinions. You listen when they are a bit boring. You listen when it's not convenient. You listen because you are not full of yourself and your time and opinions, but you have humbled yourself and learned to regard others more highly than yourself, as Jesus did and as Paul commanded.

These marks could easily be multiplied, but the list needs to be manageable. We may not call them tests, but we give them to people as a way of checking themselves out. We deliberately aid self-examination. The tests we provide may arise directly from the text we are dealing with or from wider reflection on the particular issue. We may provide positive tests that look for evidence of true spirituality, or negative tests that expose false spirituality.

Encouraging/exhorting. The final purpose of God's Word is much more familiar to most preachers. Exhortation is the most common mode of application. Paul's letters are full of exhortations and he also urged believers to exhort one another: "And we urge you, brothers, warn those who are idle, encourage the timid, help the weak, be patient with everyone" (1 Thess. 5:14).

Curiously, however, many expository preachers find it easier to exhort than to encourage. It seems easier to rebuke than to build up, to tell people what to do than to commend them for what they are already doing, to challenge than to comfort. We more easily sting than sing; we more readily wound than heal. We feel we have done good application when we have hit them hard. And some people like to be hit hard and feel the sermon has been well applied only when it has hurt! Preaching becomes like a boxing match; the best sermon is a knockout.

Why are we often less comfortable with gently spurring people on? It is certainly not due to a lack of biblical modeling. Paul repeatedly commends churches for their faith, hope, and love. He assures them of both his deep thankfulness and his genuine love for them. Perhaps our reticence stems from a reaction against people-pleasing pulpits that give congregations what their itching ears want to hear. We know Paul's warning against that and we don't want to go anywhere near it. It may also stem from the awkwardness too many men have in expressing affection or admiration of any kind. Somehow it feels difficult and unmanly to tell people that we love them, as Paul does.

Most likely, however, our inability to bring extensive comfort and encouragement stems from a deficient view of the gospel. Too easily we lapse into thinking that a free preaching of grace and too much gospel comfort and encouragement will incline people toward being lax. So we keep the heat on them lest they presume on grace. And people lap it up because they are, at heart, legalists.[17] But the gospel, while bringing us warnings and urging us to work out our salvation with fear and trembling, motivates us chiefly by grace, not by law.

17. Graeme Goldsworthy, *Preaching the Whole Bible as Christian Scripture: The Application of Biblical Theology to Expository Preaching* (Grand Rapids: Eerdmans, 2000), 118.

Preachers need to be almost dangerous in their proclamation of the free grace of God.

This point is made powerfully by Martyn Lloyd-Jones in his comments on Romans 6:1. In addressing Paul's question, "Shall we go on sinning so that grace may increase?," Lloyd-Jones contends that true gospel preaching will nearly always invite precisely this objection.

> There is no better test as to whether a man is really preaching the New Testament gospel of salvation than this, that some people might misunderstand it and misinterpret it to mean that it really amounts to this, that because you are saved by grace alone it does not matter at all what you do; you can go on sinning as much as you like because it will redound all the more to the glory of grace.[18]

He argues that the doctrine of justification is in a sense a dangerous doctrine, because it is always liable to this misunderstanding. But it is a misunderstanding that we ought to be open to for the sake of the gospel.

> I would say to all preachers: If your preaching of salvation has not been misunderstood in that way, then you had better examine your sermons again, and you had better make sure that you really are preaching the salvation that is offered in the New Testament to the ungodly, to the sinner, to those who are dead in trespasses and sins, to those who are enemies of God.[19]

This is a valuable warning. We need to be prepared to preach the gospel so fully and freely, and to bring such hope, encouragement, and comfort from the work of Christ, that we are open to the charge of going too easy on people. Yet far from encouraging laxity, this will often motivate greater godliness. Haddon Robinson has

18. Martyn Lloyd-Jones, *Romans: An Exposition of Chapter 6: The New Man* (Grand Rapids: Zondervan, 1973), 8.

19. Ibid., 10. Note that he is using the device of testing the preaching of preachers—the third purpose of the Word we have considered.

rightly noted that guilt is not actually a good motivator.[20] Over the years, I have taught each of my children the piano for a few years before passing them on to more competent teachers. At times, I've been much too tough. I have reduced more than one of my kids to tears as I criticized them for their lack of practice, their silly mistakes, or their appalling technique. But a tough lesson doesn't produce anywhere near the progress generated by genuine praise and encouragement. They have always done their best, practiced the hardest, and taken the greatest strides forward when they have been on a positive roll. Sure, every lesson requires teaching and rebuking, training and correction, testing and conviction. But the greatest aid to progress is genuine encouragement. Paul wisely told fathers not to exasperate their children. Similarly, pastors should not exasperate their congregations.

If we take our lead from Paul, then, we will at times tell our congregation how much we love them and how we miss them when we are away; we will tell them of how encouraged we are by their gospel work and how thankful we are for their ministry; we will tell them about what we pray for them; we will tell them of ways in which we see them as wonderful examples to others; we will publicly praise God for them and for his work of grace among them. Of course, we can do this only if we mean it, so it may well turn out to be a test of how healthy the pastoral bond really is.

WORKING WITH THE LIVING WORD

As we sit down to begin work on a sermon, we should begin with the consciousness that God's Word has work to do. We do not want to merely analyze the text; we want to hear it speak. We are not simply to work on our sermon; we are to let the text work on us. Our exegetical work must be undertaken with a desire to discern the intended applicatory purpose of the text.

20. Haddon Robinson, "Preaching That Opens Ears and Hearts," in Haddon W. Robinson and Craig Brian Larson, eds., *The Art and Craft of Biblical Preaching: A Comprehensive Resource for Today's Communicators* (Grand Rapids: Zondervan, 2005), 260.

So we can ask of any text, "What is this text doing?" Is it teaching, training, rebuking, warning, convicting, testing, comforting, encouraging, strengthening? What teaching is given, what warnings are sounded, what tests are suggested, what encouragements are provided?

Particular texts will usually be oriented toward perhaps one or two of these in particular, though all may be present by implication. We should look for the main things a text is doing and major on them. Romans 8:28–30 ("And we know that in all things . . ."), for example, teaches, but in particular it encourages. To teach doctrine from these verses and not greatly encourage people is to miss the applicatory boat. Deuteronomy 16:1–8 clearly commands and exhorts: remember the Passover. The applicatory thrust is that God's people must never forget how they were saved. Application here will urge and encourage, giving reasons and motivations for never forgetting the source of our salvation. By contrast, John 13:35 ("By this will all men know that you are my disciples") immediately suggests a test. It invites us to ask whether people see in our lives the true evidence of discipleship. 1 Timothy 3:1–7 teaches about the qualities necessary for church leaders. It provides clear teaching that churches need to hear about who is qualified for leadership. By implication, it tells us who is not qualified; and by further implication it urges us to strive for these qualities.

In considering the purpose of a text in this way, we reflect the fact that application is not adding something to the text but drawing out what is in the text. Every text has applicatory intent, and asking about the purposes of the text will help unearth it. This approach will also reinforce that application is more than telling people what to do. It will help us resist the temptation to think we are only applying when we are commanding or exhorting. Sometimes there is nothing more pertinent and relevant than doctrinal teaching; sometimes there's nothing more opportune than training; sometimes there's nothing more helpful than tests for self-evaluation; and sometimes there's nothing more needed than encouragement.

This approach also alerts us to the reality that an application frequently has two sides. We can present many applications both positively and negatively. There is a truth to teach but also errors to rebuke; there is right behavior to nurture but also wrong behavior to correct; there may be something to exhort people to but also something to praise them for. When we make applications, we should ask ourselves if there is a flip side to address as well. We may speak, for example, of the wonder of grace, as Paul does in Romans. But then we may also ask, "Shall we go on sinning so grace may abound?" Paul addresses the flip side of free grace so as to avoid the error of antinomianism.

WHAT DOES IT LOOK LIKE IN PRACTICE?

There are no mysteries or tricks to approaching a text in this way. It is simply adding another useful set of questions to our exegetical study of the Bible. Examples from three very different kinds of texts will help to show what working with the living Word looks like in practice.

First, let's return to Haggai 1. I suggested earlier that the *here and now* truth in this chapter is that *God challenges our priorities because Christ's glory is at stake.* As we apply that truth, we should ask, What is this text doing? Which purposes of God's Word are most prominent here? The flavor of the passage is that of convicting the people of wrong priorities. This is a text that will, above all else, test and convict. It will ask of us the question, are our priorities right? This is not so much a teaching chapter leading to a sermon on the temple or on the historical context of Israel after the exile. That is but the backdrop. The focus will be on testing our life priorities against the priority of serving God.

Along with this dominant line of application, the chapter contains some other purposes of the Word. There is rebuke for the people's sin; there is, at least, the implied exhortation to get on with the work; and there is encouragement given after the people have responded. These are suggestive of lines of application we are likely to use as well. Later, we will consider how different kinds of application may suit different people and churches. We ought not to assume that our congregation is in the same place as the people of Haggai's day. But these are the purposes of God's Word for them, and they will inform the applications we shape for today.

Given that the prominent focus of the text is to test whether our priorities are right, we could usefully develop some tests for today. The tests could include some indicators that people are living with right priorities before God. One indicator might be that they prioritize time with God and his people even when they're busy; another might be that they budget to give generously to Christian work even though that affects the realizing of some other dreams; a third might be that they are currently engaged in some activity for God that has taken them out of their comfort zone. Such tests will help reinforce the purpose of the text.

Turning to a second example, there is a somewhat different applicatory flavor to Psalm 73. The psalm is replete with diverse and telling applications, though it contains no imperatives, rules, or exhortations. In undertaking careful exegetical work, the preacher will seek to determine both the textual theme and the timeless truth of a passage. The textual theme, in "there and then" terms, may be something like this: "The psalmist nearly lost his faith when he envied the prosperity of the wicked, but he came to realize that far greater security and satisfaction in life is found in living close to God." The timeless truth takes that theme and puts it in "always" terms, taking into account the wider scope of biblical theology and redemptive history. It may be something like this: "True satisfaction and security are found not in the lifestyle of the ungodly, but in a close relationship with God through his Son, Jesus Christ."

This timeless truth starts to sound preachable, but it needs to be more grounded in life *here and now* if it is going to pack a punch. The preacher must determine the main impact, big idea, or central proposition of the sermon.[21] There is never one right way of wording this, and

21. Terminology varies, with *proposition* being a hallmark of older homileticians such as Robert Lewis Dabney in *Sacred Rhetoric* (1870; repr., Edinburgh: Banner of Truth, 1979). The most common term currently is Haddon Robinson's *big idea*. However, there is great merit in adopting Quicke's preferred expression, *the main impact*. He usefully comments: "Terms such as idea, central idea, proposition, or thesis statement sound too cerebral, as though they are concepts for the head alone. Instead, I want to emphasize that both head and heart are involved, for Scripture both *says* and *does* through its focus and function." Michael J. Quicke, *360-Degree Preaching: Hearing, Speaking, and Living the Word* (Grand Rapids: Baker; Carlisle, UK: Paternoster, 2003), 156.

a precise wording is not absolutely essential,[22] but one possibility would be: "We'll never find satisfaction when we chase after things in this world, but only when we chase after closeness to God." A preaching proposition like that ensures that the sermon, as a whole, is applicatory in focus. But the statement must be unpacked in terms of the purposes of the text itself.

What *teaching* should be given? We can see, in this wisdom psalm, many life truths that are embedded in the experience of the psalmist. There is the plain truth that the lifestyle of the wicked often seems most attractive. There is also the reality that our view of the lifestyle of the wicked tends to be highly selective (in reality, the ungodly are not always healthy, wealthy, and carefree). There is the truth that ungodliness never stands still, but advances, as the sinfulness of the wicked is shown to be progressing in verses 4–11. There is the fact that unbelief on our part can lead others astray (v. 15). There is the truth that the fortunes of the godly and the ungodly will eventually be reversed, that a day of accounting is coming, that ultimately all that we have in this world will be taken from us, and that life is fleeting and brief. There are truths about God's grace: he grasps us by the hand, he guides us, he glorifies us. There is the truth that God alone can truly satisfy the deepest desires of the human heart and his comfort alone can last beyond the grave.

These truths all fit the category of truth that is immediately relevant and applicable. But there is also *training and correcting* to be done. The psalmist sees his folly (v. 22), recognizing himself to have been a spiritual beast when he envied the prosperity of the wicked. This prompts us to warn against the dangers of envy, to rebuke spiritually brutish behavior, and to challenge people who have come to a point where they view their Christian commitment as a raw deal. We will warn against viewing life only in terms of things now and ignoring eternal realities. We will want

22. There need not be only one way of expressing the main point of a sermon. Preachers should be able to say what they are preaching on in multiple ways, either briefly and simply or in a more detailed way. The issue is not so much to have a great one-liner but to have mental clarity on what the message is about and overall unity in the message. It is also possible that a message will be about more than one thing. Homiletic rules ought to be servants, not masters.

to train people to draw near to God, to find joy and satisfaction in him, and to live in terms of eternity.

The experience of the psalmist, therefore, invites a *testing* of our own experience. Here we may suggest tests by which we may know whether we are living as spiritual mongrels or living spiritually sane lives. Or we may provide tests by which people may know whether they are in danger of falling as the psalmist was. The psalm itself supplies the substance of such tests. It suggests that we are in danger of falling if we are envious of what others have materially or physically; if we have come to see our Christian commitment as a raw deal; if we have distanced ourselves from God, his Word, and his people; and if we seldom ponder the realities of heaven, hell, and eternity.

These tests could be very convicting. We must not, however, lose sight of the fact that the dominant tone of the psalm is immensely *comforting and encouraging*. It assures us that God will honor and bless his people, that losing all in this world for the sake of Christ is no real loss at all (cf. Phil. 3:7–8), that God takes us by the hand and can satisfy our souls in such a way that the things of this world pale into insignificance. These comforts must be brought in the light of the fullness of the gospel of Jesus Christ.

In these ways the teaching, training, testing, and encouragement of the psalm open up a host of applicatory possibilities, all in line with the central theme. Later in the living application preaching process, we will find ways of sharpening these applications; we will discover ways of working them into the fabric of people's lives. But the biblical text itself sets the trajectory, determining the kinds of applications to be made.

In Ephesians 1:3–14, we again encounter a very different kind of text. It is a didactic passage loaded with substantial doctrine. Of the four purposes of the Word, the teaching function is clearly dominant. There are no imperatives in these verses.

The textual theme may be stated as follows: "God is to be praised for including us in his glorious plan of salvation, initiated by the electing love of the Father, effected by the redeeming grace of Christ, and sealed to us by the powerful work of the Holy Spirit." The timeless truth is essentially the same since the text applies directly to us today. In fact, the preaching proposition could be the same as well, though it would be more helpful to state it in fewer words and make it as direct as possible so that it is memorable and eminently preachable. The preaching proposition might be: "We must praise God—Father, Son, and Holy Spirit—for embracing us in his glorious plan of redemption."

This proposition helps us avoid the danger of treating the doctrines of the text in a way that detaches them from the lives of believers. The teaching is about a plan of salvation in which we have been included, and the result is to be that we praise God for his glorious grace that is being worked out in our lives. The text does not deal with election in an abstract way, but teaches that we, who are in Christ, were chosen by the Father. He set his love on us and predetermined that we should be adopted as his children. His intent was not that this immense privilege give us freedom to sin as much as we like, but rather that we be set apart for holiness. So, in preaching this, we need to teach the doctrine of election in such a way that people see it as a great blessing and an incentive to godly living. We should oppose both the error of viewing election as a harsh, unloving doctrine and the error of seeing it as a license for sin. We should challenge not only those who despise the doctrine of election, but also those who, in embracing it, have misused it to bring themselves false comfort while leading an unholy life.

Such an approach immediately combines several core purposes of the Word. We will be teaching truth, rebuking error, correcting wrong behavior, comforting and encouraging believers, and exhorting people to holiness. Paul's praise here may also, indirectly, demonstrate to us how to praise God. It is, in a sense, a model of praise.

The text proceeds next to the redemptive work of Christ. Teaching is now called for concerning his propitiatory death and his central place in the redemptive purposes of God. Christ is the centerpiece of God's age-long purposes. All things are being brought together under his headship. The doctrinal teaching is again rich, but it is all couched in personal terms. We have been redeemed and forgiven (v. 7), grace has been lavished on us (v. 8), and the mystery of God's purposes has been made known to us by the apostles (v. 9). In terms of the purposes of the Word, we again have a pairing of teaching and comfort.

The same is true in the third section of the text, where the work of the Holy Spirit is emphasized (vv. 13–14). It is we, believers, who are sealed by the Holy Spirit who now lives in us as a foretaste of eternity and a guarantee of our future inheritance. Teaching on the baptism and indwelling of the Spirit must be given here in the most personal terms. Wrong views, such as a two-stage Christian experience, may here be opposed.

It should be apparent that this text, which invites teaching/rebuking coupled with encouraging/exhorting, has only a limited focus on training and correcting behavior and virtually no intent to test or convict of sin. In fact, to use the passage to test and convict (for example, to raise the questions, "Are you praising God enough?") may capture the theological truth of the text but miss the applicatory thrust of the passage. Viewing the text in terms of the four main purposes of the Word helps us to see a message that will seek to apply great biblical doctrine to people as personally as possible, with the purpose of comforting them with God's grace and exhorting them to praise and glorify God for such a great salvation.

This first stage of our preaching process—discerning the intended purposes of the living Word—has allowed us to see many applicatory possibilities in the biblical text. By asking questions about the text in terms of the purposes of God's Word, we are not leaving application to a later addition but are, from the very beginning, seeking to understand the text in terms of what it is intended to do in the lives of those who hear it.

But identifying the purposes of the living Word will not, by itself, enable us to preach sermons that sting and sing. The purposes of God's Word need to be pressed against the realities of people's lives. And the first life they must be pressed against is the preacher's. So next we will look at how the truths of the text are transmitted via the life of the preacher. Only as the purposes of the Word are put through the grid of the preacher's own life can they be communicated to people today with personal force, warmth, and reality. The preacher must be the first to live the application.

DISCUSSION QUESTIONS

1. How can you help your congregation develop an appreciation for biblical *teaching*? What will help them become convinced of the importance and relevance of right doctrine?
2. In recent sermons what "how to" applications have you given to help train your people in areas of Christian living? How could you have expanded that "how to" training?
3. Practice the skill of developing *tests* by outlining several marks of (a) a healthy prayer life and (b) genuine conversion.
4. In what ways have you *encouraged* your congregation recently? What have you praised them for? What strengths of your church have you highlighted?
5. Of the four purposes of God's Word, which ones do you tend to gravitate to and which ones do you find the hardest? Why?
6. Are there other key purposes of God's Word that you don't think are covered by the four categories suggested in this chapter?

| 3 |

THE LIFE OF THE PREACHER: A FULL RESERVOIR

FOR SEVERAL YEARS drought besieged the region in which I live. Despite strict water restrictions, storage levels plummeted to a low of close to just 18 percent of capacity. The effects were devastating for those who lived on the land. Tragically, suicide rates among farmers soared. When the farm is unproductive, the mortgage is huge, and no one wants to buy your land, what do you do? But, over the last two years, the drought has broken. Rains have fallen abundantly and the reservoirs are over 90 percent full. God has been good, though the state government doesn't tend to put it in those terms.

God is also good when he allows a preacher to preach from a full reservoir. Then his people are refreshed and there is a richness and fullness to the preaching ministry. By the reservoir, I mean all that lives within a preacher. All the preacher has read, learned, thought about, observed, suffered, processed, and experienced has the potential to form a rich reservoir out of which much powerful preaching and penetrating application can flow. I say it has the potential to do so. It is not automatic. It is possible to live a full life yet have the reservoir remain almost empty. It is also possible to preach week after week with an empty reservoir, and the result is that people experience drought conditions from the pulpit.

In thinking about a preacher's reservoir, we come to the second stage of the living application preaching process (see diagram 5). The preacher is the conduit through which the message of the living Word is passed to God's people today. If, as a person, the preacher is narrow, warped, twisted, or spiritually malnourished, the truth will get squeezed and distorted as it passes through the conduit. It will be like a blockage in a pipe preventing water from flowing freely.

As a preacher examines the biblical text, there is a very real sense in which it examines him. As he explores the purposes of the Word, those purposes are pressed against his life and all he has experienced. If his reservoir is full, he will begin to shape rich and penetrating applications. It is this stage in the process that makes us recognize that a sermon doesn't take two, ten, or twenty hours to prepare, but two, ten, or twenty years. A sermon is the fruit of who we are as a person, as well as of the study we have done in the week leading up to its preaching.

TEXT AND RESERVOIR

There are really two sources of input for every expository sermon. First, there is the text itself that we squeeze hard for all its juice. We try to extract every drop of truth it contains. We read it, analyze it, pore over it, meditate on it, and savor it in order to bring from it the riches God would have us preach. But central as the text is to expository preaching, it alone does not give us a sermon. We must also pour into the message our own heart and life. Our life reservoir is the second source of input. We speak from the reservoir not by talking lots about ourselves and our experiences, but by interfacing with the truth of the text all that we know about life, so that what we say about the text is grounded in reality, connected to life, and made concrete and specific.

If we have a large reservoir, our mind will be brim full of ideas. When we see a biblical truth, possibilities will start to buzz. We make connections to people, books, events, doctrines, experiences, life. We have, quite spontaneously, illustrative material and applicatory possibilities. We feel the text's sting or balm as we press it against our own experience. And not only does the text lead to the resources in our reservoir, the reservoir leads us to texts and suggests to us themes for sermons and series. Tim Keller comments,

> I believe *many of the best sermons are discovered, not developed.* In other words great sermons often suggest themselves to you—they have a life of their own. Most preachers do virtually all of their study in a completely task-oriented way. They are always studying simply to find material for the next talk or sermon. Instead, there should be lots of "non-directed" study of a variety of areas. It is as you study broadly that new sermon topics and ideas can come to you.[1]

Diagram 5: Stage Two—The Life of the Preacher

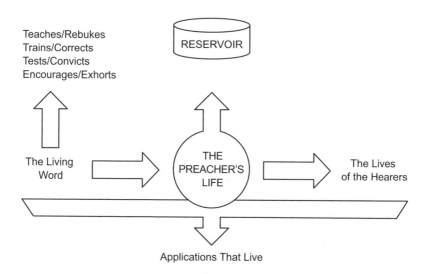

Have you ever wondered how some of the great preachers of the past managed to preach six, eight, or ten times a week? Most of us struggle with two sermons. I suspect they managed to because they had

1. Timothy Keller, "A Model for Preaching (Part One)," *Journal of Biblical Counseling* 12, no. 3 (1994): 39 (italics in original).

huge reservoirs from which to draw. They interfaced their study of the Bible with a profound grasp of theology, depth of pastoral experience, and significant insights into the human heart, backed by voluminous reading that made them men of learning. Their reservoirs were massive and they kept them topped up.

Filling the Tank

If we are to prepare sermons from these two sources week after week, we will need to keep the reservoir full. There are, I believe, four main ways in which we can fill the tank.

First, it is filled by our own walk with God. Older works on preaching always placed immense emphasis on the preacher as a person. Understanding, as Phillips Brooks so famously put it, that preaching is truth conveyed through personality, they believed that the forming of the person was of paramount importance.[2] It is so significant that Keller contends, "A man's spiritual vitality is such a critical aspect of preaching that it can create great preaching despite a poor sermon. On the other hand, the lack of this personal vitality can destroy preaching despite the presence of a good sermon."[3]

The nineteenth-century Scottish preacher James Stalker presented the *Yale Lectures on Preaching* in 1891. He put the case for spiritual vitality in a most compelling way, and in a way typical of how older works speak of preaching. I will quote him at length despite his rather quaint language:

> Valuable as an initial call may be, it will not do to trade too long on such a memory. A ministry of growing power must be one of growing experience. The soul must be in touch with God and enjoy golden hours of fresh revelation. The truth must come to the minister as the satisfaction of his own needs and the answer to his own perplexities;

2. Phillips Brooks, *Lectures on Preaching: Delivered Before the Divinity School of Yale College in January and February 1877* (London: Allenson, 1895), 8.

3. Timothy Keller, "A Model for Preaching (Part Three)," *Journal of Biblical Counseling* 13, no. 2 (1995): 51.

and he must be able to use the language of religion, not as the nearest equivalent he can find for that which he believes others to be passing through, but as the exact equivalent of that which he has passed through himself. There are many rules for praying in public, and a competent minister will not neglect them; but there is one rule worth all the rest put together, and it is this: Be a man of prayer yourself; and then the congregation will feel, as you open your lips to lead their devotions, that you are entering an accustomed presence and speaking to a well-known Friend. There are arts of study by which the contents of the Bible can be made available for the edification of others, but this is the best rule: Study God's Word diligently for your own edification and then, when it has become more to you than your necessary food and sweeter than honey or the honeycomb, it will be impossible for you to speak of it to others without a glow passing into your words which will betray the delight with which it has inspired yourself.[4]

These emphases on prayer, Bible study, and personal experience of God are too easily lost by our can-do ministry attitude, our rich array of Bible and church resources, and our constant busyness. Eugene Peterson, in *The Contemplative Pastor*, refreshingly spoke of "the unbusy pastor" who refuses to let his worth be evaluated by how busy he is or allow other people to set his agenda. In place of the endless string of meetings and commitments to which most pastors succumb, he argues for a pastor being given to praying, preaching, and listening.[5] Unless we are prepared to deal with the relentless pace of church leadership, we will most likely find that our own soul slowly withers and our body wears out. While complete burnout may not be inevitable, spiritual leanness in our preaching is.

The point of stressing Bible reading and prayer is not to enforce evangelical duty for the sake of it but to promote intimate dealings with God. We need to know God as well as we can. We seek to know his discipline and admonition, his grace and favor, his typical ways of dealing

4. James Stalker, *The Preacher and His Models: The Yale Lectures on Preaching, 1891* (London: Hodder and Stoughton, 1891), 53–54.

5. Eugene H. Peterson, *The Contemplative Pastor: Returning to the Art of Spiritual Direction* (Grand Rapids: Eerdmans, 1989), 17–23.

with us, his power, patience, gentleness, and sternness. We want to be familiar with him but never overly familiar. We covet the kind of soul experiences Paul describes—inexpressible joy, the hope of glory, power in weakness, the sufficiency of God's grace, and the secret of contentment.

If our walk with God is slight and superficial, most likely our dealing with biblical texts will be slight and superficial. This is simply a natural consequence that applies in every sphere of life. My knowledge of cars is abysmal. Recently, someone asked me whether my car was a twin cam. I knew I should know the answer but, to be honest, I haven't a clue and I can't remember what that even is. Pathetic, for sure, but that's the truth. I can't talk cars for ten minutes, because I don't know cars. Some people can't talk heart religion for ten minutes, because they don't know it. But that should never be the case with a preacher.

A close walk with God leads not only to knowing God but to knowing ourselves. This is one of the greatest aids to application. Our own heart becomes our main index for looking up the things other people need to address. If I preach to my own sins, I usually connect with other people because "no temptation has seized you except what is common to man" (1 Cor. 10:13). If I understand my own heart, I have a good sense of how other people's hearts work.[6] If I know the varying conditions of my own soul, I have greater insight into the conditions of other people's souls. We will know from experience the way temptation works, the deceptiveness of the heart, the difficulty of staying on course, the joy of sins forgiven, the peace that comes from being right with God, the joy of seeing people saved, and a thousand other spiritual realities.

The second means of filling the tank is experiencing life richly. Thankfully, God does not have a utilitarian approach to life. In the beginning,

---

6. Dale Ralph Davis quotes Alexander Whyte, who said, "Look into your own sinful heart, and back into your sinful life, and around on the world full of sin and misery, and open your New Testament, and make applications of Christ to yourself and your people." Davis then adds, "If a preacher has a lively sense of his own depravity, he won't have much trouble applying Scripture." George Freeland Barbour, *The Life of Alexander Whyte* (London: Hodder and Stoughton, 1923), 307–8, quoted in Dale Ralph Davis, *The Word Became Fresh: How to Preach from Old Testament Narrative Texts* (Fearn: Christian Focus, 2006), 93.

he placed Adam and Eve in a garden, not a desert. They were surrounded by beautiful trees, rivers, and animals. They needed to eat to sustain their bodies, but they weren't just given tablets to take each day; they were given exotic fruits. They were to procreate, but God made the sexual relationship immensely pleasurable. They were to work the garden, but their work was good and rewarding. In time, as the couple became a family and then a people, they formed relationships, made musical instruments, fashioned tools, and developed cultures. Of course, after the fall, every pursuit was tainted by sin, but the pursuits still bore the stamp of pleasure, beauty, and value. Much later, Paul could impress upon the pagan crowd at Lystra that God "has shown kindness by giving you rain from heaven and crops in their seasons; he provides you with plenty of food and fills your hearts with joy" (Acts 14:17). In a similar vein, the psalmist had written,

> He makes grass grow for the cattle,
>   and plants for man to cultivate—
>   bringing forth food from the earth:
> wine that gladdens the heart of man,
>   oil to make his face shine,
>   and bread that sustains his heart. (Ps. 104:14–15)

Therefore, God intends us to enjoy this world and all he has provided for us. Paul teaches that everything is to be received with thanksgiving, to the pure all things are pure, and God provides us with everything for our enjoyment. There is a right and holy way of enjoying everything God has given us: music, food, drink, sex, clothes, movies, sports, recreation, the outdoors, hobbies . . . everything. Of course, idolatry always stands knocking at the door, taking that which is good and so exalting it that it replaces the God who gave it to us. But, while that danger lurks, it should not prevent us from seeking to enjoy life in the right way.

Our own enjoyment of life can bring richness to our preaching in two ways. The lesser way is that it allows us to speak of those things that every other person in the congregation also experiences. If they are all watching movies, eating great food, making choices about fashion, enjoying the great outdoors, traveling to exotic locations, and experiencing the ups and downs of friendships, they will warm to our preaching when it relates to life as they know it. We are not to act as if it is more holy to be cut off from aesthetic beauty. A life lived richly will allow us to connect to listeners, illustrate truths, warn of dangers, and encourage enjoyment of God's good world. Jesus' preaching did just that. His parables were drawn from the world his hearers knew: wedding feasts, losing and finding possessions, farming, fishing, parenting, partying, and so on.

But there is a second and more significant way in which our enjoyment of life can enrich our preaching. When we live life to the full, we more consistently live with a view that embraces the world and all of life as being God's domain. We are not operating as cloistered monks who think it is more holy to be in church than in the workplace, more spiritual to pray than to play, more godly to avoid the world than to engage it. Rather, we live a worldview that confesses God's sovereign reign over all of life so that there is no divide between sacred and secular. All of life is an offering to God. As Abraham Kuyper famously said, "There is not a square inch in the whole domain of our human existence over which Christ, who is sovereign over *all*, does not cry: 'Mine!'"[7] There is no activity or place that is not to be consecrated to him. He owns and claims all.

Preachers must both believe and live this theology, and then it must filter through into all their preaching application. Because a kingdom worldview is so important to holistic life application, I will return to this theme in chapter 7. For now, we should simply note that living life richly is reflective of God's kingdom purposes in this world. And if we are going to preach it, we must also live it.

The third way to keep the tank full is by learning to be close observers of life. A lady I know, who before her conversion was a scriptwriter for

---

7. Abraham Kuyper, "Sphere Sovereignty" (lecture, Free University of Amsterdam, Amsterdam, Netherlands, 1880), in *Abraham Kuyper: A Centennial Reader*, ed. James D. Bratt (Grand Rapids: Eerdmans, 1998), 488.

TV soaps, said that every conversation, every relationship, every party, every activity became grist for her story-writing mill. In a way this is true for preachers as well. Preachers must be keen observers of life. From their marriage, their children's lives, their friendships, pastoral work, one-off interactions with people at a shop or business, engagement with others in sports or hobbies, preachers can observe how life actually goes for people. They can see the things people struggle with, the passions they pursue, the choices they make, the problems they encounter.

When we speak of spiritual truth in relation to real life, people resonate with what we say. We may speak about different ways in which temptation may come to us, and people think, "Okay, I'm not the only one who struggles with that." As we speak with some reality about people's struggles with pride, the difficulty of pure motives, or the joys of deep friendship, people find that we're putting into words their own experiences. If we speak of anxiety, stress, and pressure, or fun, love, and success, people appreciate the fact that we live in the same world as they do and that we can relate the world of the Bible to it.

Life experience and observation also enables us to offer seasoned advice. Preachers often need to say things that are neither absolute biblical commands nor invariable rules or requirements. They are just advice from someone who is not completely wet behind the ears. People go to their doctor expecting sound advice about health, diet, and lifestyle; they go to their lawyer expecting sound advice about legal matters, estates, and wills; they go to a mechanic expecting good advice about what to look for in buying a used car; and they should be able to go to a preacher expecting sound advice about life—how to live and die well.

So how is life for Joe and Jane Average? Well, for one thing, unless they are in a retirement village, it is probably busy. Juggling responsibilities is hard, work hours are long, commuting times can be excessive, kids are demanding, and sometimes the pressure is immense. Life is expensive, too. Mortgages and other debts, driven by compulsive consumerism, pressurize marriages and call for excessive working hours. Life is also complicated. The array of choices that confront us in every arena of life is bamboozling. We can but dream of the simple life. Relationships are complicated, too. When they are good, they are very, very good; when they are bad, they are horrid. I remember visiting a man for a long period of time who had suffered a complete mental and emotional meltdown after the breakup of his marriage. Divorce rates may be up, but that does not mean that it's all water off a duck's back when someone goes through one. So, another reality is that life for many is depressing. We have a higher standard of living than ever before, but we also consume antidepressants at a disturbing rate. And then there are the kids on Ritalin, the women having HRT, and the men bombarded with ads for Viagra. Life is also technologically driven: the Internet, emails, iPods, mobile phones, Twitter, Skype, movies, pay TV. . . . The ways in which people engage with technology is seemingly endless. Teenagers will most likely use half a dozen of these at the same time while they do their homework.

We could go on. These are just a few of the realities people live with from day to day. Sermons need to be connected to life as it really is for people in the pew. This is precisely why topical preaching has become so popular. It connects. It has relevance. It is practical. But if the expository preacher will connect biblical truth to the realities of people's lives, it can be just as connected, relevant, and practical. This is done by holding up our contemporary experiences alongside the experiences described in the biblical text.[8] If our preaching doesn't do so, we shortchange our hearers. We need not become pop psychologists, dispensing three steps here and four there for happiness, success, or victory. But we do want people to live well, to cope with life, to make right choices, and to live countercultural gospel lives. If we can't connect the dots between biblical truth and life as it really is, what makes us think our people will after the sermon?

8. Zack Eswine, in *Preaching to a Post-Everything World*, speaks of the "under the sun" realities of the seasons and situations contained in the biblical record: towns, cities, families, and traditions; angels, demons, languages, and sickness; health, love, relationships, and governments; art, technology, wealth, and poverty; law, justice, injustice, and nature; weather, feasting, celebration, and institutions are the "under the sun" realities he identifies in the book of Ecclesiastes. If we look for such realities in the text we are dealing with and compare them to similar realities today, we begin to ground the world of the text in our world today. There is, after all, nothing new under the sun. See Zack Eswine, *Preaching to a Post-Everything World: Crafting Biblical Sermons That Connect with Our Culture* (Grand Rapids: Baker, 2008), 27.

Older writers called this *experimental preaching*. Joel Beeke explains it well.

> Experimental or experiential preaching addresses how a Christian experiences the truth of Christian doctrine in his life. The term experimental comes from *experimentum*, meaning trial, and is derived from the verb, *experior*, to know by experience, which in turn leads to "experiential," meaning knowledge gained by experiment. Calvin used experimental and experiential interchangeably, since both words indicate the need for measuring experienced knowledge against the touchstone of Scripture. Experimental preaching seeks to explain in terms of biblical truth how matters ought to go, how they do go, and what is the goal of the Christian life. It aims to apply divine truth to the whole range of the believer's personal experiences as well as in his relationships with family, the church, and the world around him.[9]

The entire living application model is designed to produce this kind of experimental application; and consideration of life as it actually is, as we draw on our own close observation of life, is a key element of such preaching.

The final way in which we can fill the tank is through our knowledge of theology, church, and culture. Preachers are usually readers for good reason. They study and learn from others. One of the benefits of attending a theological college or seminary is that it gives a head start on filling the reservoir. Students are immersed in the study of God's Word and theology, in church history and practical theology. They are forced to read. They are given a biblical-theological framework within which to work.[10]

9. Joel R. Beeke, "William Perkins on Predestination, Preaching, and Conversion," *The Practical Calvinist*, ed. Peter A. Lillback (Fearn: Christian Focus, 2002), 207, quoted in James M. Garretson, *Princeton and Preaching: Archibald Alexander and the Christian Ministry* (Edinburgh: Banner of Truth, 2005), 3.

10. Phillip Jensen argues well for the place theology has in shaping preaching. It is impossible for us to come to a text without a theological framework with which to approach it, and, while each text must test and refine our theology, theology inevitably shapes our

Following formal study, ministers of God's Word ought to continue a disciplined program of reading and study. Keller recommends reading in five core areas: the Bible (he advocates reading the Bible at least once a year and also studying books of the Bible for ourselves), theology, church history, sermons and "experimental" works (which he says are "an absolute must!"), and cultural analysis and apologetics (including reading magazines on contemporary trends and viewing key movies).[11] Preachers should aim at an appropriate balance in these five areas and make time to do so. The plethora of books on church leadership, for example, could easily absorb all of a pastor's reading time. But if that happens, imbalance will develop in his preaching ministry because of his neglect of theology, church history, and perhaps even the Bible itself. The time required to read broadly is considerable, and unless it is locked in to a pastor's schedule it is unlikely to happen. So preachers should allocate some fixed time, whether it be a morning a week, or an hour a day, or some other time slot of several hours, knowing that such time is not wasted but is an investment for the long haul. We must be "unbusy" enough to do so.

Working from a Full Reservoir

A full tank helps to produce sermons full of insight, perspective, and wisdom. This stage of the preaching process encourages us to examine the biblical text from the perspective of our own walk with God, our experience of life, our observations of people and the world around us, and our study of theology, church, and culture. With a full reservoir, we begin to think both more broadly and more specifically about the application of biblical truth.

With our reservoir, however, it is never a case of once full, always full. We are constantly drawing on the supply, and that which we don't draw on stagnates or slowly seeps away. We cannot minister effectively

---

interpretation. Without a strong theology, a preacher is ill-equipped to preach. See Phillip D. Jensen and Paul Grimmond, *The Archer and the Arrow: Preaching the Very Words of God* (Kingsford, New South Wales: Matthias Media, 2010), 65–84.

11. Keller, "A Model for Preaching (Part One)," 39.

from past spiritual experiences, past reading, or merely prior knowledge. Freshness and vitality come from continually replenishing the supply. Once we stop growing, our ministry ceases to have an impact. Weekly, monthly, and annual deposits need to be made into the reservoir, or drought will return even after seasons of blessing.

If our reservoir is full, the interface of the text and our life should be like the rubbing of metal against metal. Sparks should fly. The text will prod and prompt us, speak to us, and stir us. We need to engage with the Bible spiritually, not just technically. Similarly, our lives will bring issues to bear on the text. Our reservoirs will supply us with questions, illustrations, and examples. The result is that text and reservoir together will prompt richer life application.

But this does not happen automatically. The four ways of filling the tank discussed above must be combined with a measured reflectiveness. It is not by chance that a fair proportion of preachers, past and present, have been introverts. Preachers need to reflect on their own walk with God, on life and all it offers, on the experiences of other people, and on what they read. You can live a full life, read many books, meet lots of great people, and do many things, but if you never stop to think and process, your reservoir will be drained, not replenished. It is as we reflect on life that experience is turned into wisdom and observation into insight. Great preaching is marked by both. Without spiritual processing of all we see and do, we will likely remain shallow and superficial.

It is also necessary that we take time during the sermon preparation process to consciously interface the text and our reservoir in a prayerful way. We have seen that the development of living application in preaching cannot be rushed. Saturday night is not a good time to begin. For me, the crux moment in sermon preparation is often somewhere in the middle of the process, after I have exegeted the text and before I have begun to write my sermon notes. Often I take a long walk. I am a strong believer in peripatetic sermon preparation! That is my favorite time for thinking, praying, processing, drawing from the reservoir, and interfacing text and life. It is frequently the point at which the message starts to come together. Sometimes whole sermons form during my walk and I rush home to make some notes.

As we are preparing in this way, interfacing the text and our life reservoir, we will have on our mind the people to whom we will speak. We must not be confined to how the text speaks to us, though it is an essential starting point. Our chief concern is with how God is going to speak to his people. So, next, we will turn to where the entire preaching process is headed: the lives of those who hear God's Word. In studying God's Word and mining it for ourselves, we must not be selfish. We've been set aside to mine the text for others, too. James Stalker again put this in a wonderful way:

> I like to think of the minister as only one of the congregation set apart by the rest for a particular purpose. A congregation is a number of people associated for their moral and spiritual improvement. And they say to one of their number, Look, brother, we are busy with our daily toils and confused with domestic and worldly cares; we live in confusion and darkness; but we eagerly long for peace and light to cheer and illuminate our life; and we have heard there is a land where these are to be found—a land of repose and joy, full of thoughts that breathe and words that burn: but we cannot go thither ourselves; we are too embroiled in daily cares: come, we will elect you, and set you free from our toils, and you shall go thither for us, and week by week trade with that land and bring us its treasures and its spoils. Oh, woe to him who accepts this election, and yet, failing through idleness to carry on the noble merchandise, appears week by week empty-handed or with merely counterfeit treasure in his hands! Woe to him, too, if, going to that land, he forgets those who sent him and spends his time there in selfish enjoyment of the delights of knowledge! Woe to him if he does not week by week return laden, and ever more richly laden, and saying, Yes, brothers, I have been to that land; and it is a land of light and peace and nobleness: but I have never forgotten you and your needs and the dear bonds of brotherhood; and look, I have brought back this, and this, and this: take them to gladden and purify your life![12]

12. Stalker, *The Preacher and His Models*, 282–83.

DISCUSSION QUESTIONS

1. Do you feel that you are currently ministering from a full reservoir, or are you running on empty? What accounts for the current state of your reservoir?

2. How are you developing your own relationship with God? Are there measures you need to take to prioritize it and ensure that it is not swamped by ministry demands?

3. What activities, friendships, interests, and pursuits do you have that help to enrich your experience of life and your preaching about life?

4. What did older writers mean by the term "experimental preaching"? Why is this kind of preaching so important?

5. How well are you doing in being regular and intentional in serious reading that includes theology, church history, and cultural analysis?

6. What militates against the deeply reflective approach to life and sermon preparation that is necessary for rich application in preaching?

| 4 |

THE LIVES OF OUR HEARERS: THE HEART IS THE TARGET

I HAVE A FRIEND who regularly goes deer hunting. Not just for the fun of it, he tells me, but to keep the freezer well stocked with venison. From time to time, he turns up at our home group with another hunting adventure to report on. So I asked him one night what part of a deer he aims at when he's shooting. Not being a hunter, I wondered whether you aim for the head or the heart. I learned that while you could aim for the head, it is a low percentage shot; it's too risky. It's better to aim behind the shoulder, or at the chest or the neck, where your chances of hitting vital organs are much higher. A shot into the heart or lungs will drop the deer.

As a preacher, however, I don't have to choose between shooting for the head or the heart. That's because biblical anthropology is rather different from deer anatomy. In biblical thinking, the heart is not the physical organ that pumps blood around the body, nor is it simply the emotional center of our being, as we often think of it in the West. In Hebraic thought, the heart is the core of our entire being. It is the center and soul of who we are, comprising the seat of all our thoughts, feelings, and actions. The heart is the real us. So when you shoot at the heart, you are shooting at the whole person, including their thinking and their feeling. In other words, shoot at the heart and you get the head as well.

Diagram 6: Stage Three—The Lives of the Hearers: Faculties of the Heart

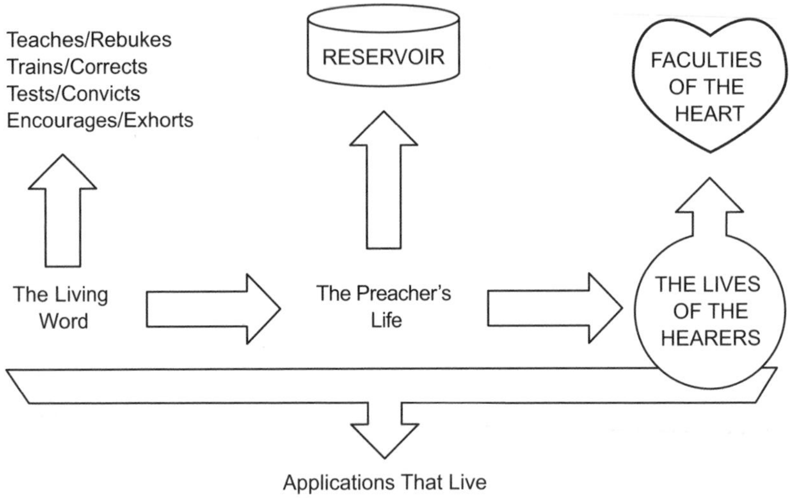

THE HUMAN HEART

In considering the human heart we come to the third part of the living application preaching process (see diagram 6). The intended applications of the living Word, spoken by the preacher in the light of his own experience, must be pressed on the lives of those who hear the Word. To do this effectively, a preacher needs, with the enabling of the Spirit, to "get inside" people. He does not want to speak in a way that makes people feel that the truths are largely detached from them, but in a way that shows the truths to be real and relevant.

Two things will aid that. First, preachers need to understand the human heart and how to address it. The Bible repeatedly talks about the heart, and it is essential that we understand what it really is and how to preach from the heart to the heart. This chapter will explore that in some detail. Second, preachers need to think broadly and deeply about the life situations into which they speak, with a particular focus on the spiritual conditions of individuals and churches. That will be the concern of the next chapter.

Our first concern, then, is with understanding the human heart, and, in particular, with how to speak to the faculties of the heart.

In Matthew 22:37, Jesus identifies the first and greatest command of the Bible as that which is found in Deuteronomy 6:5—"Love the LORD your God with all your *heart* and with all your *soul* and with all your *strength*." When he cites this, however, he says God is to be loved "with all your *heart* and with all your *soul* and with all your *mind*." *Strength* is replaced with *mind*. In Mark and Luke, *mind* is added to the other three, and so he speaks of loving God with heart, soul, mind, and strength.

These four words together speak of the sum total of our being. With all that we are physically, emotionally, and intellectually we are to love God. Our thoughts, affections, strength, abilities, and passions are to be bent toward him and his glory. We are to love him with all that we are and all that is within us. The shorthand for this is to say that we are to love him "from the heart" and, if that is the greatest command, it is surely the great thing at which preaching should be aiming. The end goal of preaching is to draw people to love God with all their heart.

True gospel living is always driven from the heart. Christianity is not a religion of mere external practice or outward ritual, but a faith that revolves around personal relationship with God—a relationship in which all our thoughts, motives, desires, and actions are increasingly directed toward him and his glory. The heart, however, is naturally in a state of spiritual deadness. It is not calibrated to love God as it ought but is desperately corrupt and inclined toward evil. The great need of every man, woman, and child is a new heart that is completely reprogrammed. We need God's law to be written on our hearts so that we both desire and are enabled to obey God sincerely.

This is not only our great need but also the great work of the gospel. By the power of the Holy Spirit and through the work of Jesus Christ, God is able to give us a new heart that is capable of responding to him with love and faithfulness.

There are no fewer than 858 occurrences of the Hebrew words for heart (*leb* and *lebab*)[1] in the Old Testament and 160 uses of the Greek equivalent (*kardia*) in the New Testament. The vast majority of these uses refer to the central core, the inner being of the person. From this extensive usage, some dominant themes and emphases stand out. Early in the biblical narrative we are told that

> The LORD saw how great man's wickedness on the earth had become, and that every inclination of the thoughts of his heart was only evil all the time. (Gen. 6:5)

However, God's covenant people were called to set their hearts on God.

> But if from there you seek the LORD your God, you will find him if you look for him with all your heart and with all your soul. (Deut. 4:29)

> Love the LORD your God with all your heart and with all your soul and with all your strength. These commandments that I give you today are to be upon your hearts. (Deut. 6:5–6)

> Circumcise your hearts, therefore, and do not be stiff-necked any longer. (Deut. 10:16)

Samuel was reminded that the Lord is concerned about the heart of a man, not his external appearance.

1. See Sinclair B. Ferguson, "Preaching to the Heart," in *Feed My Sheep: A Passionate Plea for Preaching*, ed. Don Kistler (Morgan: Soli Deo Gloria, 2002), 192.

But the LORD said to Samuel, "Do not consider his appearance or his height, for I have rejected him. The LORD does not look at the things man looks at. Man looks at the outward appearance, but the LORD looks at the heart." (1 Sam. 16:7)

The Psalms and Proverbs speak often of the heart in terms such as these:

I will praise you, O LORD, with all my heart;
    I will tell of all your wonders. (Ps. 9:1)

Create in me a pure heart, O God,
    and renew a steadfast spirit within me. (Ps. 51:10)

Trust in the LORD with all your heart
    and lean not on your own understanding. (Prov. 3:5)

Above all else, guard your heart,
    for it is the wellspring of life. (Prov. 4:23)

The prophets speak of the new heart that God will give his people.

"This is the covenant I will make with the house of Israel
    after that time," declares the LORD.
"I will put my law in their minds
    and write it on their hearts.
I will be their God,
    and they will be my people." (Jer. 31:33)

I will give you a new heart and put a new spirit in you; I will remove from you your heart of stone and give you a heart of flesh. (Ezek. 36:26)

Jesus himself often referred to the heart, highlighting its centrality to our entire life and our response to God.

You brood of vipers, how can you who are evil say anything good?
For out of the overflow of the heart the mouth speaks. (Matt. 12:34)

These people honor me with their lips,
    but their hearts are far from me. (Matt. 15:8)

Don't you see that whatever enters the mouth goes into the stomach
and then out of the body? But the things that come out of the mouth
come from the heart, and these make a man "unclean." For out of
the heart come evil thoughts, murder, adultery, sexual immorality,
theft, false testimony, slander. These are what make a man "unclean."
(Matt. 15:17–20)

On the day of Pentecost, Peter preached powerfully from the
prophet Joel and from Psalm 16, and the impact was felt at the level
of the heart.

When the people heard this, they were cut to the heart and said
to Peter and the other apostles, "Brothers, what shall we do?"
(Acts 2:37)

Acts also records Lydia's conversion in these words:

One of those listening was a woman named Lydia, a dealer in purple
cloth from the city of Thyatira, who was a worshiper of God. The
Lord opened her heart to respond to Paul's message. (Acts 16:14)

Paul repeatedly speaks of the heart in his epistles, calling always
for a heart response to God.

A man is a Jew if he is one inwardly; and circumcision is circumcision of the heart, by the Spirit, not by the written code. Such a man's
praise is not from men, but from God. (Rom. 2:29)

If you confess with your mouth, "Jesus is Lord," and believe in your
heart that God raised him from the dead, you will be saved. For it is

with your heart that you believe and are justified, and it is with your mouth that you confess and are saved. (Rom. 10:9)

I pray also that the eyes of your heart may be enlightened in order that you may know the hope to which he has called you, the riches of his glorious inheritance in the saints. (Eph. 1:18)

Finally, the epistle to the Hebrews speaks of the heart as that which is searched and known by God and cleansed by him.

For the word of God is living and active. Sharper than any double-edged sword, it penetrates even to dividing soul and spirit, joints and marrow; it judges the thoughts and attitudes of the heart. (Heb. 4:12)

Let us draw near to God with a sincere heart in full assurance of faith, having our hearts sprinkled to cleanse us from a guilty conscience and having our bodies washed with pure water. (Heb. 10:22)

This litany of verses clearly highlights the central place the heart has in biblical anthropology and, therefore, in biblical spirituality. Clearly, any preacher who wants to make an impact will want to preach to the heart. But how is that done? What will enable access to the human heart? How do you preach so as to touch, move, or stir the heart?

The most helpful tool for the preacher aiming at the heart is to consider the various faculties of the heart. The human heart is best understood as consisting of the core faculties of mind, conscience, will, and passions. In diagram 7, these four faculties are depicted in a particular configuration. The *mind* is at the top as the entrance point of the soul; the *passions* are at the bottom as the deepest part of the soul. In between are the *conscience* and *will*, which are affected by the mind and the passions. An understanding of these faculties and how they work together will aid the preacher in aiming at the heart.

Diagram 7: Faculties of the Heart

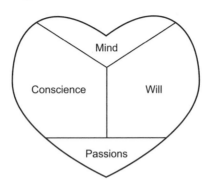

THE MIND

We have already seen that in Hebraic thinking the heart includes the mind—the rational center of our being. It is not surprising, then, that in the New Testament, heart Christianity has a strong focus on our minds, which are depraved and darkened before conversion, but renewed and focused on God afterward. Paul graphically describes the state of the unregenerate mind:

> Furthermore, since they did not think it worthwhile to retain the knowledge of God, he gave them over to a depraved mind, to do what ought not to be done. (Rom. 1:28)

> The mind of sinful man is death. (Rom. 8:6)

> Once you were alienated from God and were enemies in your minds because of your evil behavior. (Col. 1:21)

> So I tell you this, and insist on it in the Lord, that you must no longer live as the Gentiles do, in the futility of their thinking. They are darkened in their understanding and separated from the life of God because of the ignorance that is in them due to the hardening of their hearts. (Eph. 4:17–18)

It is interesting that, in this last verse, a close connection is made between a darkened, futile mind and a hard heart. The former is a part of the latter. Similarly, the two are simultaneously changed in regeneration.

104

Once we have been given a new heart, our entire life is transformed by the renewing of our mind:

> Do not conform any longer to the pattern of this world, but be transformed by the renewing of your mind. Then you will be able to test and approve what God's will is—his good, pleasing and perfect will. (Rom. 12:2)

> Set your minds on things above, not on earthly things. (Col. 3:2)

> Finally, brothers, whatever is true, whatever is noble, whatever is right, whatever is pure, whatever is lovely, whatever is admirable—if anything is excellent or praiseworthy—think about such things. (Phil. 4:8)

The renewed mind reflects the mind of Christ. It thinks new thoughts, dwells on new things, and has new understanding. It is for this reason that we find so much reasoning and teaching in the New Testament epistles. Paul, in particular, wanted people to understand the truth and be transformed by it. He didn't want them to be ignorant, because godly living flows from right understanding. His chief concern was to speak intelligently, to the mind, so that people would be edified:

> For if I pray in a tongue, my spirit prays, but my mind is unfruitful. So what shall I do? I will pray with my spirit, but I will also pray with my mind; I will sing with my spirit, but I will also sing with my mind. If you are praising God with your spirit, how can one who finds himself among those who do not understand say "Amen" to your thanksgiving, since he does not know what you are saying? You may be giving thanks well enough, but the other man is not edified.
> I thank God that I speak in tongues more than all of you. But in the church I would rather speak five intelligible words to instruct others than ten thousand words in a tongue. (1 Cor. 14:14–19)

It is not somehow spiritual to bypass the mind. An intellectual understanding of God and of revealed truth is the entrance point to the other faculties of the heart. The mind comes first, but we must always go further.

THE CONSCIENCE

> To the pure, all things are pure, but to those who are corrupted and do not believe, nothing is pure. In fact, both their minds and consciences are corrupted. (Titus 1:15)

Alongside the problem of a depraved mind, Paul here places the evil of a defiled conscience. The conscience is the faculty of the heart that bears testimony to God's law within us, either condemning us with feelings of guilt or defending us with a sense of our righteousness:

> (Indeed, when Gentiles, who do not have the law, do by nature things required by the law, they are a law for themselves, even though they do not have the law, since they show that the requirements of the law are written on their hearts, their consciences also bearing witness, and their thoughts now accusing, now even defending them.) This will take place on the day when God will judge men's secrets through Jesus Christ, as my gospel declares. (Rom. 2:14–16)

The conscience is the smoke alarm of the heart. At home, we have a smoke alarm in the kitchen that goes off frequently. The slightest burning of the toast and it blares. It's annoying, but far better than a smoke alarm with no batteries. A fire could be raging and such a smoke alarm wouldn't raise the faintest bleep. Some people's consciences are like oversensitive smoke alarms, making them feel guilty when they have done nothing wrong. Other people's consciences are like alarms with no batteries. They have seared consciences, allowing them to act in the most evil ways without any scruples.

> The Spirit clearly says that in later times some will abandon the faith and follow deceiving spirits and things taught by demons. Such teachings come through hypocritical liars, whose consciences have been seared as with a hot iron. (1 Tim. 4:1–2)

The more frequently people act against their consciences, the more the sound of the alarm will be dampened, until eventually they can sin without wincing. But in regeneration, that suddenly changes. The conscience is awakened as the Holy Spirit works within us to convict us of sin and to show us our true standing before God.

> When he comes, he will convict the world of guilt in regard to sin and righteousness and judgment. (John 16:8)

That was what happened on the day of Pentecost when the Jews were "cut to the heart" (Acts 2:37), realizing that they had murdered the promised Messiah. The Spirit also convinces us of the truth of the gospel so that we do not merely believe in an intellectual way, but are utterly persuaded of its truth. The gospel becomes for us a deep conviction, as in the case of the Thessalonians.

> We always thank God for all of you. . . .
>   Because our gospel came to you not simply with words, but also with power, with the Holy Spirit, and with deep conviction. (1 Thess. 1:2, 5)

Even among believers the state of the conscience varies. Some believers have a "strong" conscience, allowing them to exercise greater Christian liberty. The alarm doesn't go off for toast. Others have a weaker conscience, feeling less freedom in matters not clearly defined by God's Word. The alarm goes off very readily. Paul addresses this in Romans 14.

> One man's faith allows him to eat everything, but another man, whose faith is weak, eats only vegetables. . . .
>   One man considers one day more sacred than another; another man considers every day alike. Each one should be fully convinced in his own mind. . . .
>   Therefore let us stop passing judgment on one another. Instead, make up your mind not to put any stumbling block or obstacle in your brother's way. . . .

So whatever you believe about these things keep between yourself and God. Blessed is the man who does not condemn himself by what he approves. But the man who has doubts is condemned if he eats, because his eating is not from faith; and everything that does not come from faith is sin. (Rom. 14:2, 5, 13, 22–23)

As long as we remain sinners, the conscience is not an entirely accurate gauge of our relationship to God's law. Nonetheless, it is an important gauge and we are not to act contrary to it. We must allow God's Word to guide and inform our conscience so that it increasingly conforms to his will. We can then live with a clear conscience before God and man, as Paul often claims to do, and we can also put our hearts at rest as we depend on Christ's grace. John writes,

This then is how we know that we belong to the truth, and how we set our hearts at rest in his presence whenever our hearts condemn us. For God is greater than our hearts, and he knows everything. (1 John 3:19–20)

We have seen, then, that truth enters the heart via the mind and must be pressed on the conscience so that it is felt. But heart work goes further and elicits a response, which is the domain of the will.

THE WILL

The Bible views us not as robotic beings but as people with the God-given capacity to choose, to make decisions, and to act. Our choices and actions are a function of our will, but our will always reflects the state of our heart. As Jesus said, "Out of the overflow of the heart the mouth speaks" (Matt. 12:34). The unregenerate heart is always expressed in choices and actions that are, at the end of the day, wicked and rebellious. It chooses for self and against God. After regeneration, we are enabled to live in increasing conformity to God's will and we are constantly urged to do so. We are called to "put off" the old self and "put on" the new:

You were taught, with regard to your former way of life, to put off your old self, which is being corrupted by its deceitful desires; to be made

108

new in the attitude of your minds; and to put on the new self, created
to be like God in true righteousness and holiness. (Eph. 4:22–24)

Putting off the old self and putting on the new is an act of the will, but here
it is again connected to the state of our mind. As our minds are renewed and
our hearts are recreated in the image of God, our actions change. It is, therefore, to be expected that as people hear biblical preaching and their minds are
renewed with the truth, action will follow. James rightly says, "Do not merely
listen to the word, and so deceive yourselves. Do what it says" (James 1:22).

Similarly, Jesus also urges action in response to his preaching. At
the end of the Sermon on the Mount, he warns his hearers that not to
put his teaching into practice is to be like a foolish person building on
sand. Wisdom is to hear and then put into practice what he says.

Repeatedly, the New Testament calls us to action: to pray, to serve,
to love, to give, to grow in godly virtues, to obey God's law, and so on.
We are to offer our bodies as living sacrifices to God and, with renewed
minds, we are to live transformed, not worldly, lives. The law written on
the heart is the law that teaches us not to steal, nor to commit adultery,
nor to bear false witness, nor to hate, nor to covet. And, with renewed
hearts, we begin to walk in the new life God has created for us, "For
we are God's workmanship, created in Christ Jesus to do good works,
which God prepared in advance for us to do" (Eph. 2:10).

Preachers will frequently aim their applications at the will. In fact,
many preachers aim their applications only at the will, forgetting the
other faculties of the heart. They reduce application to telling people
what to do. Living application will lead us to address the other faculties
of the heart as well, but the will must never be neglected.

Yet even when the mind, conscience, and will have been addressed,
the work of speaking to the heart is not complete.

THE PASSIONS

The final core faculty of the heart to remember in developing
holistic application is the capacity God has given us to feel things deeply.
We are people who love and hate, who hope and fear, who rejoice and

grieve, who are bold or cowardly, who strongly desire some things and inwardly recoil from others. We find in our hearts deep passions, strong drives, and powerful affections.

These passions have the power to overwhelm reason. Think of the gambler who knows that his addiction is bringing him to ruin, but he can't stop. Think of the lustful lover who knows his affair will lead to the destruction of his family and the blackening of his name, but he refuses to stop. Against all reason, and with the guiltiest of consciences, the passions of the heart have taken control. They now dictate to the will what course of action will be taken.

This is a sure sign of a thoroughly distempered heart. But it is the norm before regeneration just as it is the norm of our society as a whole. The advertising industry, for example, does not usually appeal to our minds but to our passions. It typically places a product (soap, toothpaste, a car, alcohol, furniture) alongside a lifestyle (usually the lifestyle of the young, sexy, carefree, and wealthy), and the advertisement is designed to attract us to the lifestyle, hoping we will buy the product with which that lifestyle is now (irrationally) associated. It is a blatant appeal to our passions and desires.

Biblical Christianity works the opposite way. It always begins with the mind and, as our minds are renewed, our passions are engaged and changed. What we once loved, we now hate; what we once hated, we now love. New desires, hopes, and dreams begin to drive us. Our foremost passion becomes loving God with all our heart, mind, soul, and strength. Every other pursuit, relationship, and achievement will now be rated differently. Like Paul, we must come to count all else as rubbish compared to the surpassing greatness of knowing Christ. Other passions cannot live alongside this passion as equals. We can no longer live all out for this world, chasing after money, popularity, or human wisdom. We are to hate evil, we are not to make a god of the stomach, we are to resist the Devil, we are to avoid every kind of impurity, we are to fear God's wrath, we are to flee temptation. Such exhortations, and many others, speak not just of a cerebral rejection of what is wrong, but of a heart aversion to it.

Paul frequently speaks of our passions and desires. In Romans 1, he chillingly describes God giving people over to their sinful passions.

Notice in this passage the remarkable confluence of futile thinking, foolish hearts, sinful desires and passions, and ungodly actions:

> For although they knew God, they neither glorified him as God nor gave thanks to him, but their *thinking became futile* and their *foolish hearts* were darkened. Although they claimed to be wise, they became fools and exchanged the glory of the immortal God for images made to look like mortal man and birds and animals and reptiles.
>
> Therefore God gave them over in the *sinful desires of their hearts* to sexual impurity for the degrading of their bodies with one another. They exchanged the truth of God for a lie, and worshiped and served created things rather than the Creator—who is forever praised. Amen.
>
> Because of this, God gave them over to *shameful lusts*. Even their women exchanged natural relations for unnatural ones. In the same way the men also abandoned natural relations with women and were inflamed with lust for one another. Men committed indecent acts with other men, and received in themselves the due penalty for their perversion.
>
> Furthermore, since they did not think it worthwhile to retain the knowledge of God, he gave them over to *a depraved mind*, to *do what ought not to be done*. (Rom. 1:21–28)

This is the sinful heart at its wicked worst. But as we have seen with the other faculties of the heart, in regeneration there is a complete change. New desires and passions begin to take root:

> Those who belong to Christ Jesus have crucified the sinful nature with its passions and desires. Since we live by the Spirit, let us keep in step with the Spirit. (Gal. 5:24–25)

> For the grace of God that brings salvation has appeared to all men. It teaches us to say "No" to ungodliness and worldly passions, and to live self-controlled, upright and godly lives in this present age. (Titus 2:11–12)

The passions are the deepest part of the heart and often the most powerful of the faculties. Wrong passions can destroy us; right passions are a power for great good.

THE WHOLE HEART

In summary, we have seen that Christianity is a heart religion. The gospel calls for the response of our whole being to the living God who has saved us from our sinful rebellion. Heart Christianity embraces what we think, feel, do, and desire. It is focused not on outward ritual but on inner reality, which produces fruit in our lives.

Our hearts lie open before God and he sees all—our motives, desires, intentions, and actions. Mercifully, he is the God who, by the gracious work of his Son and his Spirit, changes hearts, giving us a renewed mind, an awakened conscience, a transformed will, and godly passions and desires. In the unregenerate heart, the mind is darkened, the conscience is seared, the will is rebellious, and the passions are ungodly. In regeneration, we are given a new heart: the mind is enlightened, the conscience awakened, the will transformed, and the passions turned toward God and godliness (see diagram 8).

Diagram 8: Heart Change in Regeneration

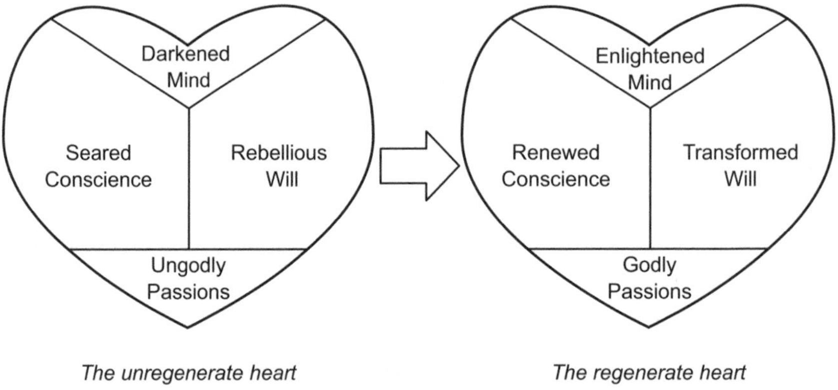

The unregenerate heart

The regenerate heart

Preachers can examine biblical texts in terms of these faculties. Living application will always aim at the whole heart. In deficient preaching, we see some faculties of the heart addressed to the virtual exclusion of others. This always produces damaging distortions. If preaching really only addresses the mind, it leads to arid intellectualism, with its attendant dangers of pride, hypocrisy, and hardness of heart. Mind-only Christianity, without an awakened conscience, changed behavior, and godly passions, makes for cold, heartless religion. It also makes for quite boring preaching! If preaching aims chiefly at the conscience, it easily descends into manipulation. People are motivated by guilt rather than by love for God and an understanding of what he requires of us. Frequently, such preaching will be distressing and depressing. If preaching chiefly addresses the will, it easily produces legalism or the kind of "decisionism" in which "making a decision" for Christ is seen as a sufficient response to the gospel, regardless of whether there is real heart change. Actions are called for without people being given a clear understanding of why, without right convictions, and without true affections for God. Such preaching produces shallow activism. Finally, if preaching aims chiefly at the passions, it can give rise to an empty emotionalism in which people feel much but know, and perhaps do, little. It produces light, fluffy Christianity that cannot stand in times of great testing.[2]

Living application aims at all four faculties of the heart. But it does so in a particular order. It drives from the top down (see diagram 9). The mind comes first. Biblical Christianity is rational. It presents biblical truth as clearly as possible and seeks to persuade and convince people of it so that they grasp and embrace it for themselves.

Diagram 9: Heart Order

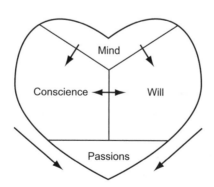

2. See also my treatment of this in Murray A. Capill, *Preaching with Spiritual Vigour: Including Lessons from the Life and Practice of Richard Baxter* (Fearn: Christian Focus, 2003), 99–100.

From there, truth is impressed on the conscience and the will. By pressing truth on the conscience, we help people measure themselves against the truth. By pressing it on the will, we give assistance to them in responding to the truth. But both must be addressed with a view to going deeper. We do not merely want people to do the right thing; we want them to feel the right thing. The passions, or affections, are really the deepest recess of the human heart. Christian experience at its best is always about a felt faith. We should not be content with knowing what sin is, but should come to feel the burden of sin and utterly hate it. We want not only to know the facts of the gospel, but to feel its comfort and be filled with thanks and praise to God for his amazing grace. We want not only to know that Jesus is Savior and Lord, but to feel the excellence of Christ and long to be closer to him.

True Christianity is *felt*, and many ordinary Christians intuitively sense that. When they come to hear God's Word preached, they don't just come to receive information about God or the Bible, nor do they come simply to be told what to do. They come to be encouraged and inspired, to have their love for God rekindled, their hearts reordered, their minds set on things above, and their zeal for the gospel renewed. As preachers, we want them not only to know God's Word better but to find it sweeter than honey and more precious than anything this world can offer.

ASKING THE RIGHT QUESTIONS

How do we handle God's Word in such a way that it speaks to the whole heart? How can we develop heart-oriented application? We must be careful not to seek heart impact by pragmatic means rather than by depending on the power of God's Word and Spirit. It is possible to give inspiring, motivational talks that stir the passions without ever really taking God's Word seriously. Expository preachers will shun such shortcuts, knowing they will yield only superficial results. While we will want to use stories and illustrations to aid clarity and impact, our primary concern must be not with clever illustrations but with the heart impact of the biblical text itself.

114

To unearth the Bible's heart impact, we should again ask questions of the text. In exegesis, we ask questions about context, intent, meaning, grammar, syntax, interpretation, and so on. In considering the purposes of the Word, we ask questions about what the text is doing—is it teaching/rebuking, training/correcting, testing/convicting, exhorting/encouraging? Now, in developing heart application, we can ask questions of the text about the human mind, will, conscience, and passions.

When we ask "mind" questions of the text, we ask what are the central truths of the text that people must know and believe. And then we ask, How can I make those truths clear? How can I demonstrate their importance? What wrong ways of thinking about this truth should I oppose? How will these truths help people? What might stop people from believing this? Will they buy it, and, if not, how can I help them to do so? These questions are similar to the teaching/rebuking purposes of God's Word, but there is a difference in emphasis. The concern is not just with identifying the truths to be taught, but with getting those truths implanted into people's minds. Our concern is not merely to state truth, but to convince and persuade, to teach and make those ideas memorable.

Next we can ask "conscience" questions of the text that will help us develop the convicting, testing, warning purposes of God's Word. What in the text should convict and challenge? What truths do people need to become deeply convicted of? What failures, sins, or omissions should people be convicted of? In what ways should people be testing and examining themselves? What would justify a clear conscience in regard to the text? How might people have an oversensitive conscience on this matter? How do I give such people peace? How might people have a seared conscience in these matters? How can I bring conviction?

After that we can ask "will" questions of the text. We want to identify any key actions and responses the text calls for. We ask ourselves, What response do I want to see people make? What practical difference should this make? What should this look like in practice? What am I going to ask people to do in response to this text? And what motivations and incentives can I give them? What help can I give them? There is, again, overlap with the purposes of the text. The will has close correlation to the task of training and correcting. But as we ask "will" questions, we sharpen our training and correcting.

It's possible, of course, that we will ask "will" questions of a text and largely draw a blank. The passage may have no imperatives, and not even implied exhortations. But we still want people to respond to God's Word. We must steer away from bolt-on application (somehow, surely, they must need to pray more, read the Bible more, give more, or serve more!). Instead, we will explore what a heart response to the text will look like.

Finally, we ask questions about the *passions* of the text. What are the passions of the biblical writer? What are the deep desires of the heart this truth should stir? How ought this text to make people feel, and how can I help them feel that? What impact should this truth have on them? In what ways should people be stirred, moved, inspired, or humbled by this truth? What drives and ambitions should this cultivate or inhibit?

We should not expect every text to yield answers to all these questions. In fact, if a text did, we would be overwhelmed with far more applicatory grist than our preaching mill could cope with. Many texts will be aimed predominantly at just one or two faculties of the heart. Since we want to let God's Word do its own work in people's lives, we will gladly work with the grain of the text and not impose on it what is not there. But the value of asking these questions is that we are more likely to unearth what is there and we will more consistently preach to the heart.

While it is useful to ask these questions, the reality is that the four faculties work together rather than independently. Our task is to speak to the heart as a whole, not just to separate faculties of the heart. We don't want four-point sermons that speak to the mind, will, conscience, and passions in turn. We want to aim at an overall impact by which people's minds are convinced, their consciences convicted, their wills persuaded, and their passions stirred.

IDOLS OF THE HEART

Perhaps the most significant clue to accessing the heart as a whole is to realize that the fundamental heart problem is idolatry. Paul Tripp, in

Instruments in the Redeemer's Hands, addresses heart ministry in counseling, but what he says applies to preaching and other areas of ministry as well.[3] He reminds us that our hearts were made to love and worship God, but, since the fall, human beings have turned away from God and replaced him with a multitude of substitutes. When we turn from God, we do not stop worshiping. We can't. We are hardwired to worship. The human heart is made to reach out beyond itself and so, as G. K. Chesterton is alleged to have said, when people reject God they do not worship nothing, they worship anything.[4] Calvin rightly said our hearts are "idol factories." Tripp defines an idol of the heart as *anything that rules me other than God*."[5] We may serve the god of image, or the god of possessions, or the god of sexual lusts, or the god of the stomach, or the gods of pleasure and entertainment, or the god of self-image—in fact, almost anything.[6]

Preachers aiming at living application need to understand some of the inner dynamics of heart idolatry. Tripp reminds us, for example, that we need to understand that idolatry is subtle.[7] Seldom do these idols look like idols. We are not so blatant as to carve idols out of wood and stone. Rather, we carve them out of our passions and desires, subtly moving away from finding our hope, security, and purpose in God alone. These subtle idols of the heart can live alongside a seemingly decent Christian life. So subtle can idolatry be that we can even make an idol of gospel ministry, church growth, or effective preaching. Idols mostly don't look like idols—they look more like legitimate passions and pursuits. The things we pursue are often not wrong in themselves.

3. See Paul David Tripp, *Instruments in the Redeemer's Hands: People in Need of Change Helping People in Need of Change* (Phillipsburg, NJ: P&R, 2002).

4. G. K. Chesterton is often quoted, without reference, as having written, "When a Man stops believing in God, he doesn't then believe in nothing, he believes anything." The source of this quotation in Chesterton's writings, however, has not been identified and is invariably cited unreferenced.

5. Tripp, *Instruments in the Redeemer's Hands*, 66 (italics his).

6. Preaching that targets heart idolatry is a hallmark of Keller's approach to application. His approach is helpfully discussed in Dennis E. Johnson, *Him We Proclaim: Preaching Christ from All the Scriptures* (Phillipsburg, NJ: P&R, 2007), 54–61.

7. Tripp, *Instruments in the Redeemer's Hands*, 67.

The problem is they have assumed a wrongful place in our lives. They have become God-substitutes, so that our sense of well-being, joy, and purpose is found in these things rather than in God. No matter how much we confess the right theology, God has been shunted out of the central place.

We also need to understand that idols always demand sacrifices. Idols take time, money, focus, and attention. As we serve our idol, we cheat God. If money has become our idol, we accumulate wealth and spend lots of time and energy thinking about how to gain and/or spend money instead of how to invest in the work of the gospel. If entertainment is our god, we spend far too much time watching movies, listening to music, and surfing the Internet, and far too little time with God. If image is our god, we spend far too much time and attention on how other people perceive us and what they think of us and far too little time focused on what God thinks of us. Tripp says idolatry is, therefore, always "moral thievery."[8] It takes from what is rightly God's and gives it to someone or something else.

The idols of our hearts also tend to grow over time. It is very hard to keep an idol down to size. Our appetite for pleasing an idol increases. That's why it is so dangerous to give an idol a foothold in your life. Give an idol an inch, and it will take a mile. The man who begins with a little pornography is soon gripped by it and wants more and more. The woman who finds some solace and comfort in eating finds that it becomes harder and harder not to eat. Just as God should become greater and greater in our lives, so God-substitutes also increase. Yet if we know that the substitutes are wrong, they will most likely incline us to go underground even as we sacrifice to them more and more. We become deceptive, furtive, covert.

Another crucial dynamic to note is that idols always fail us.[9] They promise much but deliver little. Strangely, that is why we go back for

8. Ibid.
9. Johnson summarizes Keller as identifying two reasons why idols fail us: they do not forgive "sin" committed against them ("sin" being defined by the idol as behavior that prevents us from receiving the idol's promised "blessings"), and they will eventually be torn from us. See Johnson, *Him We Proclaim*, 58.

more. They don't satisfy. Food doesn't satisfy the deep longings of our heart; neither does golf, sex, money, or success. The heart has been made for God, not for lame substitutes. So, no matter how much of our idol we get, we never get enough to feel it is really good. The thrill is fleeting. The sense of satisfaction is only momentary. More often than not, the aftertaste is appalling. We are left feeling empty and cheated. But the sinful heart is foolish enough to go back for more. We think that next time it will be more satisfying. Or we think that momentary pleasure is enough.

These are heart realities we need to understand both for ourselves and for those to whom we minister. But how do we address the issue of idolatry in preaching? How do we speak to this most entrenched sin of the human heart? It is not enough for us simply to throw the word *idolatry* around a few times. We need to do more to help people understand, face up to, and dispense with their God-substitutes.

To expose heart idols, we need to go to the bottom of the heart and address people's passions: what they desire, love, serve, chase after, treasure, enjoy, and delight in. The passions are, as we have seen, the most powerful forces of the human heart and so we should probe them often. What excites people? What motivates them? What gives them a reason to live? What would break their heart if it were to be taken from them? People must learn to sift rigorously their own desires and affections, taking an honest look at what is driving them.[10]

Once people are thinking about their deepest passions, we need to expose the danger of idolatry. We need to help people understand the dynamics of idolatry with a clear mind. We will show that things that are not wrong in and of themselves easily assume a wrongful place in our lives. We will remind people that the joy of sex, food, material gain, fame, or anything else in this world is temporary and fleeting. We will warn people about the grip such things can assume in our lives. We will show how easily they rob God of his place in our lives. We will

10. See Timothy Keller, *Counterfeit Gods: When the Empty Promises of Love, Money and Power Let You Down* (London: Hodder & Stoughton, 2009), 167–70.

119

demonstrate that idols always leave us shortchanged, never delivering what they promise.

The point of such teaching is to bring conviction of sin. People must see idolatry for what it is. Without such conviction (of the conscience), there will be no incentive to change (the will). Only with such conviction will the call to repentance gain traction.

This, then, is the preacher's next great task in ministering the Word to idolaters. We must urge true repentance, which consists of both confession and change. Confession is not merely the acknowledgment that something has become an idol in our life, but owning up fully to the fact that this thing has a grip on us that has effectively dethroned God. Confession must not be compromised by minimization or shifting of blame, by self-justification or denial. Nor should it be confined to private confession alone. Idolatry thrives in secrecy, and very often the only way to address it is to tell someone else the idol of our heart and seek help in dealing with it. Confession must also focus on the heart impact of idolatry. Idolaters must admit that, because of their idolatry, they have not loved God as they ought to have but have allowed something else to seize their affections and begin to rule them. They must confess that they have looked elsewhere for love, security, joy, hope, and purpose.

We must tell people, however, that even such full and free confession is only one half of true repentance. Repentance demands change, and that is the hardest part of the job. The idolater must turn from the idol back to the true and living God. Worship of the idol must be replaced with worship of God. The idolater needs help to cultivate renewed dependence on the Lord, renewed love and passion for him, and renewed vigor in serving him and putting him first. Idolaters must be trained to focus on him, rejoice in him, treasure him, and delight in him. He must resume the place the idol has stolen. One of our key tasks, then, is to present a compelling view of the beauty and excellence of God. We need to help idolaters see that there is something more precious than what they currently cling to. They need to see not only their own sin, but the surpassing greatness of Christ Jesus our Lord. Without leading people to see the supremacy of God and the joy and hope found in him alone, we will leave them not merely convicted but condemned.

As we help people to reinstate God as King, we must also help them to smash their idols. That will mean different things in different situations, and we must be careful not to be overly prescriptive. For some, it will mean decisive and radical change as they cut off an idol completely. For others, it will mean changed priorities, new account-abilities, or rigorous self-monitoring. We should reassure people that this is seldom quick or easy. It is a journey on a difficult road. But the road leads to life.

It should be clear that addressing idolatry requires serious, heart-searching preaching. This is what gospel ministry demands. Jesus came to seek and to save the lost, to search out sinners, to find those who had turned from God and given themselves over to a thousand other plea-sures and treasures. Christ came and bore in himself the punishment for the sin of idolatry so that all who turn to him can be set free from not only the guilt but also the power of idolatry. Christ is in the busi-ness of setting people free from idols that bind so that they can serve the living and true God with all their heart. The end goal of a ministry that exposes and addresses idolatry is to see many people, both within and outside the church, freed to serve God with all their heart, mind, soul, and strength. No one can serve two masters. The idols of our hearts must go in order that we might set apart Christ as Lord and live all-out for him.

WORKING WITH THE HEART

Living application always calls for heart change. The third stage of the living application preaching process has prompted us to exam-ine the living Word in the light of how the human heart functions so that we can call people to wholehearted allegiance to Christ. To anchor these ideas, we will return to the three passages we have previously considered when examining the purposes of God's Word: Haggai 1, Psalm 73, and Ephesians 1.

What faculties of the heart and what heart idols are particularly in view in Haggai 1? It is not hard to see the impact of the passage on all four faculties of the heart. First, there are truths and spiritual realities that need to be understood and accepted intellectually. One fundamental truth is that God cares about what we prioritize. Another is that God may well bring physical consequences for spiritual sin. These "mind" truths need to be explained so that people are persuaded of their reality, but they must also be pressed against the conscience. People need to be convicted of any wrong priorities in their lives and convinced of the supreme importance of putting God and his kingdom first. The tests suggested earlier when we considered the purposes of the Word will be powerful tools in working on the conscience.

But conviction is not enough. The will must then be persuaded to prioritize the things of God above the things of self. Preachers might need to be quite explicit in calling for the priorities of the kingdom of God to trump all other interests. People may face some hard choices: spending money on an overseas vacation, or on a kingdom project the church is promoting; pursuing a career that will be comfortable and secure, or opting for a vocational pathway that is less safe but will open many more doors for serving God. The reality is, kingdom choices will be made only if people have a passion for the things of God that exceeds their passions for self, comfort, money, and other things in this world. At the end of the day, the issue Haggai was raising was the issue of where the people's passion lay—their houses or God's house? What were they serving? What was their heart set on? Since the return from exile they had quickly returned to idolatry, but not now the idolatry of Baal worship. They had succumbed to the more subtle idolatry of selfish, comfortable materialism.

Significantly, when they resolved to obey the Lord, he "stirred up the spirit" of the leaders and the people (Hag. 1:14). I take that to mean that he gave them a renewed passion for the work. In preaching this, our desire will be that the Lord stirs a similar passion in our hearers' lives—a passion for the work of the Lord that outshines all else.

There are some similar themes in Psalm 73. An examination of the psalm in terms of the faculties of the heart again leads us to see an overlap with the purposes of the Word. But this angle will help sharpen our application. Beginning with the mind, we see that the truths previously identified must now be considered with regard to the question of how to persuade and convince people of these things. The preacher will ask, "How can I convince people that envy is spiritually dangerous? How can I show them that there is an inevitable slide from basic hedonism to total God-rejection? How can I impress upon them the transitory nature of this life, the comfort of the gospel, and the reality of ultimate judgment in which the believer will be secure and the unbeliever lost?" At the end of the day these are *mind* issues. They are not things people must do, but things they must see, grasp, and "take to heart."

For this psalm to gain traction in people's hearts, we will need to show them how remarkably contemporary these truths are. It will be helpful to look at contemporary materialism, exemplified most clearly in the advertising industry. It will be valuable to consider contemporary Christian forms of envy and ways in which we might think our Christian experience is something of a raw deal. It will be useful to find current examples of the brevity of life and the messiness of the lives of the rich and famous, whom we too easily idolize. It will also be helpful to impress upon people the truth that closeness to God is of far greater worth than the very best things this world has to offer, not because it looks or feels better but because it is the only track to eternal security.

Some of these truths might also be pressed on the conscience. The preacher can ask people whether they are in danger of slipping, as the psalmist was. The tests developed in relation to the purposes of the text will add bite to this question. Ask them to assess where they are finding their security, whether they live with reference to eternity, whether things in this world have lost their grip on them in the light of the surpassing greatness of God's love in Christ. The preacher should be aware, however, that some people may have very sensitive consciences and others seared consciences. While tests and questions will hopefully make some impact on the more hardened conscience, those with sensitive consciences will too readily feel convicted of their failings. Yes, they do struggle with envy, and they have sometimes lost heart as Christians, and they know that they are spiritual beasts a lot of the time. They hate themselves for it and wonder if they can ever experience what the psalmist eventually did. To such people the free, full, rich grace of God must be preached. It is God who grasps us, guides us, and glorifies us. It is not we who take hold of him but he who takes hold of us. Besides, even when the psalmist was living as a brute beast, he was still a child of God. His feet had nearly slipped yet God had held him.

Is there anything in Psalm 73 for the will? Does it call for action, for decision, for response? Absolutely. While there are no express commands, there is throughout an implied response. The preacher will urge people to resist envy and covetousness in practical ways, which might mean putting up the "no junk mail" sign, not going window-shopping, and not looking through display homes. More than that, it might mean overcoming the grip that material possessions gain on us by deliberately giving away money saved for some precious acquisition. Envy is a sin to fight, not a weakness to tone down.

Because the mind and will must work together, it will be helpful to arm people with motives for resisting worldly temptation. In the second half of the psalm, we find a man much more at peace, feeling more secure and experiencing greater enjoyment of God. People need to be shown that being an envious Christian is really the worst of both worlds, not the best.

But action against the pull of a worldly lifestyle is only half the deal. It was when the psalmist entered the sanctuary of God that he came to his senses and saw the insecurity of those living only for the goodies of this world. Here it is tempting to go straight to "more" applications. We need to go to church more, read the Bible more, pray more. But the reality is that Asaph was doing all that, and yet his spiritual disciplines were a burden to him as he eyed the seemingly carefree living of the wicked. We need to dig deeper for a solution. What Asaph needed was not just more devotional activity but spiritual sanity. When spiritually sane, he would treasure his relationship with God above all else and the disciplines would become a delight.

If our chief applicatory concern is to draw people to the excellence of a relationship with God, we have also found the key to preaching this psalm in a distinctly Christian way. Our relationship with God can only be in and through Christ. While the psalmist went to the sanctuary, we go to the One who is the presence of God with us. It is in Christ that God grasps us, guides us, and glorifies us. It is in him that he satisfies us most deeply.

The language of satisfaction, of desires fulfilled and of a profound sense of security, is the language of passion. It is seldom difficult to find passions in the Psalms. Poetry is the language of emotion. This psalm turns from the strong passion of envy to the stronger passion of delight in God. In preaching this psalm, we will almost inevitably speak of the deep drives and affections of life. Our goal must be to stir in our hearers a greater passion for God than for the things of this world. They need a picture of how satisfying a relationship with God can be. They need to be reminded that Christianity is not about the performance of spiritual duties but about a relationship with God. They need to be drawn afresh by the love, grace, goodness, faithfulness, and mercy of God. Ultimately, we cannot draw them; the Spirit must. But the Spirit will use our words as we paint a picture of the excellence of Christ.

The aim in considering mind, conscience, will, and passions in this way is to ensure that we move from explaining the psalm to impressing it upon people's hearts. This psalm affords great opportunity to challenge one of the classic idols of our day—the glamour of a carefree, moneyed lifestyle—holding up next to it the rewards of forsaking that idol for pleasures that only God can give.

Ephesians 1 is, as we saw earlier, a very different kind of text from Psalm 73. As we examine it in terms of the human heart, we are less likely to see the specter of idolatry rise from the page. There is much less here to convict the conscience and little to directly urge on the will. Instead, it is a text laden with substance to feed the mind and stir the passions. That is a significant combination. Although there is immense doctrinal content in these verses, Paul has not written this as a theological text. He has written about these doctrines to stir praise to God for our glorious salvation. The passage begins with praise and the refrain reminds us that all is "to the praise of his glory." The text contains no imperatives, though the strongly implied response is to praise God.

The goal when preaching this passage, therefore, needs to be to help people grasp these truths with their minds in such a way that their passions are stirred to praise God. The goal must be for doctrine to be felt. The grand truths Paul packs into these verses are designed to warm believers' hearts, drawing men and women to a doxological response. Election, redemption, and sealing with the Spirit are reasons for praise. God's grand, age-long plan of redemption, which has culminated in the coming of his Son and the outpouring of the Holy Spirit, has been crafted by him for his own glory. It is his intent that those who dwell on it fall to their knees in adoration. These doctrines are presented not for theological debate but for worship.

In preaching this on one occasion, I began by describing a flight I took in New Zealand from Wellington to Christchurch. It was a perfectly clear day, and I had a window seat allowing me to take in the glorious view of the snow-laden southern Alps. On that flight I didn't read any books or work on my laptop. I just gazed out the window and soaked in the glorious sight. Some of the peaks I recognized from my earlier climbing days. I knew that any one of them would have made for a challenging climb. But this was a moment to fly above them all and just enjoy the splendor of snow-capped mountains. I then said that Ephesians 1:3–14 was really the same. I wanted them just to look at the glorious display of our salvation and soak it in. I encouraged them to sit back and marvel at it. See what God has done. Each verse could be a sermon in itself, but for now just enjoy the scene as a whole. I told them that I would not be asking them to do anything other than realize that God is a God greatly to be praised for his plan of redemption. By beginning that way, I sought to make clear from the start that this was intended to be doctrine for the affections. There was no work to be done on the conscience or the will—just on the mind and the passions.

But how do you do that? How do you preach doctrine to the passions? And, for that matter, how do you preach so as to convince, persuade, convict, move, motivate, and inspire? If our task is to take aim at the heart, how do we learn to shoot straight? We will consider that shortly, but first there is another vital dimension of speaking into the lives of our hearers that we must consider. The human heart is, as we have seen, found in many different conditions. Preachers therefore need to think not only about how the heart works, but also about the varying spiritual conditions of people and churches. Living application doesn't assume that every heart is the same. It differentiates from person to person, church to church, and season to season, as we will see in the next chapter.

DISCUSSION QUESTIONS

1. What are the preaching implications of the Bible's teaching that the mind is a key faculty of the heart and is the primary way in which the other faculties are to be addressed?
2. Why must preachers aim at heart conviction? How do you try to do this?
3. How can you address the will, urging people to right action, without sinking into moralism or legalism?
4. Why is it that faithful expository preaching has often failed to stir godly passion?
5. What are the dominant individual and cultural idols that you need to address in your preaching context?
6. Review your last sermon: Was the text particularly aimed at one or more of the faculties of the heart? Did you shape the sermon in a heart-oriented way?

| 5 |

THE LIVES OF OUR HEARERS: ONE SIZE DOESN'T FIT ALL

I HATE SHOPPING. True to the male stereotype, I find clothes shopping especially to be a wearying chore. When the time comes to buy a new article of clothing, I'm in and out of the store as quickly as possible, trying on as few items as I can, hoping something will fit right the first time and be marked down considerably. If only one size would fit all! But one size doesn't fit all. Not all clothes suit all people, and things aren't always on sale. Life's hard.

Application is hard, too, for some of the same reasons. There is no one-size-fits-all way of applying God's Word. Not all applications suit all people or all churches, and good applications seldom come at cut prices. So, even when we have discerned the intended purposes of the living Word, have processed them for ourselves by drawing from our life reservoir, and have discovered how the truths of the text should impact the human heart, we need to go further and focus on the actual people to whom we will be speaking.

Living application must speak to the real-life issues of our hearers. But their lives differ. Their heart conditions differ. Their needs, desires, aspirations, sins, and triumphs differ. So to speak the living Word into

129

the lives of our hearers, we need not only to understand how the human heart works, but to understand the varying life circumstances of our hearers. This is the second essential dimension of the third part of our preaching process, as diagram 10 shows.

**Diagram 10: Stage Three—The Lives of the Hearers:
Spiritual Conditions**

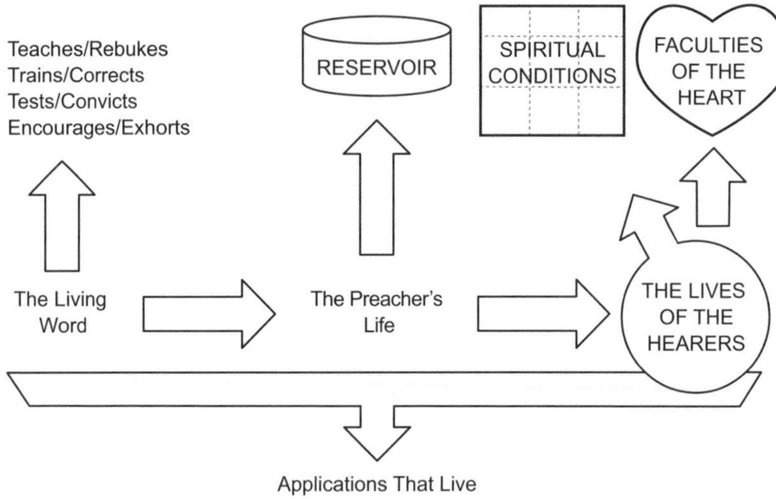

THE DIVERSITY OF THE CHURCH

When you think about it, the variety of people in most churches on any given Sunday is quite astounding. It is one of the wonders of the church. God pulls together into his new covenant community the most diverse array of people, many of whom would otherwise probably have nothing to do with one another. In the church to which I belong, there are several lecturers alongside several people with intellectual disabilities; there are some successful businessmen, a number of professionals, quite a few tradesmen, and a few people on welfare benefits; there are some fit young guys who enjoy working out and others with debilitating long-term physical and mental illnesses. Then there is the age range, from 0 to late 80s; there is the ethnic range—not large in our church, but certainly several nationalities represented; there are singles and couples; there are variations in family size and in the educational choices being made for children (homeschooling, state schools, private schools, Christian schools); there are many different hobbies and interests pursued, from classical music buffs to surfers to computer gamers to scrapbookers, to name a few.

This is how the church is meant to be. It is not meant to be a homogenous group of people who are all basically the same age, with the same IQ, the same interests, the same appetites, and the same incomes. Such a church may be easier to handle, but it is far less reflective of the astounding work God is doing in assembling a people for the glory of his name.

Yet these variations only begin to scratch the surface of diversity in the church. More significant are the varied experiences of the hundred or so people I am thinking of—their diverse life journeys, their differing joys and sorrows, their varying pains and griefs, their particular successes and blessings, their unique hopes and desires. They may have good or bad marriages. They may struggle with depression or anxiety. They may be trying to deal with the effects of abuse from years back. They may be eternal optimists who never think things could go wrong.

These realities often run much more deeply than one's job, lifestyle, education, and health. But even they are not the deepest level at which people vary. The most profound differences are in their varying spiritual conditions. Some are saved; some aren't. Some are growing while others are backsliding. Some are enjoying victory over a particular sin while others are about to be felled by some compelling temptation. Some are complacent while some are full of zeal and passion; some are babes in Christ while yet others are preachers in the making. The list could go on, but the point is clear: not all people are the same so, in application, one size doesn't fit all.

In this regard, there's been an interesting change over the years in preaching. It used to be that preachers would think chiefly in terms of the varying spiritual conditions of their hearers. Today it is more common for the focus to be on people's social, economic, personal, and cultural circumstances. If the former is the focus, then an emphasis will be found on the preacher being a pastor who knows and loves his people. If the latter is the focus, the emphasis will fall on the preacher being someone who understands culture, studies demographics and sociology, and knows how unchurched Harry and Mary think.[1]

This should not be an either/or choice. Both are important considerations. We need to understand the world in which people live. We want to know something of the culture we are speaking into. But cultural and sociological awareness will not, by itself, produce heart-oriented application. The deepest level of people's lives is their relationship to God, irrespective of where they live, the color of their skin, and what kind of car they drive. Sociological factors give a certain spin to spiritual realities, but the spiritual realities are core business for the preacher. For that reason, "our best target research is done in the Scriptures,"[2] where we come to understand the human condition and God's remedies for it. And target research is done also in everyday pastoral work as we get to know our flock. Christopher Ash wisely observes,

> It can be daunting to hear a speaker imply that unless we all become equipped to give deep and perceptive analyses of everything from the fashion industry to climate change, we cannot preach. We cannot each become experts in every aspect of culture and contemporary issues. What we can and must do is to love the people we serve and the people we seek to reach. And if we love people we will listen to them and begin to understand them. And if we do that thoughtfully we are bound to get insight into culture.[3]

We do need to understand the times in which we live, because culture shapes people and people shape the church. Cultural change in

1. See Lee Strobel, *Inside the Mind of Unchurched Harry & Mary: How to Reach Friends and Family Who Avoid God and the Church* (Grand Rapids: Zondervan, 1993).
2. Phillip D. Jensen and Paul Grimmond, *The Archer and the Arrow: Preaching the Very Words of God* (Kingsford, New South Wales: Matthias Media, 2010), 94.
3. Christopher Ash, *The Priority of Preaching* (Fearn: Christian Focus, 2009), 56.

the West over the last thirty years has been massive, and any preacher or church that has ignored it will most likely be operating in an antiquated and irrelevant mode. There is no virtue in being dated and it is not spiritual to be old-fashioned. Neither is it helpful to the advance of the gospel to be culturally anachronistic. But, at the end of the day, the preacher is a pastor not a sociologist, a spiritual doctor not a cultural analyst. Cultural awareness should feed into our understanding of people, but our understanding of people is developed not chiefly from reading books on culture but from reading God's Word and interfacing it with the real stories of people's lives. Cultural awareness sharpens our focus on what God's Word tells us about people and what they tell us about themselves.

CONDITIONS OF THE SOUL

The historic interest of preachers in people's varying spiritual conditions led them to think in terms of different categories of hearers. Their categories were not sociological: men and women, old and young, rich and poor. They were spiritual. The most fundamental distinction was always between the saved and the unsaved, or the regenerate and the unregenerate. These categories have been fudged in much of our church language today. We talk about the churched and the unchurched, about Christians and seekers. But not everyone who is churched is saved, and not every non-Christian is a seeker. We need more nuanced categories if we are to speak to people pointedly.

One of the earliest categorizations in English homiletics was given at the end of the sixteenth century by William Perkins.[4] He spoke of seven categories of hearers. First, there were unbelievers who were "both ignorant and unteachable." We might call them hardened sinners. Next there were those who were "teachable, but ignorant," then those who "have knowledge, but have never been humbled." Fourth, there were those who have already been humbled. Here, Perkins notes, "We must carefully consider whether the humbling that has already taken place is

---

4. William Perkins, *The Art of Prophesying and The Calling of the Ministry* (1606; repr., Edinburgh: Banner of Truth, 1996), 191. First published in Latin in 1592.

complete and sound or only just begun and still light and superficial." It is only with his fifth category that he comes to those who believe, followed by those who are backsliding, and finally a congregation that has a mix of believers and unbelievers.

A more extensive categorization is found in the great nineteenth-century work of Charles Bridges, *The Christian Ministry*.[5] He begins with "the infidel," who is marked by impatience with all moral restraint and defiance against God's rule. Such people love sin and either believe there is no God or wish it were so, giving in to love of sensual desires, self-conceit, or intellectual pride. Second, there are ignorant and careless people. This is the condition of many who simply do not know or understand the gospel. So Bridges is not harsh with them, but gentle and gracious. They must be treated with "the greatest mildness" as we urge them to be reconciled to God. His third category concerns the self-righteous, as exemplified by the rich young ruler. Then comes "the false professor," who has listened to the gospel and been persuaded of it, but who has not embraced it. Such a person has "no dread of self-deception, no acquaintance with his own sinfulness, no assault from Satan, because there is no real exercise of grace, or incentive to diligence."[6]

With his fifth category, Bridges turns to those who have come under conviction, but he notes that natural and spiritual convictions do not necessarily equate with salvation. There is a difference between "a sight of sin, and a loathing of its sinfulness." It takes great skill to discern the real spiritual condition of those convicted of sin. Next comes "the young Christian." Such a person is awakened and excited but not yet greatly enlightened. Repentance is sincere but partial, faith is genuine but often confused, love is real but not yet strong or deep. Such a person needs milk, not meat, as he or she is established not only in the truth but in the Christian way of life. Bridges treats this condition more fully than any other. It is followed by three further conditions in which believ-

5. Charles Bridges, *The Christian Ministry* (1830; repr., London: Banner of Truth, 1967), 361–82.
6. Ibid., 367–68.

ers may be found: the backslider, the unestablished Christian, and the confirmed and consistent Christian.

Bridges's treatment is striking not simply for the categories he develops but for the kind of ministry he prescribes for each one. His discussion is full of reflection, using scriptural examples, on what must be done to address each particular spiritual state, whether the need is for pointed preaching to the conscience, basic teaching, exhortations and encouragement, strong meat, a setting forth of the glories of Christ, giving of counsel and advice, or some other remedy.

Though these examples come from the sixteenth and nineteenth centuries respectively, it is not only preachers of the past who have thought in these terms. Tim Keller develops application with a similar grid in mind. In his series of articles on preaching he presents a list of "Possible Spiritual Conditions in an Audience."[7] He begins with non-Christians, identifying conscious unbelievers, non-churched nominal Christians, churched nominal Christians, awakened sinners, and apostates. He then itemizes Christians in seven groups: new believers, mature and growing Christians, the afflicted, the tempted, immature believers, the depressed, and the backslidden. For each category he has further description. For example, the afflicted include the physically afflicted (the sick, the elderly, the disabled, the dying), the bereaved, the lonely, the persecuted/abused, the poor, and the deserted.

The point of thinking in such categories is to help us deliver applications that are truly useful to people. We target our application of the text to people's real spiritual experience. We begin to ask ourselves, Where is this person at? What does she need? How can I get inside him? How can I help her advance spiritually? Such questions will help us generate varied application as we realize that different people need different medicine. I don't want to go to a doctor who automatically prescribes penicillin for every patient. I want to go to one who diagnoses before she prescribes. Careful diagnoses will then ideally lead to a range of holistic remedies. They won't be just about what medicine to take,

7. Timothy Keller, "A Model for Preaching (Part Two)," *Journal of Biblical Counseling* 13, no. 1 (1994): 43.

but about exercise, sleep, diet, mental well-being, relaxation, and so on. Preachers must do the same.

A couple of years ago, when I was teaching this material, one of my students came up with another categorization of hearers that is simple but extremely helpful.[8] First, there are those who are *not going well and they don't even know it.* This is a dangerous place to be, and can be the condition of both believers and unbelievers. Such people think they are fine, but they do not know that they are wretched, poor, blind, and naked (cf. Rev. 3:17). They may be arrogant in their unbelief or smug and complacent in their immature faith or wayward Christian living. Either way, they need to be shaken up and called to repentance.

Next there are those who are *not going well and they know it.* Again, this group may embrace both believers and unbelievers. Some believers are not going well and they know it. They are backsliding, slipping, struggling with sin and temptation. They believe but they long for God to help them overcome their unbelief. They know their life is not what it should be and they want help. Or they may just be young in the faith and know they have much to learn. These saints need biblical teaching and counsel coupled with gospel incentives and motivations. Some unbelievers may also fall into this category. They know that they do not know God but they want to. They sense the emptiness of their own life and have found that idols do not satisfy. They are genuine seekers who are ripe for the gospel.

Third, there are those who are *going well but they don't know it.* These are the tenderhearted saints who always feel inadequate. They have sensitive consciences that incline them to worry about themselves, doubt their faith, feel great guilt for their sin, and see their own faults very readily. These people need much encouragement and consolation. They need the load to be lightened. They need to hear Jesus say, "Come to me, all you who are weary . . . and I will give you rest" (Matt. 11:28). They do not need the teaching of the Pharisees that tied heavy loads on people.

8. My thanks to Karl Deenick for his helpful interactions on this.

Finally, there is the best category of all: those who are *going well and they know it*. Such people know and believe the gospel, they love the Lord, and they respond warmly to God's Word. They are positive, active, grateful believers. The truth means much to them and it makes a difference in their lives. They are great people to have in the church, and we want to encourage and spur them on. They are ready for meat, and we should give it to them.

Diagram 11: Spiritual Conditions Grid

	Not Going Well	**Going Well**
Don't Know it	Arrogant/Complacent → Challenge/Confront	Struggling/Discouraged → Comfort/Spur on
Know it	Backsliding/Seeking → Help/Advise	Positive/Grateful → Encourage/Teach

SPEAKING TO DIFFERENT KINDS OF PEOPLE

In preparing to preach, a preacher can cast his mind around the congregation, thinking of which of his people may be in these different categories. The categories can form a grid in the preacher's mind, as shown in diagram 11. Of course we do not know people's hearts, but a pastor will generally know his people well enough to have some idea of their varying spiritual conditions. We want to bring to them a timely word. We want the truth of the text we are opening to hit the spot. Daniel Overdorf recommends that we "imagine individual faces, expressions, smiles, and tears."[9]

Considering our hearers in this way is not done with a view to tickling itching ears. Paul warned Timothy against giving people what

9. Overdorf is strong on this aspect of thinking about particular people as we apply God's Word. However, his focus is more on life situations than on spiritual conditions. Daniel Overdorf, *Applying the Sermon: How to Balance Biblical Integrity and Cultural Relevance* (Grand Rapids: Kregel, 2009), 124–25.

they want to hear. Congregations develop certain appetites, and savvy preachers learn how to give people what will get them "Amening." There may be certain doctrines they love, stories they warm to, humor they appreciate, controversy they thrive on. But giving people what they want seldom leads to their growth. If there is growth, it is usually of their egos. The kind of preaching that speaks pertinently to people's spiritual conditions gives people not so much what they want as what they need. It speaks not to their felt needs, but to their unfelt needs.

But how do you do that if, within a congregation, there are people in many different places? How do you, within one congregation, hit the proud hard while comforting the vulnerable? How do you simultaneously stir up sinners and soothe the souls of troubled saints? Might not people listen to the wrong part? And don't we all tend to listen on behalf of others instead of for ourselves?

Hazards abound and there is no fool-proof strategy. But the best policy is that of being direct. If applications are specifically targeted, say whom they are for. Identify them, not by name but by type. Describe them. This can often be done by lead sentences such as these:

Maybe some of you are just visiting today, looking in, checking out this church and checking out what Christians are all about. That's great, and I'd like to suggest two things to you this morning . . .

I know some of you have been believers for years. You were raised in a Christian home, attended a Christian school, have been to church all your life. If that's you, let me say . . .

There might be some people here who, as I say this, are thinking, "This is just what Mrs. So-and-so needs to hear." But if that is what you are thinking, if you are listening for someone else, then you above all people need to take this to heart . . .

Maybe you find yourself thinking, "This is all too hard. The standard is too high. I can't possibly live this way . . ." If you think that, then you have understood me precisely. This is too hard! Jesus' standards are too high. And that is precisely why we need him. Don't let the impossibly high standards turn you away from Christ. Let them drive you to him.

Perhaps some of you are feeling hopelessly condemned as I say this. If so, you are not really the kind of person I am speaking about. My concern is with those of you who never seem to feel condemned about anything. Every sermon is like water off a duck's back. You nod in agreement but you never take anything to heart. Those of you who feel smitten are in a much healthier place than those of you who feel smug!

I want to speak for a few moments to those of you who feel that you have nothing much to offer God . . .

I know some of you just love this doctrine. That's great! Not everyone has a taste for this, but you know that it is pure gold.

Such lead sentences capture the people we want particularly to target with an application. We might even say whom an application is not for. If you say, "I want to speak for a few moments to the men, and, to be honest, I wish there were no women in the room . . . ," you can guarantee that you have the ears of every man *and* woman, and probably the kids too.[10] I have occasionally said, "I want to go a bit deeper for the next few minutes and so if you want to switch off, feel free. This is tough meat. I'll cue you back in when it's over." Chances are, by giving people an out, they will actually opt in to see what is so hard. That's human nature!

Another way to speak to different kinds of people is to do so by means of a story. Think, for example, of the way Jesus targets the arrogance of the Pharisees in Luke 15. In verses 1–2 we are told that the Pharisees and teachers of the law were muttering unhappily about the way Jesus was spending time with tax collectors and sinners. They had no understanding of the grace of the kingdom and the Father's love for

10. Haddon Robinson astutely observes that "information overheard can be more influential than information received directly." Haddon W. Robinson, *Making a Difference in Preaching: Haddon Robinson on Biblical Preaching* (Grand Rapids: Baker, 1999), 122–23.

sinners whom Jesus had come to save. So Jesus addresses them directly in an indirect way. The series of three parables that follows sets up the pattern of lost-found-rejoicing, three times over. But at the end of the third cycle there is an addition: lost-found-rejoicing-grumbling. Here the Pharisees were to see themselves as older-brother types with no grasp of the grace of God. Jesus' preaching was well targeted and there can be little doubt that the Pharisees felt its sting.

Preachers should not try to address every kind of hearer in every message. But over a period of time, we will address a whole range of spiritual conditions among our hearers. One fruit of this will most likely be that our people feel increasingly at ease to bring along their friends. They will know that we speak to unbelievers as well as believers. They will know that we are aware of people's pains, their differing perspectives, their alternative beliefs. People gain confidence in preaching that applies the Word to the real lives of real people.

SPEAKING TO DIFFERENT KINDS OF AUDIENCES

Just as people differ, so do audiences or congregations. Again, we tend to think most naturally in terms of sociological differences. We look at the demographics of a church; is it white, middle class, educated? Is it racially mixed? Is it working class, or rural? Are they old or young? Are there many children? These are relevant questions for any speaker or preacher. The answers substantially affect the applications made. Think of the difference between applying a text to a group of preschoolers, and applying the same text to a youth group or in a retirement village. The same truth needs to cut into the lives of each group in different ways.

But important as these considerations are, they are not the most significant questions to ask. The most profound differences from one group to another are spiritual. The reason there is a difference between bringing application to preschoolers and bringing it to retirees is not simply that they are in different stages of life, but that those different stages bring about different levels of spiritual maturity and varying spiritual realities. Of course, assumptions must not be made. The older audience is not necessarily spiritually mature. You can be an old babe in Christ. You can be old and foolish. You can be old and hardened in sin. But the older audience must face the reality of eternity, of pending judgment, of past regrets or missed opportunities, or of a lifetime of blessings and provisions, in a way that a five-year-old never can.

It is evident from the letters of Jesus Christ to the seven churches of Asia Minor that he knew the spiritual condition of each church and addressed words specifically suited to those conditions. Two of the five churches receive no criticisms at all; one receives no commendations; four receive both praise and rebuke. The all-seeing Lord knows both the condition of the church as a whole and the individuals within it. So he can challenge the congregation in Sardis hard, knocking their reputation of being alive by the bald fact that they are spiritually dead. Yet they are not completely dead. There are "a few people in Sardis who have not soiled their clothes" (Rev. 3:4). The church as a whole is, therefore, challenged, while a few individuals are encouraged. Not so with Laodicea. The whole church seems to be living in complacent compromise. The Lord knows the people's real condition even though they don't. They think they are rich, but in reality they are wretched, pitiful, poor, blind, and naked. What kind of application do they need? They are counseled (Rev. 3:18), rebuked (v. 19), invited (v. 20), and promised blessing if they respond (v. 21).

The spiritual conditions addressed are not isolated from the sociological setting of each church, yet the latter may well stand in stark contrast to the former. The church in Smyrna lives in poverty and experiences great affliction. Outwardly it is not a church that looks to be thriving. But Jesus, who knows the people's circumstances, also knows that their spiritual condition is healthy despite their difficult setting.

Interestingly, the theme tune of Christ's application to the churches with problems is encapsulated in one word: repent (Rev. 2:5, 16, 21–22; 3:3, 19). But the call to repentance is made specific. The sins they ought to repent of are exposed and the particular changes they need to make are identified. Repentance is a turning around, not just individually but corporately, and there needs to be clarity in what a church is to turn from and what it is to turn to.

Jesus' "preaching" to these churches encourages us to be specific in speaking to particular audiences about their spiritual condition while recognizing that one size doesn't fit all. The same can be seen in Paul's preaching to varying groups in Acts. In Acts 13, at the synagogue in Pisidian Antioch, Paul's audience is largely Jewish along with some Gentile God-fearers. So he is speaking to people who know the Scriptures and value their heritage as children of Abraham. He therefore presents the gospel message in terms of Old Testament history. He leads them from their beginnings in Egypt through to the reign of King David. From there he moves to Christ, proclaiming him as the fulfillment of what God had promised to their forefathers. He then proclaims to them the good news of forgiveness of sins in Christ and calls them to believe. He also warns them of what will happen if they don't.

This presentation of the gospel is very different from the message recorded in Acts 14, where Paul is confronted by a raving mob of pagans set upon offering sacrifices to him and Barnabas. This rural, polytheistic crowd, operating in terms of their own local myths, could not present a starker contrast to the previous setting. Paul, not surprisingly, begins and ends in a completely different place. He speaks of the creator God who has given testimony of himself in the world around us. He doesn't quote a single Bible verse, neither does he speak specifically of Jesus. His appeal is to general revelation alone. Admittedly this was not a "sermon" as we think of it but a spontaneous speech given in a unique situation. (When did people last try to offer sacrifices to you?) But while this situation is unique, it is instructive that Paul does not walk around with a four-point gospel outline in his pocket, presented to all people in the same way.

His audience in Acts 17 is entirely different again and so is his message. He now speaks to philosophers who love debating ideas, have a religious mindset, and are open to discussion of new perspectives. This setting, it has been noted by many, is perhaps more like our contemporary postmodern context than any other in the New Testament.[11] What

---

11. See, for example, Don Carson, "The Worldview Clash," *Southern Cross Quarterly*, Summer 1998, available online at http://www.facingthechallenge.org/carson.php; also Dean

was Paul's approach? First, it is important to note the depth of burden and passion out of which he speaks. His own heart is grieved by what he sees in Athens. He is disturbed by their terrible idolatry and intelligent ignorance. Yet, while disturbed and burdened, he doesn't begin by lambasting them for their folly. Instead, he builds bridges into their culture, observing realities (vv. 22–23), quoting their literature (v. 28), commending their religious passion (v. 22), and zooming in on a point of self-confessed need (v. 23). This was a brilliant combination of sociocultural awareness and spiritual diagnosis. It led him to proclaim, as he did in Lystra, God as Creator, who doesn't need us but has graciously given us life and assigned our places. This God is to be sought and known. He is no mere idol that we make, but the true God who made us. Therefore we should repent of the sin and ignorance that leads us to ignore God and we should prepare for the day when he will judge us. He will judge us through the one he raised from the dead.

Although Paul built strong bridges to his audience, he didn't flatter them or give them what they wanted to hear. He was prepared to speak of their ignorance, of their need for repentance, and of future judgment. The response was typical of what we might expect in evangelistic preaching: some sneered, some sought more teaching, and some were saved.

This brief consideration of audience adaption strongly advises against our hawking our favorite sermon around a number of churches, making assumptions about the state of a congregation, or slapping some standard call for response onto each message. Biblical preaching has far more nuance.

SPEAKING TO THE CHURCH AS A WHOLE

In the New Testament, most application is to the body of Christ as a whole in the first place and to individuals only secondarily. We tend to miss that when we read our English translations, because we have no way of distinguishing between "you" singular and "you" plural. But

---

Flemming, "Contextualizing the Gospel in Athens: Paul's Areopagus Address as a Paradigm for Missionary Communication," *Missiology* 30, no. 2 (2002). It is interesting that two leading megachurches in the USA are called *Mars Hill*.

in Greek you can distinguish the two, and the plural is more common. Paul, for the most part, writes to churches, and even when he writes to individuals (Timothy, Titus, and Philemon), the church is usually in view as well.[12] Many of his applications are, therefore, to be taken up in the life of the church as a body, family, or household. These corporate images are his prime focus.

A quick perusal of 1 Corinthians, the letter in which Paul most fully addresses trouble in a church, readily demonstrates this. Paul begins by assuring them that they have been enriched in every way (1:5). That does not mean that each individual has been enriched in every way, but the church as a whole has been fully supplied with all that it needs to live for Christ. Tragically, however, the church has broken into factions, focusing on human leaders: Paul, Apollos, Cephas. The body has been divided. Paul talks to them, therefore, about what the church really is. It is a rather motley collection of pretty ordinary people who have been called together by the seemingly foolish message of Christ crucified. In the church, God has mocked human wisdom. Together, they are now servants working in a field (3:5–9); they are a building, founded on Christ (3:10–15); they are a temple indwelt by the Spirit of God (3:16–17).

As God's new covenant community, they are to expel from their fellowship those who are immoral (chapter 5), they are not to take each other to court as if they needed to depend on unbelievers to help them live in community together (chapter 6), and they are not to live immorally with one another as if they had not been washed, sanctified, and justified. When they decide whether or not to eat meat from the local market that has previously been sacrificed to idols, their chief consideration is to be the effect it will have on other believers (chapters 8–10).

12. For example, the final "you"s of 1 and 2 Timothy and Titus are plural, despite the letters being written primarily to individuals. Peter Adam writes, "Most of the Bible is addressed to churches (e.g. Old Testament books, Romans, Corinthians, Galatians), to the people of God, or to leaders of churches for the benefit of the churches (Timothy, Titus). . . . This means that the primary question is not, 'What is God saying to me?' but 'What is God saying to the church?'" Peter Adam, *Hearing God's Words: Exploring Biblical Spirituality*, New Studies in Biblical Theology (Downers Grove: IVP, Apollos, 2004), 175.

When they come together to celebrate the Lord's Supper, they are not to go ahead and grab whatever they can, ignoring their brothers and sisters (chapter 11). When they exercise spiritual gifts, it is not to be for the selfish display of individual spirituality but for the building up of the body as a whole (chapters 12–14).

Obviously, individuals have to think about what each challenge means for them personally. But the applications are about the formation of the church as the holy bride of Christ, not just the maturity of individual Christians. We need to bear this constantly in mind when we are applying God's Word. As well as asking, "What does this mean for *me?*," we should ask, "What does this mean for *us?*" As well as thinking about the spiritual condition of individuals, we should think about the spiritual condition of churches.

This will prompt preachers to speak rather personally to the flock as a whole. We may commend a church that is going well and should know it. "I want to commend you, friends, for being one of the most loving, caring, thoughtful churches I have ever seen." We may also challenge a church that thinks it is going well when it is not. "Let's be honest. We have fine buildings and well-organized rosters and a pretty good reputation. But there are too many individuals who come into this church for a Sunday service and never come again. They are lost in the crowd while we talk to our friends and busily go about our duties . . ."

WORKING WITH VARYING SPIRITUAL CONDITIONS

Living application means taking the lives of people seriously, and, as we have seen, not everyone is the same. So how does this angle on application help in preaching the texts we have considered in previous chapters?

In Haggai 1, the prominent spiritual condition being addressed is that of a people who are not going well and they don't know it. They can't understand why they are experiencing such negative physical conditions. It doesn't seem to have dawned on them that it is because they have been disobedient, neglecting the house of God and preferring their home construction projects. They need to wake up to reality.

It may well be that the people to whom we preach are in the same place. Then again, they may not be. It is an applicatory fallacy to assume that our congregation is in the same place as the original hearers. If the text speaks to apostate Israel, we ought not to assume that our congregation is apostate; if the recipients of the text have wrong priorities, we ought not to assume that our congregation has wrong priorities. We will have to nuance our application according to the diversity of spiritual conditions present in the church and take into consideration the spiritual condition of the church as a whole. But even if the church is going well in terms of its priorities, this passage still speaks relevantly. It warns of the danger of complacency and encourages those who have responded with wholehearted zeal for the Lord.

When we preach Haggai 1, it is also worth noting that the message was presented to God's covenant people (plural), not to a disparate bunch of individuals. While the issues raised have bearing on our individual choices and preferences, this text should primarily prompt us to think corporately about our priorities.

Psalm 73 is much more the story of an individual believer as the psalm depicts three distinct spiritual conditions. The first and most prominent condition is that of the psalmist in the first half of the psalm. He is not going well and he knows it. He is backsliding. He is slipping from his commitment to the Lord. Sins of jealousy and envy grip his heart. Faithfulness to God is looking less and less attractive and spiritual disaster is just around the corner. That, then, is a spiritual condition that we ought to discuss openly as we preach. It's easy for people to find themselves in a similar place even if they have had a strong faith in the past. We ought to describe this condition in contemporary terms, explaining how we can get to such a perilous place and warning people against going or staying there.

The second spiritual condition depicted in the psalm is that of the arrogant unbeliever. This is the kind of person the psalmist is envying. The picture is of people who seem to have it all together: strong, young, fit, healthy, carefree, living it up. They wear trendy clothes, hang out in cool bars, drive fast cars, and have good-looking friends. They don't seem to have a care in the world, and they certainly don't care for God or anything religious. Why do they need to? They've got it all. All except one thing. They haven't got a secure eternity. Though it may not look like it, they are not going well at all, and the tragedy is that they don't know it. We need to warn people who are living this way, or those who aspire to, that it is a perilous lifestyle.

The third soul condition in the psalm is that of the psalmist after he has come to his senses. Now he's going well and he knows it. He knows that it is good to be near God. He enjoys God's presence and treasures true security. He has peace. He has a sound perspective on life. He has all he desires and this world's pleasures look tawdry in comparison with what he has now seen in Christ. This, surely, is where we want all our people to be. We should paint an attractive picture of the true blessedness of living close to God. We want to give people every incentive to trade this world's pleasures for the surpassing greatness of knowing Christ.

On one occasion, when I preached this psalm, I concluded with these three spiritual conditions. I asked people where they were: were they in the first part of the psalm, backsliding like the psalmist; were they in verses 4–11, living the life of the arrogant ungodly; or were they living in the second half of the psalm, secure in the grace of God? I tried to press on them that only one of those places was a healthy place to be. Another time, however, I didn't finish that way because I was preaching at a theological college where I assumed there were few, hopefully none, in the place of the ungodly. I worked descriptions of the other two conditions into the body of the sermon and concluded by asking them how their walk with God had been in the past semester. Had they drawn closer to him or drifted from him? Had they increased not only in their knowledge of God but in their sense that it is good to be near God, and not good to be far from him? Because Psalm 73 is the testimony of an individual, the application is rightly targeted at individuals.

Such varying soul conditions are not so prominent in Ephesians 1. The opening phrase—"Praise be to the God and Father of our Lord Jesus Christ, who has blessed us in the heavenly realms with every spiritual blessing in Christ"—prompts the church to reflect on

147

its glorious position in Christ. Whether the Ephesians fully grasped their position or not is unclear, and it is not the focus. These words are written with a view to urging the church to rejoice in its God-given privileges and blessings as a result of having experienced the power and grace of the gospel. Both Jews and Gentiles have been brought into one body, having been saved by the electing love of the Father, through the redeeming work of the Son, and sealed with the indwelling of the Spirit. They have been caught up in the grand redemptive purposes of God. If, as a church, they are in the spiritual condition they ought to be in, they will rejoice in the truths Paul outlines here. They will bask in the warm glow of the doctrines of election, redemption, and Spirit-baptism. They will value the work of each person of the Trinity. They will feel richly blessed and will readily praise God and give him all the glory.

But not everyone may be in that place. Some among them may accept the doctrine of election yet fear that they are not among the elect. Some may hate that doctrine and see it as an affront to the exercise of their own free will. Some may think they are elect but use their election as an excuse for spiritual laxity, presuming on grace rather than living in its glorious grip. Some may reject Christ altogether. They have no interest in him at all and make no claim to be among his redeemed people. All the blessings stated are for those "in Christ," but these people are clearly not in him. They were dragged along to church by their persistent Christian friend.

The wise preacher, then, will not assume that all his hearers are "going well and know it." The main thrust of the message will be to the church as a whole, urging them to be a community of people who rejoice in the grace of God's redemptive plan and praise him for it. But it will be helpful to address, along the way, people in other places spiritually. Pause and talk to the person presuming on God's grace. Spend a few minutes addressing the concern of those who fear they are not among the elect. Stop and challenge the person who has no relationship with Jesus and is, therefore, missing out on the rich blessings that come only through him.

Taking the time to connect the text to the varying realities of life, and especially the spiritual conditions of different individuals and congregations, does much to increase the impact of application. It is the very opposite of the bolt-on approach that assumes a few fixed applications will suit every text and every person. Picturing our hearers helps us drive God's Word much more specifically into the lives of the different men, women, and children who have come to hear God speak.

By this point in the living application process, a preacher has given massive thought to how the text speaks today. The God-intended purposes of the living Word have been identified, insight has been poured into the message from the preacher's life reservoir, thought has been given to how the applications bear on the four faculties of the human heart, and the applications have been honed to address the specific life situations and soul conditions of the hearers. But, as we have said earlier, words must now be found to achieve these ends. How can we package this application so that it hits home? How can we make it interesting so that our hearers don't drift? How can we make it telling so they sense that it speaks pertinently to them? How can we make it both forceful and winsome?

It is possible for a preacher to have great lines of application but an ineffective means of making the applications strike home. You might know how the text should be applied but not actually know how to do it. So we will turn now to nine ways of making applicatory truth sting and sing—nine ways of making all these applications really live.

DISCUSSION QUESTIONS

1. Create a list categorizing the various spiritual conditions represented in your congregation. Consider both those going well and those not going well.

2. For the next sermon you prepare, fill in the spiritual conditions grid, noting the kind of spiritual conditions the text particularly addresses.

3. Take one application you intend to make and try shaping it for people in at least three different spiritual or life situations.

4. How would you describe the spiritual condition of your church as a whole? What are your church's most pressing spiritual needs? What are your church's greatest spiritual strengths?

5. When you shape sermon application, do you tend to think individually or corporately? Why?

6. What are the strengths and weaknesses of ending a sermon by addressing a few words to several different kinds of people?

|6|

APPLICATIONS THAT LIVE: SHOOTING SHARP ARROWS

ONE OF MY FAVORITE regions for climbing and walking in New Zealand is Lake Wanaka. Surrounded by beautiful mountains, the lake is picture perfect. For those not into serious mountain climbing but wanting to go to some higher ground to take in the magnificent views, Mt. Roy is a great option. Two or three hours will see you to the top, as you wind up a long zigzag track through sheep-grazing farmland. But the trip down takes only a fraction of the time. There are many well-worn shortcuts, formed by dozens of people and sheep who have cut corners in the race to the bottom. Although it is jarring on the old body, the shortcuts are almost irresistible.

In preaching, too, there are some almost irresistible shortcuts. The most tempting when it comes to application is the shortcut from explanation to exhortation, with nothing in between. When training preaching students, I urge them to do four things with biblical truth: state it, ground it, impress it, and apply it. We need to state truth as clearly and compellingly as possible. Then we need to ground it in the text, showing where in the text we found it and explaining, proving, and reinforcing it, often calling on other Scriptures in the process. Next we need to impress that truth upon people so that, at a heart level, they are convinced, persuaded, and moved by it. Finally, we apply it to their lives, giving them an understanding of how to respond to the truth. The tempting shortcut is to roll "state" and "ground" together into a longish explanation of the text, and then move briefly, at the end of the sermon, to some application, usually in the form of a few commands or exhortations. We are long on explanation (the climb up) but, on the way down, we omit impressing the truth on people, and we are reductionistic in the applications we make. We take a shortcut to exhortation.

If we are aiming at the heart, the "explain-exhort" formula is inadequate. It is a shortcut that misses the heart. What we need to do is to spend precious sermon time impressing the truth upon people so that it touches the mind, conscience, and passions as well as the will. We need to remember that explaining truth doesn't necessarily mean people will accept it, and commanding response doesn't necessarily mean people will do it.

Bald exhortation following extensive explanation can actually disempower people in an unfair way. Think, for example, of the preacher who has opened some text of Scripture at length, explaining it in detail and producing from it a profound truth, which he then applies by saying, "Isn't that encouraging! What a wonderful comfort this is. In fact, if this doesn't encourage you, I wonder if you have even begun to understand the grace of God. This should make all of us full of joy and thankfulness." Old Mrs. Black sits in the third pew from the front thinking, "Well, I'm sorry, young man, but it didn't encourage me at all. And I do happen to understand the grace of God rather well. You can't command me to feel encouraged; you need to encourage me. You can't tell me to feel comforted; you need to comfort me. You can't put the guilt trip on me, saying that we should be full of joy and thankfulness; you need to make me feel joyful and thankful." Mrs. Black just happens to be pretty savvy in her response. Many others will not be so sharp. They will feel discouraged because the application has not only failed to comfort them but has actually called into question their own understanding of the gospel.

This issue struck me with particular clarity after reading some words C. S. Lewis addressed to other writers. "Instead of telling us a thing is 'terrible,' describe it so that we'll be terrified. Don't say it was a 'delight,' make us say 'delightful' when we've read the description. You see, all those words ('horrifying,' 'wonderful,' 'hideous,' 'exquisite') are only saying to your readers, 'Please, will you do my job for me.'"[1] Frequently, I fear, we as preachers leave the congregation to do our job for us. But how unrealistic that is. If we don't know how to bring encouragement and comfort from the text, what makes us think they will be able to when they have come to the text without the hours of study and prayer we have had? *We* need to do the hard work of application and bless our people with it.

So the question is, how? How do we impress the truth on people so that they are convinced, convicted, and stirred? How do we form applications that penetrate the heart? How do we shoot straight? The answer is found in drawing some sharp arrows from the preacher's quiver. There are nine arrows that preachers regularly use with good effect in impressing truth on people's hearts. We will not use all the arrows in every sermon, but we should endeavor to select the right ones to get the job done in each case. In most sermons, we will need to fire quite a few if we are to make a heart impact.

1. APPEAL TO PEOPLE'S OWN JUDGMENT

In seeking to convince people of a certain truth, we can call on their consciences as a witness. We appeal to what they know, believe, accept, can see, or can't deny. Phrases like, "Don't you find that . . ." or "I'm sure you'd agree that . . ." usually indicate that we are making an appeal to our people's own judgment and intuition.[2]

A preacher might, for instance, be speaking of the doctrine of original sin and he knows that for some this is a hard truth to accept. So

---

1. *Letters of C. S. Lewis*, ed. W. H. Lewis (New York: Harcourt, Brace, and World, 1966), 271, quoted in Timothy Keller, "Reformed Worship in the Global City," in *Worship by the Book*, ed. D. A. Carson (Grand Rapids: Zondervan, 2002), 209.

2. Robert Dabney, in *Sacred Rhetoric*, spoke of there being two sources for all our mental convictions: self-consciousness and intuitive judgments. The former concerns our innate knowledge of our self, the latter universally admitted truths. See Robert Lewis Dabney in *Sacred Rhetoric* (1870; repr., Edinburgh: Banner of Truth, 1979), 182–83.

he says, "Maybe you don't like the idea that babies are born hard-wired to sin. You think of them as innocent. But let me ask those of you who are parents: did you ever have to teach your little fellow how to lie? Or did you ever have to sit little Daisy down and say, 'Okay, sweetheart, it's a big bad world out there and you are going to have to learn how to be selfish, how to stand up for yourself, how to grab toys back, how to scream when you don't get what you want'? You never had to do that, did you? That all came very naturally and easily to dear little Daisy. And it came to her without any lesson, or without her ever seeing you kick and scream; and it came very early in her life because she was hard-wired to be selfish."

Such an appeal to experience and life observation is much harder to argue with than the theological definition of original sin. Used well, this can be a sharp and effective arrow to fire now and then.

2. ANTICIPATE AND ANSWER OBJECTIONS

The previous example overlaps with this next arrow. The preacher can anticipate people struggling to accept the doctrine of original sin. With his first arrow he appeals to their own experience. With his next arrow he addresses their objections quite directly. People will often fully understand what we say, but they won't agree with us. We must help them accept what we are saying by anticipating their objections and answering them straightaway.[3]

A classic way of doing so can be seen in the following scenario. A preacher dealing with the command to "rejoice in the Lord always" might say,

> Maybe you're thinking, "That's all very well for you to say. You're in Christian ministry. Your life is sorted out. You can see God's hand so

3. Donald Sunukjian suggests that there are three main reasons people do not accept what we are saying: they fail to see the cause-effect connection that is characteristic of much biblical truth, they think that the truth is contrary to real life, or they simply have something else that is more important to them. He offers helpful advice for how each of these objections may be addressed. See Donald R. Sunukjian, *Invitation to Biblical Preaching: Proclaiming Truth with Clarity and Relevance* (Grand Rapids: Kregel, 2007), 92–106.

clearly. Try rejoicing in the Lord with mental health issues, a broken marriage, and unemployment. It's not so easy." I'm sure that's true. I'm sure that's not so easy. Your situation may well be far harder than mine, and I don't know all the things you're going through. Maybe your situation is harder than anyone else's in this room. There might be little, if anything, in your life that you feel happy about.

But it helps to remember, Paul didn't write this from a nice hotel room on the Mediterranean coast. He wrote this from prison. And in his life he was stoned, shipwrecked, flogged, and maligned. Okay, maybe your life has been harder than Paul's. That's possible. But the point is this: Paul is talking about not a joy that's related to our circumstances but a joy that rises above them. He's talking about a joy that is precisely for people like you—people who've been hurt, and who are struggling, and who don't know how to cope. He's talking about finding joy in the Lord when you can't find it in people, or paychecks, or personal achievements. God isn't calling you here to something impossible—he's calling you to himself. He's calling you to find joy in him when there's no joy anywhere else.

This kind of dialogue with people serves a number of purposes. It increases our credibility as we acknowledge the realities of their experiences and the limitations of our own. It shows that we take them and their situations seriously. It proves that we have thought about some of the hard issues of life and are not offering merely slick, theoretical answers. It suggests that there is a way through some of their good questions. Most importantly, though, it forces us to sit down and think hard about how applied truth looks in the real-life situations of our people. We are much more likely to speak to the heart when we do that.

3. GIVE REASONS, MOTIVATIONS, AND INCENTIVES

We've seen that the mind and the will work together. If we want people to take action, rather than simply demand it of them, we need to convince them that it is best. Pastors are to be not coercive but persuasive. Preachers who berate, nag, and scold fail to produce mature gospel-hearted believers. By contrast, Paul constantly presents gospel motivations and reasons for the actions he requires of people. Sexual purity, for example, is urged on the Corinthians not just because it is morally right, but because God has washed them, sanctified them, and justified them and their bodies are now God's temples, indwelt by his Holy Spirit (1 Cor. 6:9–20). On the basis of their gospel status, he urges them to a life of sexual purity because impurity would be a contradiction of their standing in Christ.

The gospel is full of motivations and incentives to respond to God and, as we set them forth, we fire off the next arrow. Ultimately, the twin eternal realities of heaven and hell stand before us. There is a heaven to be won and a hell to be avoided. There is divine reward and divine retribution. But even short of those ultimate realities, the gospel provides many incentives for godly action. They may be stated in the text or they may be deduced from a wider Christian worldview. As we ask the right questions, we will be able to draw on our biblical-theological understanding to provide helpful answers. So we must ask, Why should they do this? What rewards accompany it? What blessings will follow? What will the benefits be in their life and the lives of others? How will this glorify God and aid the work of his church and his kingdom? Why have saints in the past done this? What will they miss out on if they don't do this? Where could disobedience lead?

To illustrate the use of this arrow, I will briefly suggest to preachers five motivations for using motivations! First, by providing motivations you will encourage your people to take what you are saying more seriously. They will not just receive a bald command but will have to reckon with compelling reasons for acting on that command. Second, by providing motivations you will more keenly engage their minds. You will speak to the will via the mind. You will force them to think about their action or lack thereof. Third, motivations will often resonate with their experience and make the demand seem more reasonable. People will frequently know the incentives or warnings to be true. Fourth, motivations will help them realize that how they respond to the message has consequences. It is not "take it or leave it." Motivations help spell out positive and negative consequences. Finally, and perhaps most importantly, providing motivations will enable you to link moral calls to gospel truths more clearly. If your motivations are rooted in the gospel, then what you call people to do will be grounded in the gospel and not in some kind of sub-Christian, self-improvement pop psychology.

4. BE SPECIFIC, POINTED, AND DIRECT

The aim of application is to be helpful. We want to help people respond to the text we are expounding, and most people will find it helpful if we are specific rather than general, pointed rather than vague, direct rather than indirect. If we leave our applications in vague generalities, they will respond in vague generalities. In other words, they will do nothing. We fire the fourth arrow when we are specific, pointed, and direct.

If, for example, we are speaking of some area of sin and we want people to be convicted of that sin, we need to get specific. Rick sits near the back of the church with his family, and he can fudge it when the preacher warns against the danger of sexual temptation. The preacher warns that we live in a sex-saturated society and we all need to be on our guard. Rick nods in agreement. But the application has not gripped his conscience because it is general. Since it has not gripped his conscience, he's less likely to make any concrete changes that will help him avoid such temptation. He understands with his mind, but no arrows have pierced his heart.

But then, just when he's feeling okay, the preacher moves up a gear. "Let me speak to the men here for a few moments. Guys, it's been said that men easily fall for one of three temptations: girls, gold, or glamour. I want to speak for a few minutes to those of you who know that your weak spot is girls. You're not about to commit adultery but you know that your eyes easily stray. You push the boundaries in what you watch on TV and at the movies. You click on the mouse and go places on the Internet you don't want anyone else to know about. You play in your mind with fantasies that are blatantly immoral. And you try to reason that it is under control and it is only a fantasy. But, men, don't think that you can easily draw the line and stop there. Sin in the mind is exactly where most marital unfaithfulness begins. In fact, Jesus says it *is* marital unfaithfulness. It is adultery in the heart. And many of you know that such heart sin gets a grip on you and you just can't shake it off . . ." Now the preacher is hitting hard because he has become specific. Rick's conscience begins to burn. An appeal to change will begin to gain far more traction in his life.

In calling for specific action, however, we need to distinguish between action that is biblically commanded and action that is, perhaps, a useful possibility. Specific applications should include a range of possibilities if there is not only one right way. For example, if you are encouraging personal prayer, while the evangelical norm might be a morning quiet time, that is not the only option. Suggest other times that might work for the mom with young children, for the shift worker, for the retiree. Suggest possible aids to personal prayer: perhaps a prayer list, or a prayer diary, or journaling, or praying while you take a walk in the evening. There is no one right technique, so we should try to give a range of options that may well prompt further ideas on the part of our hearers.

Speaking directly to people is also important. The question is often asked, Should we speak in first or second person when preaching? Is it "we" or "you"? The answer is, yes! If you look at the New Testament, you'll see that both are used. We can change from one to the other quite easily, sometimes including ourselves with the congregation because together we sit under God's Word and hear what he has to say to us. At other times we can speak very directly to God's people because we know we are his herald, speaking his Word to them. The more you push into pointed application, the more helpful it will be to use the second person. Preachers should feel free to use both, as I have in this paragraph, paying particular attention to what message the use of either pronoun will send. Does the first person make it too weak? Does the second person sound too arrogant? Will it allow us to speak candidly?

One final aspect of direct, specific application is to make good use of questions. While they can be overused and should by no means be our only applicatory device, questions are useful for pressing a matter on people. Ask them straight. To illustrate, let me ask preachers a few straight questions right now: Do your applications get specific or do they remain vague and general? When you speak of sin, do you name specific sins that you know are real issues for your people? When you encourage your congregation, do you tell them why you love them, value them, and always speak highly of them to others? When you develop your applications, do you do so in a hurry, hoping they will come together when you preach, or do you labor as carefully over how to get inside your people's hearts as you do to get into the heart of the text?

5. USE ILLUSTRATIONS FOR BOTH CLARITY AND IMPACT

As with each arrow, there is a danger here of overuse. Some preachers feel that their power and impact depend almost entirely on effective illustrations. The sermon becomes a string of stories, jokes, and anecdotes. The preacher feels inordinate pressure to be clever, humorous, and fascinating. We are, however, easily given to the swing of the proverbial pendulum, and too many expository preachers fail to use illustrations to good effect. I have heard some able expository preachers almost apologize for an illustration as if they were descending to the lowest trick of the trade.

Illustrations, used judiciously, are of immense help in impressing truth upon the heart. They help because they put truth in a more tangible, concrete form. Instead of seeing clothes on a rack, we see them on a person. Instead of examining a jewel in the dark, a light is thrown on it and we see it clearly. Illustrations help people see and feel truth as well as know it. That means that they allow the preacher to access more of the heart. They speak to the mind by triggering the mental faculty of imagination, but they can also speak to the conscience and to the passions. They tend to speak least directly to the will and, given our propensity to overly address the will in application, this makes illustrations a valuable aid.[4]

4. Note, however, Bryan Chapell's argument that illustrations address not only the heart (by which he chiefly means the emotions) but also the will, because we make decisions and responses on the basis of not only what we know but how we feel about what we know. Bryan Chapell, *Using Illustrations to Preach with Power* (Wheaton: Crossway, 2001), 37–40.

The value of a story speaking to the whole heart is seen compellingly when the prophet Nathan confronts David with his sin with Bathsheba. He tells the story of a rich man who steals the little pet ewe lamb of his very poor neighbor in order to provide a meal for guests who have come his way. David is immediately incensed at the injustice of the situation and demands that the man should die. The story has made an impact on David; his passions have been stirred. But the main impact is still to come. Nathan turns to him and says, "You are the man!" (2 Sam. 12:7). Now the story is cast on David's conscience. He's been caught from behind and there is no escape. He has condemned himself.

This powerful use of parable was what Jesus also did repeatedly. His stories, or illustrations, were not merely pleasant entertainment to lighten the sermon. They were the means of bringing deep conviction and confronting people with truth in a way plain statement would not achieve.

Of course, not every illustration will do that. It is incredibly hard to use illustrations half as well as Jesus did. But even in our less convicting stories, illustrations help us bring truth to life, anchor it in reality, and make it clear and memorable. Paul uses "ordinary" illustrations when he urges Timothy to endure hardship like a good soldier, to compete according to the rules like a good athlete, and to work hard like a good farmer. Each image is loaded and can easily be unpacked. They put flesh on the bones of endurance, obedience, and effort.

6. PROVIDE TESTIMONIES TO THE TRUTH

Closely related to illustration is the "real life" illustration of a person who in some way reinforces the truth of which we are speaking. Testimonies may come from our own life, the lives of other people we know, or the lives of those we've read about. But with each, there are dangers. The danger in using our own life is that we become too prominent and, if the testimony is a positive one, we appear proud. Generally, self-deprecation works and self-congratulation doesn't. The danger with using the testimonies of people we know is that it may give the impression that anyone who shares his or her life with us may provide the next sermon illustration. Pastoral ministry requires us to keep many confidences and to give people assurance that what they say to us stays with us. So I find that many people whose lives illustrate the truth I am speaking of simply cannot be used. The danger with illustrations from our reading is that too often our reading is of historical figures or preachers, whose lives, while fascinating to us, are often far removed from the lives of the people to whom we are preaching.

These dangers will limit the use we make of personal testimony. But limitation is not elimination. When an appropriate testimony can be added, it has the value of clothing in flesh and blood the principles of which we are speaking. This invariably brings the matter closer to people's hearts. Some stories will inspire, some will expose, some will excite, some will sober us.

7. SHOW WHAT IT LOOKS LIKE IN PRACTICE

The arrows we are considering each aid the preacher in drilling biblical truth down into real life. The seventh arrow does so by describing in story form what the response we are calling for actually looks like in practice. We may use a fictional but "real" scenario, drawn from the realities of life, in order to give a mental picture of how the truth we are describing or the application we are calling for works in practice. Donald Sunukjian says, "Unless the listeners get a mental picture of some real-life situation, the biblical truth remains an abstraction. Unless they see a video running in their minds, the biblical concept remains vague and unhelpful. The message has no apparent bearing on their lives until they visualize some person, event, or circumstance in their everyday world."[5]

What does this approach look like in practice? Consider the following introduction to a sermon on our need to listen to God's preached Word:

5. Sunukjian, *Invitation to Biblical Preaching*, 106. For further examples see 106–24.

Picture Tom. He's had a huge week with long hours at work, a few minor crises with the kids, and a great party to go to on Saturday night. Sunday morning he wakes late, feeling terrible. He gulps down some breakfast and chases the kids to get ready for church. Driving slightly over the speed limit all the way, they arrive only five minutes late—about par for the course. Tom and his family shuffle in to the back row, where he takes about five minutes to settle the kids, catch his breath, and tune in to the service. But no sooner has he settled than his young son needs to use the restroom. Out he goes, only to return just as his daughter drops her pencil case. There is a quiet skirmish to gather pens and pencils from under the seats in front. With relief, Tom eventually hears the kids called to go out to Sunday school. He settles back in his seat for the start of the sermon.

Do you think Tom is in a good state of mind to hear a sermon? Is his heart ready? Is he expectant of what God might say to him? Is he keen and hungry for God's Word? Forget it! Unless the sermon is astoundingly relevant, phenomenally interesting, and remarkably dynamic, Tom is going to drift mentally, physically, and spiritually for the next thirty minutes. It will be the most peaceful half hour of his week. And the preacher will scarcely disturb him at all.

Tom is not a real person, but his situation is real. People understand what he is going through. They may well relate to him and will listen further to see what he should do about his situation. Such a fictional, but real, scenario helps anchor truth in life.

8. USE FRESH, VIVID WORDS

Words are our tools. They can be sharp or blunt, fresh or bland, insightful or pedestrian. They can grab our attention or wash over us. They can be unhelpfully complicated, overly simplistic, or well chosen for clear effect. They are worth choosing well because people's minds will be more captivated by apt words, and even their affections can be stirred by graphic ones.

Too often, preachers are wordy. We have a reputation for being verbose. Often, our higher education has extended our vocabulary and given us a facility with grammatically complicated sentences. So our preaching sounds like a commentary or an essay. We fail to note adequately the difference between written and oral communication.

How do we develop effective word usage? First, we need to expunge from our preaching words that are not easily understood. The issue is not whether words are large or small, but whether their meaning is clear or not. Use the most interesting word that can easily be understood by everyone. Second, use words in short sentences. In public speech, it is awkward to have sentences comprising multiple clauses. Use mostly single-clause sentences. Third, assign yourself some banned words, and think up alternatives for them. My youngest daughters, who are homeschooled, use a resource for helping them develop their writing style. They are given a list of banned words for which they must always find substitutes. Some of their banned verbs are *said, thought, go, went, see, saw,* and *like.* Some banned adjectives are *good, bad,* and *fun.* For each banned word they have a list of alternatives. Instead of *said* they can use words like *exclaimed, whispered, howled, ejaculated, screamed, murmured, uttered, croaked, gasped, squeaked, stated, expressed, chattered, scoffed, whined, jeered, grumbled, moaned,* or *muttered.* They have to think about how the person said it. It is amazing what a difference that makes to their writing.

A fourth way of developing good word usage is to employ precise, descriptive words. It is much more colorful to speak of a rusted, blue 1982 Ford Escort than simply a car. This very brief description creates a mental picture. Finally, use brief analogies and images. The Puritans excelled in doing so, refraining from the telling of stories but employing many striking word pictures. They used words like hammers to nail the truth into people's minds. They used them as bellows to fan the affections into flame.

The difficulty for the preacher is to know when and where to develop these word skills. The pulpit is the worst place to try. There, we want our mind to be on biblical truth, not on rhetorical skill. One possibility is to work at these skills by preparing a sermon manuscript. While preaching from a full manuscript tends to hinder freedom and effectiveness, the discipline of writing will help preachers think about how to express thoughts clearly and compellingly. Writing a manuscript and then discarding it has value, especially for the young preacher. Another helpful discipline is to engage in other forms of writing. Producing brief articles and papers can help us think carefully about how to use words. We should also practice verbal skills in everyday conversation. If we deliberately focus on using clear, crisp words in brief sentences, and employ as many deft descriptions and figures of speech as possible, it will become more natural for us to use words effectively in the pulpit. But most likely none of this will be possible if we have not trained our minds by exposing them to the words of others. By reading great literature and the best of speeches, by studying the arguments and rhetoric of others, by enjoying poetry or drama, by delving into history or philosophy, we train our minds to appreciate precise words and rigorous argument. This develops our capacity to use words well ourselves. Whether our education is formal or informal, an educated mind produces better speech than an uneducated one.

Does this really help us shoot straight? Absolutely. The human heart is much less easily penetrated by mundane, complicated, flat speech. And it is never penetrated by incoherent, incomprehensible words.

9. SPEAK PERSONALLY AND PASSIONATELY

Richard Baxter wrote, "The best matter will scarcely move them, if it be not movingly delivered."[6] He also observed that "It seldom reacheth the heart of the hearer, which cometh not from the heart of the speaker."[7] It is a vital point. To speak to the heart, we must speak from the heart.

6. Richard Baxter, *The Reformed Pastor* (1656; abridged by William Brown, 1892; repr., Edinburgh: Banner of Truth, 1974), 149, quoted in Murray A. Capill, *Preaching with Spiritual Vigour: Including Lessons from the Life and Practice of Richard Baxter* (Fearn: Christian Focus, 2003), 163.
7. Richard Baxter, *Compassionate Counsel to All Young Men*, in *The Practical Works of Richard Baxter* (London: George Virtue, 1986; repr., Ligonier, PA: Soli Deo Gloria, 1990), 4:19, quoted in Capill, *Preaching with Spiritual Vigour*, 163.

This cannot be feigned. Passion must be genuine. The passions of the text must have worked their way into our own heart. The message we speak must have stirred us. We must have become convinced that what we are going to say is truly important. Stuart Olyott says, "Spiritual urgency is the fruit of a single conviction. . . . It is *that I have the truth that men and women need to hear.*" He maintains that "this conviction is the mother of all true eloquence."[8]

If we are dispassionate, cold, detached, or aloof in our public speech, we communicate that the message is not so important. People are unlikely to take it to heart. Similarly, if our passions are contrary to the text, we make our hearers onlookers rather than participants. When they see us speaking coldly of love, lightly of hell, or academically of Jesus, they are more likely to latch on to our manner than on to our subject matter. They will learn to relate coldly, lightly, or academically to these things.

Speaking passionately cannot be separated from speaking personally. That does not mean that we must always speak of ourselves and how we relate to the truths with which we are dealing. We must do that somewhat sparingly so that we are not the focus of our preaching. But it does mean that when we speak of any biblical truth, we speak of it as something that we know, love, value, hold to, and believe in. When we speak of God, for example, we speak of him as someone we know and love—someone whose honor matters to us, whose Word delights us, whose grace amazes us. Then, when we preach, it will be patently obvious to our hearers that we are not detached commentators engaging in post-match analysis, but ardent fans who wear the team colors and cheer loudly.

Speaking personally also means speaking with love for the people to whom we speak. Paul spoke freely to people, telling them they were his joy and crown. He loved them and told them so. The preacher who comes across as cold and distant from his people, who seems to love God but not his chosen ones, who is caught up in the things of heaven but not the lives of people on earth, will have far less success in winning the hearts of men, women, and children. Love for people, as well as love for God, must drive our work.

8. Stuart Olyott, *Preaching—Pure and Simple* (Bridgend: Bryntirion, 2005), 150.

PERSUASIVE ARGUMENT

When these arrows are fired in judicious combinations, something of an assault is made on the hearers' hearts. Truth is not just taught; it is pressed against them with some force.

But (to employ the second arrow) you may be thinking, "Isn't this all just human rhetorical technique? Isn't this the kind of Greek wisdom Paul rejected? Aren't we meant to just speak the plain truth of Scripture and let the Spirit bring conviction to people's hearts?" Well, evidently, Paul himself saw no disjunction between employing these kinds of homiletical skills and depending on the Spirit to drive the truth of Scripture into people's hearts. Romans 9 provides a brilliant example of how he shapes a compelling and persuasive argument, driving it into the heart while dealing with substantial doctrine.

The issue he deals with is this: the place of Israel in God's plan of redemption. He explains God's purposes by weighing into the doctrine of election. But look at how he does so. He begins personally, exposing his own heart passion:

> I speak the truth in Christ—I am not lying, my conscience confirms it in the Holy Spirit—I have great sorrow and unceasing anguish in my heart. For I could wish that I myself were cursed and cut off from Christ for the sake of my brothers, those of my own race, the people of Israel. (Rom. 9:1–3)

He then briefly sketches a picture of Israel's privileged spiritual position by calling on truths none of his readers would have denied and so strengthening the sense of tragedy at their disobedience to the gospel: "Theirs is the adoption as sons; theirs the divine glory, the covenants, the receiving of the law, the temple worship and the promises. Theirs are the patriarchs, and from them is traced the human ancestry of Christ, who is God over all, forever praised! Amen" (Rom. 9:4–5).

So what is the explanation? Paul states the issue plainly according to the biblical narrative: "It is not as though God's Word had failed.

For not all who are descended from Israel are Israel" (v. 6). It is not God's fault, he says. God never promised that he would save every Jew. Not all Israel is Israel. But that truth may be hard to swallow, so he backs it up with two biblical examples: Isaac and Ishmael, and Jacob and Esau:

> Nor because they are his descendants are they all Abraham's children. On the contrary, "It is through Isaac that your offspring will be reckoned." In other words, it is not the natural children who are God's children, but it is the children of the promise who are regarded as Abraham's offspring. For this was how the promise was stated: "At the appointed time I will return, and Sarah will have a son."
>
> Not only that, but Rebekah's children had one and the same father, our father Isaac. Yet, before the twins were born or had done anything good or bad—in order that God's purpose in election might stand: not by works but by him who calls—she was told, "The older will serve the younger." Just as it is written: "Jacob I loved, but Esau I hated." (9:7–13)

Paul has clearly explained the reason why not all Jews are currently being saved. But in throwing it back on God, he anticipates that some may object further: "What then shall we say? Is God unjust?" (v. 14). That is the objection he now answers, appealing again to biblical examples:

> Not at all! For he says to Moses,
>
> "I will have mercy on whom I have mercy,
>   and I will have compassion on whom I have compassion."
>
> It does not, therefore, depend on man's desire or effort, but on God's mercy. For the Scripture says to Pharaoh: "I raised you up for this very purpose, that I might display my power in you and that my name might be proclaimed in all the earth." Therefore God has mercy on whom he wants to have mercy, and he hardens whom he wants to harden. (9:14–18)

Evidently people struggled with the doctrine of election then as much as they do now, so Paul does not let his case rest. He wants to win their hearts and minds. So he anticipates a further complaint: "One of you will say to me: 'Then why does God still blame us? For who resists his will?'" (v. 19). How will he answer that? He effectively closes down those who resist this doctrine by way of an illustration:

> But who are you, O man, to talk back to God? Shall what is formed say to him who formed it, 'Why did you make me like this?' Does not the potter have the right to make out of the same lump of clay some pottery for noble purposes and some for common use? (9:20–21)

It is a compelling illustration and Paul proceeds to drill its truth home by asking some questions that are addressed to the conscience as much as to the mind:

> What if God, choosing to show his wrath and make his power known, bore with great patience the objects of his wrath—prepared for destruction? What if he did this to make the riches of his glory known to the objects of his mercy, whom he prepared in advance for glory—even us, whom he also called, not only from the Jews but also from the Gentiles? (9:22–24)

Paul is backing any opponents of this truth into a corner. God has never promised that every single Jew will be saved. Moreover, he has repeatedly foretold that he will embrace the Gentiles in place of the Jews. Paul packs this final punch with a string of quotations from the prophets:

> As he says in Hosea:

> "I will call them 'my people' who are not my people;
>   and I will call her 'my loved one' who is not my loved one,"

> and,

168

"It will happen that in the very place where it was said to them,
   'You are not my people,'
they will be called 'sons of the living God.'"

Isaiah cries out concerning Israel:

"Though the number of the Israelites be like the sand by the sea,
   only the remnant will be saved.
For the Lord will carry out
   his sentence on earth with speed and finality."

It is just as Isaiah said previously:

"Unless the Lord Almighty
   had left us descendants,
we would have become like Sodom,
   we would have been like Gomorrah." (9:25–29)

Paul continues his argument in the next two chapters, but we have seen enough to make the point that doctrine can and should be pressed against the heart. Which arrows did he fire? He has made use of arrows 1, 2, 4, 5, 6, 8, and 9 at least. They are not used mechanically or for the display of rhetorical skill. They are fired to aid Paul in making a tremendously important doctrinal point with persuasive clarity.

If, under the influence of the Holy Spirit, Paul employed this kind of skill in pressing home biblical truth, shouldn't we also work hard at making truth sing and sting? Our life applications need to live. We need to shoot straight at the heart. We need to fire off these arrows frequently. No preacher can afford to travel far in a sermon without firing one of these arrows. Long stretches of explanation followed by exhortation is nothing but a dead-end shortcut for application. Succumbing to the temptation to cut this corner is homiletically disastrous. Truth must be stated and grounded, but the largest task for the preacher is impressing it upon the heart. In that task, few things will be more helpful than to carry these nine arrows in your quiver, and then draw and fire them frequently.

Diagram 12: The Living Application Preaching Process

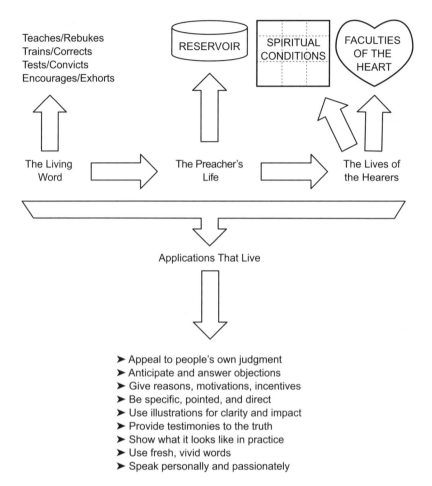

Teaches/Rebukes
Trains/Corrects
Tests/Convicts
Encourages/Exhorts

RESERVOIR

SPIRITUAL
CONDITIONS

FACULTIES
OF THE
HEART

The Living
Word

The Preacher's
Life

The Lives of
the Hearers

Applications That Live

➤ Appeal to people's own judgment
➤ Anticipate and answer objections
➤ Give reasons, motivations, incentives
➤ Be specific, pointed, and direct
➤ Use illustrations for clarity and impact
➤ Provide testimonies to the truth
➤ Show what it looks like in practice
➤ Use fresh, vivid words
➤ Speak personally and passionately

THE LIVING APPLICATION PREACHING PROCESS

The entire preaching process is depicted in diagram 12. The fruit of developing application by way of this process is a rich diversity of applications in sermon after sermon. The applicatory possibilities become almost endless. No two sermons need to sound the same. The many variables provide for endless variety. Each message is a unique fusion of text, preacher, and audience, set in the context of real life, which is itself constantly changing. Firing the applications home with many arrows brings life and vigor to the preaching and introduces further variety in tone and intensity.

While this approach yields a wealth of applicatory material, the model itself is simple. Identify the purposes of the text. Reflect on your own experiences of those things. Picture the people to whom you will preach—their heart faculties and their life situations and soul conditions—and then choose several arrows for shooting the applications to their target. Yes, it takes time, mental energy, and intense spiritual focus. But it is not impossible. This kind of application is within the reach of every expository preacher. And when you preach sermons that flow out of this process, your congregation will most likely rise up and called you blessed!

DISCUSSION QUESTIONS

1. How would you respond to someone who says that biblical truth is powerful in itself and doesn't need us to use preaching gimmicks like the nine arrows described in this chapter?

2. Take the manuscript of a sermon you have preached recently and decorate it with three color highlighters: one color for where you state and ground biblical truth (explanation), one color for where you spend time impressing the truth of the text on people (any of the nine arrows), and one color for direct application. Analyze the proportions of each. Have you spent adequate time explaining, impressing, and applying truth?

3. Which of the nine arrows do you use most easily and frequently? How many did you use in the sermon you analyzed?

4. Identify two arrows that you do not tend to fire often at all. Practice shooting these arrows by taking a recent truth you have preached on and finding ways to impress it using these two arrows.

5. Are there other arrows, not included in these nine, that you use to impress truth on people when you preach?

6. What are the dangers of using these means of impressing truth? How can they be misused?

PART 2

Putting Living Application into Practice

The living application preaching process presented in part 1 helps us see diverse applicatory possibilities in a text and enables a holistic approach to expository application. We are not left to our intuition alone when it comes to thinking about how a text applies today, and therefore we should not be so likely to settle for bolt-on applications. The process provides a systematic way of thinking about the applicatory intent of a text as it interfaces with the lives of the people to whom we preach, prompting diverse and penetrating applicatory preaching.

This process, however, raises some important questions that we need to consider if we are preaching week after week from a range of genres. There are four issues I want to address in part 2 because, sooner or later, anyone using this model will encounter each of them. The first issue is this: doesn't this model tend to produce rather narrowly pietistic preaching? How do you use this model in a way that avoids an intensely personal, introspective kind of application to the exclusion of other applicatory modes? The answer to this lies, I believe, in using this approach in the context of a broad kingdom theology. We will explore what that means in the next chapter.

A second issue to consider is how this model can aid us in applying Old Testament narratives. There are, perhaps, more pitfalls to avoid in the application of that genre than any other. Is it possible, in the light of this approach, to develop rich, varied, penetrating applications from Old Testament narratives without turning them into little more than nice stories with moral examples? In chapter 8 we will bend the living application preaching process toward the challenging task of preaching Christ-centered, redemptive-historical sermons loaded with application.

A third issue may be less prominent on the average preacher's radar, but it is essential to address if we are to use the living application model well. Sound application needs to pay attention to the distinct force of biblical indicatives, imperatives, and subjunctives. How do these grammatical forms give nuance to application? In particular, how do you apply indicatives? How do you avoid legalistic or moralistic preaching when applying imperatives? And what is the homiletical payload of subjunctives? In chapter 9, we'll think about preaching the three "ives."

Finally, we will step back and look at the preacher's work as a whole, from exegesis to aftermath. While developing application is essential, it is always part of a larger process. The model we have considered for developing living application needs to interface with all the other aspects of a preacher's exegetical and homiletical work. That will be the focus of chapter 10.

| 7 |

PREACHING
THE KINGDOM

A FEW YEARS AGO, I presented a paper at our annual preachers' conference entitled, "Confessions of a Pietistic Preacher."[1] I made five rather frank confessions. I confessed to a tendency to preach the gospel of individual salvation rather than the gospel of the kingdom, a tendency to address sin in the individual but not sin in society, a tendency to gravitate toward texts about personal spirituality but not texts about social justice, a tendency to set forth a vision for the church but not a vision for the world, and a tendency to preach a narrow view of worship and ministry rather than an "all of life" view. It's not that I always preach in this narrow way, but it can easily be my default setting.

It seemed that many preachers identified with my confessions. The reality is that preachers who are genuine in applying God's Word can sometimes do so penetratingly but not broadly or expansively. If we look at a text considering only the purposes of the Word in terms of its bearing on our own experience, the faculties of the human heart, and the varying spiritual conditions of individuals and churches, there is a danger that we will reduce the applicatory focus to matters of personal piety alone. Historically, pietism has been associated with an emphasis

1. Presented at the Preaching the Kingdom conference, Reformed Theological College, September 28, 2007.

on faith, prayer, personal godliness, the inner life of communion with Christ, the inward work of the Holy Spirit, and missions. Such emphases rightly lead to preaching that is searching, personal, spiritually challenging, and gospel focused. However, while true piety begins with personal spirituality, it must not end there.

PIETISM AT ITS BEST

Pietism predates the Wesleys, the Moravian Brethren, and even the Puritans. John Calvin is arguably the father of Protestant piety, but his pietism was broader than that of some of his successors. The word *piety* (*pietas*) or *godliness* is liberally scattered throughout his writings. In his thought, piety is rooted in a heart knowledge of God and marked by saving faith, reverential worship, filial fear, prayerful submission, and deep love for the triune God. Such godliness is "the beginning, middle and end of Christian living."[2] At the heart of such piety lies the doctrine of union with Christ. That union, in which we are in him and he in us, is realized through the Holy Spirit working faith within us and joining us by that faith to Christ. Believers are therefore animated and empowered by the secret power of Christ in them. The goal of such piety is the glory of God. We belong to him and are to live for him, as summarized in Calvin's famous motto, "I offer my heart, Lord, promptly and sincerely."[3]

The believer's life of faith is cultivated in the church by both the Word and the sacraments. Reformed piety gives priority to corporate spirituality and only after that to individual spirituality. It is a spirituality of the church gathered, the Lord's Day, the preached Word made visible in the sacraments, public prayer, and corporate singing. By these means, Calvin and the Reformers held, God's people would be edified. They would then leave the church service to go out into the world to continue their walk with God in every part of life, engaging daily in heartfelt, repentant, humble, confident prayer and seeking always to mortify the flesh and bring to life the works of righteousness.

2. Joel R. Beeke, "Calvin's Piety," *Mid-America Journal of Theology* 15 (2004): 35.
3. Ibid., 37.

For the Reformers, true godliness was not about some kind of monastic lifestyle. It was not the spirituality of celibacy, asceticism, and passivism. It was godliness for life: family life, civic life, life in the field and at the marketplace. It was the kind of godliness that drove reform not just in the church in Geneva, but in the city of Geneva. A century later, it was the piety of the Puritans who worked hard not only to reform the Church of England, but to reform English society.[4]

The danger we face, then, is that we may not take piety far enough. We make it *only* a matter of the heart, rather than *firstly* a matter of the heart. That leads us to develop pietistic blind spots. We come to a text and see implications for personal spirituality, the church, and evangelism, but little else. The antidote is to understand the vastness of God's kingdom project. Jesus' mission was to "preach the good news of the kingdom" (Luke 4:43). He proclaimed not merely the good news of personal salvation but the good news of the kingdom, which is nothing less than the world-to-come breaking into this world. God, who will eventually recreate this world, has already begun the work of restoration. In the coming of Christ, his kingdom has come into this world with power. The miracles of Jesus demonstrated this as he began to push back evil, reversing the effects of the fall and demonstrating his lordship over sin, Satan, and death. God's intention is to reclaim this whole world for himself. His dominion will stretch from shore to shore, and the knowledge of God will cover the earth as the waters cover the sea.

---

4. John Wright, however, offers an interesting analysis of the development of preaching in North America. He argues that Puritan preaching in New England displaced the biblical narrative of God's work from creation to consummation with two other narratives: that of the individual moving from sin to salvation to service (hence the narrative of Scripture was found in the order of salvation), and that of the nation (America) as God's new Israel that God would bless with prosperity in response to righteousness. These narratives, he argues, displaced the church as being central to God's redeeming purposes, and the two new narratives have shaped and reinforced the American preoccupation with the individual and the nation. "Within the narrative horizons provided by North American culture, the church exists for the salvation of the individual and the moral formation of the nation, but has no inherent theological significance itself" (75). He therefore advocates a homiletic rhetoric that begins with the narrative people usually live in (that of American culture) and then moves people to their place in the biblical narrative. John W. Wright, *Telling God's Story: Narrative Preaching for Christian Formation* (Downers Grove: IVP, 2007), 54–76.

A KINGDOM VISION

The invading kingdom is radically different from the kingdoms of this world, turning their values upside down. It is advanced not by political means or military strategy but by the preaching of the gospel. It is set up not in a particular geographic region but in the hearts of men, women, and children, both black and white, slave and free, smart and simple, rich and poor. It is established in their hearts when they repent and believe the good news of the King and the kingdom. They are then transformed both decisively and progressively. Kingdom values begin to take root in their hearts. They begin to think, act, live, and love differently.

Quite naturally, transformed kingdom citizens advance the agenda of God's kingdom wherever they live. They begin to live for God's reclamation of this whole world. Their lives become kingdom outposts in homes, schools, workplaces, and neighborhoods. They are salt and light, impacting the world through not so much political revolution as spiritual permeation. They live out the kingdom values of love, truth, justice, righteousness, mercy, and grace and, as they do so, the way is opened for further gospel proclamation. Their transformed lives also help transform communities, neighborhoods, towns, and cities, so that increasingly this world is reclaimed for Christ. This mission continues until all his enemies have been put under his feet, and the rock cut out of the mountain has dashed the kingdoms of this world to pieces and has itself become a huge mountain filling the whole earth (Dan. 2:34–35). Then the king will return, the new heaven and earth will be established, every knee will bow, and everyone will acknowledge that Jesus Christ is Lord.

KINGDOM APPLICATIONS

This kingdom perspective opens up vast dimensions in application. Living application is not about just personal life but kingdom life. When a kingdom theology makes up part of our reservoir, we will see many applicatory possibilities beyond matters of personal piety. Three arenas of application are particularly helpful for preachers to bear in mind.

A Wider View of Sin

We can never preach the good news without talking about the bad news. The more clearly we see our lostness, the more we rejoice at being found; the more we sense our impurity, the more thankful we are that we've been cleansed; the more we know our distance from God, the gladder we are that Christ has drawn us near to God. Pietistic preachers will always be aware of this and will frequently speak to the heart with a view to convicting people of their sin. But we may less readily remember that sin moves out from the individual to society. Sin doesn't remain locked up in human hearts but spreads and permeates so that our families, communities, and societal structures become infected with sin. In Genesis, sin begins in the heart of one man, but just five chapters later the whole world is filled with evil and God is grieved that he had made man. By chapter 11, we read of a city in rebellion against God, conspiring to displace him. Thereafter we encounter communities, nations, and empires that are the very embodiment of evil.

Sin spreads so deeply into the fabric of entire societies and nations that we are warned that this world is itself one of the chief sources of temptation, alongside the flesh and the Devil. We are warned not to love the world or anything in it (1 John 2:15–17). In Revelation, we are given a graphic picture of the cosmic conflict between Satan and Christ that is played out on the stage of this world with its political forces, most notably the Roman empire, depicted as a beast, and Rome depicted as a drunken prostitute.

The Bible, therefore, recognizes not only personal sin but systemic evil. Not only do individuals have idols, but cultures and countries have them.[5] Once we see that, new applications become not only possible but necessary. Preachers need to speak a prophetic word against the evils and sins of society, not just of the individual. We need, for example,

5. See Timothy Keller, *Counterfeit Gods: When the Empty Promises of Love, Money and Power Let You Down* (London: Hodder & Stoughton, 2009), xix, 97–125.

not only to convict the heart of the person who has succumbed to Internet pornography, but also to condemn the perpetration of that sin by those who have plastered the web with pornographic sites. Statistics are constantly changing and disputed, but it is estimated that 28,258 Internet users are viewing pornography every second. At $97.06 billion per annum in 2005 and 2006, the pornography industry has larger revenues than Microsoft, Google, Amazon, eBay, Yahoo, Apple, and Netflix combined.[6] The perpetrators of this evil are the equivalent of drug dealers who make vast profits while the lives and marriages of countless victims are torn to pieces. Yes, the victim is a sinner, but he or she is also caught in a vast web of evil. The same might be said of the gambling industry, much of the fashion industry, or the West's addiction to materialistic consumption.

Why should preachers speak about such sins? First, because if the church won't speak against evil, who will? Second, if preachers won't address these issues on Sunday, how will their people be equipped to do battle with them from Monday to Saturday? Third, when people who are struggling with individual sin recognize that they are caught in a wider web of evil, they face their sins differently, often finding themselves empowered to do more about it. But, most importantly, preachers should speak about these sins because the kingdom of God that has invaded this world stands opposed to all evil. Christ's kingdom is the kingdom of righteousness and, where that kingdom advances, it exposes evil and declares the righteousness of Christ. The gospel proclaims that one day every corrupt regime, every evil structure, every oppressive government, and every unjust business will be overcome and will yield obedience to Christ.

A Wider Range of Texts

Pietistic tendencies may incline us to gravitate toward texts about personal spirituality but not texts about social justice. There has been a

6. Jerry Ropelato, "Internet Pornography Statistics," Internet Filter Review, accessed November 19, 2013, http://internet-filter-review.toptenreviews.com/internet-pornography -statistics.html.

tendency over the last 150 years for personal spirituality to be the concern of evangelicals and social justice to be the domain of liberals. You go to an evangelical church to hear sermons on faith, repentance, prayer, love, joy, service, giving, evangelism, healthy relationships, personal integrity, God's grace, God's power, and God's providence. You go to a liberal church to hear sermons on family violence, the victims of AIDS, oppression of the poor, environmental issues, and the concerns of the marginalized.

But then you turn to Amos. He speaks against the false piety of a people who pray and sacrifice but do not love justice and mercy. He condemns those who live in luxury but deny justice for the poor. Similarly Isaiah writes,

> Is not this the kind of fasting I have chosen:
> to loose the chains of injustice
>   and untie the cords of the yoke,
> to set the oppressed free
>   and break every yoke?
> Is it not to share your food with the hungry
>   and to provide the poor wanderer with shelter—
> when you see the naked, to clothe him,
>   and not to turn away from your own flesh and blood? (Isa. 58:6–7)

You could be forgiven for thinking these Old Testament prophets were theological liberals with a social gospel like that. But Jesus spoke the same way:

> Depart from me, you who are cursed, into the eternal fire prepared for the devil and his angels. For I was hungry and you gave me nothing to eat, I was thirsty and you gave me nothing to drink, I was a stranger and you did not invite me in, I needed clothes and you did not clothe me, I was sick and in prison and you did not look after me. (Matt. 25:41–43)

James says, "Religion that God our Father accepts as pure and faultless is this: to look after orphans and widows in their distress and to keep oneself from being polluted by the world" (James 1:27). He summons the rich to

> weep and wail because of the misery that is coming upon you. Your wealth has rotted, and moths have eaten your clothes. Your gold and silver are corroded. Their corrosion will testify against you and eat your flesh like fire. You have hoarded wealth in the last days. Look! The wages you failed to pay the workmen who mowed your fields are crying out against you. (James 5:1–4)

It is clear from Scripture that evangelicals cannot neatly separate personal spirituality from social responsibility. The two go together. The liberal's fault is to talk about social issues without bringing the ultimate hope of healing and salvation through Christ. The evangelical's fault is to speak of salvation and healing in the lives of individuals and not to apply that to addressing the social issues of the day. The gospel should instill in us an agenda to proclaim and enact the good news of the kingdom to the poor, needy, alienated, lonely, widows, and outcasts, not only in word but also in deed.

Global issues of justice and mercy must also be on the preacher's radar. Issues of fair trade, poverty, and oppression are increasingly receiving important air time in evangelical pulpits. Given that TV and Internet news has placed us in a global village where we learn constantly of crises, oppression, and violence in other countries, it would be a failure for the church to act as if no one knew or thought about these issues. It is a healthy sign when churches embark on aid projects overseas, looking beyond themselves and putting the gospel into action in places of great need, even if they can only make the smallest of dents on enormous problems. Such action is a cup of water in the name of Christ.

To advance this broader social application, we need to resist spiritualizing all the social justice expressions in the gospel. If our text is about Jesus healing the blind, we don't tend to think about people who are actually blind, we think about those who are spiritually blind; if it is about the poor, we speak of the poor spiritually; if it is about the Gentiles, we think of the unsaved. We do this with strong biblical warrant.

But we must also remember that each of these represents real categories of people who physically, as well as spiritually, need to encounter the kingdom of God and discover its justice and mercy.

These broader applications from a wide range of texts are needed constantly in our preaching ministries if the church is ever to be a city on a hill, a light shining in darkness.

A Wider View of Serving God

One of the most helpful applicatory benefits of a kingdom view is to open up an "all of life" view of worship and ministry. This was one of the fundamental rediscoveries of the Reformation. The Reformers "affirmed the essential spirituality of the everyday, ordinary life."[7] As evangelicals, however, we easily revert to a narrow view of worship, calling, and work. We seem to be compulsively monastic in our thinking. No phrase is more indicative of this than the language of "full-time ministry." People are encouraged to leave their "secular" work to engage in "full-time Christian work." If they are not able to do so or lack the gifts to be a pastor or missionary, they can at least give themselves to some church ministry after hours and their "secular" job can be a platform for evangelism and for earning money to support gospel ministry.

Such perspectives are foreign to New Testament thinking. It is essential that preachers align their thinking to a biblical theology of worship, calling, and work. While it is not possible to explore these themes in detail now, a brief overview of each will be suggestive of the applicatory freight they carry.

First, preachers need to promote a kingdom view of worship that views the whole world and the whole of life as the setting for true worship. Worship is to be a way of life, one in which we honor and glorify God for who he is and what he has done. In true worship, we stand in reverent awe before him, acknowledging him to be our God, submitting to his sovereign rule in our life, and giving him our very best. Our lives

7. Michael P. Schutt, *Redeeming Law: Christian Calling and the Legal Profession* (Downers Grove: IVP, 2007), 48. Schutt's chapter on "Vocation and the Local Church" (46–67) superbly addresses the dualistic thinking that marks much of the evangelical world.

are offered to him as living sacrifices. All that we do is sacred, because every act is lifted up to him as an offering. Of course, there is something unique and significant about believers coming together in corporate worship. But when they leave, they do not cease to worship but rather continue to honor and glorify God wherever they go and whatever they do. Corporate worship ought to equip and encourage them to do so. Preachers will aid this by ensuring that their language conveys a broad view of worship and that their applications concerning worship relate not only to corporate gatherings but to everyday life.

Second, preachers should teach a kingdom perspective on the concept of calling. Too often, calling is seen as an almost mystical experience in which a person senses deeply that God wants him to take up some area of professional Christian ministry. This view tends to be rooted in the calling experiences of the Old Testament prophets. In the New Testament, however, every believer is called in three senses. First, there is the general call of the gospel to faith and to following Christ. Second, there is the call to live holy lives. We are to serve God and live lives worthy of the gospel. Third, we are called to particular life circumstances, which are the setting in which the first two calls are carried out. God assigns our places and circumstances (1 Cor. 7:17–24), and we are to serve him as he enables us in the situations he has assigned to us.

In our life applications we need, then, to resurrect the language of vocation. In whatever job we happen to be doing, God *calls* us to serve him there. Of course we want to be good stewards of the gifts he has given us and so we seek to work where we can be of greatest usefulness to the advance of the kingdom. For those with preaching, pastoral, or evangelistic gifts, this may well mean working for the church full time. Such people rightly speak of God calling them to that ministry, but their particular calling is only an outworking of their broader calling to serve the Lord. A lawyer, plumber, or housewife equally has a calling on his or her life and a particular context in which that calling is carried out.

Third, then, we need a kingdom view of work. If preachers are to encourage people to worship God in the whole of life and to view every job as a vocation, it is essential that they arm people with a biblical theology of work. In a dualistic theology, everyday work is seen as essentially meaningless and little more than a means to an end. Work is just one of those things we have to do in this sin-cursed world, though it may have some value as a place to witness and as a means of providing for one's family and the work of the gospel. Such a perspective does no justice to a biblical theology of work. As preachers we must remind people, probably quite often, that work was mandated by God before the fall as the means by which people would serve God in his world. Adam was to tend the garden, name the animals, fill the earth, and subdue it. With no one to evangelize and no money to be made or churches to support, his work had value in and of itself because it was the means of caring for God's world. Since the fall work has become harder, but it has not lost its innate worth. We are caretakers and custodians of the world God created. If no one did the noble work of garbage collection or cleaning, the beauty and wholesomeness of God's world would soon be lost and we would all be the worse for it. Similarly, builders, teachers, plumbers, dentists, doctors, teachers, musicians, parents, lawyers, and a host of other workers help maintain order in God's world, advance our knowledge of it, or aid our enjoyment of what God has blessed us with.

Given that many people in our congregations spend the bulk of their week in non-church work, we need to apply biblical truth regularly to those contexts so that they are encouraged and strengthened to serve God there well. That is their prime place of ministry, where their gifts are bent toward serving God, caring for his world, loving their neighbor, and representing the kingdom of heaven.

If preachers work hard to avoid narrow perspectives on these themes, they will more readily make holistic applications that connect to people's everyday world, encouraging them to adopt kingdom values in their trade, business, industry, profession, or study; equipping them to love their bosses, clients, patients, customers, or pupils; and urging them to do all for the glory of God. In these ways, preachers can begin to close the gap between Sunday and Monday.

To make these kinds of applications, however, preachers will need to have plenty in their reservoir about everyday worship, a range of vocations, and ministry beyond the walls of the church. The world of preachers is often restricted to engaging mostly with Christians and the church, and consequently their applications are narrowed as well. By engaging people in conversation about their work, by reading and thinking about Christian perspectives on key trades and professions, and by engaging in relationships and ministry outside of the church, preachers will pour into their reservoir abundant waters for kingdom applications. But they will also need to add to the reservoir a broad biblical understanding of life, gleaned from hours spent in some of the harder corners of the Word: the law, the prophets, and Proverbs.

A while ago, I listened to an address Tim Keller gave to a gathering of Christian lawyers about a biblical perspective on practicing law.[8] It was apparent that he had read extensively on the subject before speaking and that he had interfaced his reading and his general knowledge of law with his own biblical worldview. But it was also clear that he was reticent to tell the lawyers what they should be doing. He wanted to learn from them because they were the ones in the field, wrestling with the hard questions of what it means to practice law as a believer. His approach was to give broad frameworks for Christian thinking and then to allow extensive Q&A sessions to think through the issues the lawyers wanted to discuss. In a regular preaching context, something of this dynamic could be replicated if preachers laid out, from time to time, broad principles of a biblical worldview for areas such as law, politics, education, business, trade, family life, and so on, and then created forums where people could discuss and debate the application of those principles in greater detail. If the church's task is to equip people for works of service, it is time we equipped people for service in the places where God has called them to work for forty to sixty hours a week.

KINGDOM PREACHING AND LIVING APPLICATION

If our aim in holistic application is to bring the message as a whole to the person as a whole for life as a whole, we need to rec-

---

8. Timothy Keller, "Re-imagine Law," *Redeemer Presbyterian Church*, November 2, 2007, http://sermons2.redeemer.com/sermons/re-imagine-law.

ognize that we will never achieve the last part of that aim unless we have a broad kingdom perspective, or what others might call a biblical world and life view. We must resist making only narrowly pietistic applications, encouraging instead a spirituality that begins with the heart but reaches into every part of life. We realize that God rules over all. Every part of life is of interest to him, every corner of creation is being reclaimed for him, every nation is to be discipled, and every person is to submit to the rule of his appointed King, Jesus Christ. "Jesus is Lord not only of the church but of the world, not only in the religious life but all life."[9]

Most likely our hearers will thank us profusely for this. They live in the world 24/7. They want to know what it means to glorify God and enjoy him forever in all that they do. They want to know how to serve God where he has placed them. They need to know that they are not living Plan B because they didn't go into church ministry.

As we engage with the living application preaching process, therefore, we need to view each stage of it through kingdom glasses. In asking questions about the purposes of God's living Word, we must bear in mind the extent to which God addresses not only his own people but also the surrounding nations. We should remember the vast scope of what he is doing in this world and what he is redeeming. As God's Word teaches and rebukes, trains and corrects, tests and convicts, encourages and exhorts, we must bring its message to bear not only on the lives of individuals but on our world, our nations, our economies, our vocations. God has much to say about contemporary culture and society, not just about personal prayer and evangelism.

Kingdom glasses will also impact, as we have seen, what goes into our reservoir. We will be motivated to read more widely and engage with culture and society more fully if we understand that God is redeeming this world and has called us to go into all the world,

9. Lesslie Newbigin, *Truth to Tell: The Gospel as Public Truth* (Grand Rapids: Eerdmans, 1991), 34, quoted in Zack Eswine, *Preaching to a Post-Everything World: Crafting Biblical Sermons That Connect with Our Culture* (Grand Rapids: Baker, 2008), 40.

not to hide from it. Our reservoirs need to be kingdom reservoirs as well as personal life reservoirs. When a kingdom theology is part of our reservoir and rich enjoyment of the whole of life to the glory of God is fundamental to the way we think and live, we will find that we are hard-wired to see expansive applications of the biblical text. We will find ourselves talking about not only serving in the church but serving in the world; not only urging evangelistic witness but urging, alongside it, acts that bring hope and transformation to people's lives; not only spurring people on to a life of prayer and personal godliness but also spurring them on to engagement in this world with a passion to incarnate the love of God in this present darkness.

Then, as we interact with the lives of our hearers—their heart conditions, life realities, and spiritual well-being—we will broaden the scope of application to speak of their world from Monday to Saturday as well as Sunday, and to speak of their days from nine until five, not just their quiet times. Kingdom glasses will broaden the scope far beyond the weary old bolt-on applications.

If you share in some of my confessions as a pietistic preacher, maybe it is time to think much more about how far ranging God's plan of redemption really is, and the implications of that for the whole of life.

DISCUSSION QUESTIONS

1. Over the last year, have you preached on a variety of texts and topics so as to cover issues of personal spirituality, corporate church life, the believer's broad calling to serve God in the whole of life, and contemporary issues in society?
2. What current sins, idols, evils, and issues in your local community, society, and culture need to be exposed and addressed in your preaching ministry?
3. How can you address these kinds of issues in a gospel-focused way that avoids merely lambasting the failings of people outside the church?

4. When people in your church speak about worship, calling, and service, is their focus on church and ministry contexts, or on all of life?
5. In your preaching, how can you actively challenge the sacred/secular dualism that often marks evangelical thinking?
6. How could you create in your church life contexts for people to discuss together what living the gospel looks like in their particular areas of work?

8

ENGAGING WITH
STORIES

THERE'S NOTHING LIKE a great storyteller. Charles Dickens, Mark Twain, Roald Dahl, John Grisham—you can take your pick in terms of style and substance, but all can tell a gripping story. Popular novels are often described as "unputdownable." Children are stereotypically put to bed with a story. Paperbacks, frequently of dubious quality, line bookstores to satisfy the insatiable desire of adults for stories, especially when faced with a long-haul flight. And, in church, old and young alike perk up when the preacher begins a story.

The greatest storyteller of all time is God himself. He tells stories frequently and powerfully. Sidney Greidanus has said, "Of all the biblical genres of literature, narrative may be described as the central, foundational, and all-encompassing genre of the Bible. The prominence of the narrative genre in the Bible is related to the Bible's central message that God acts in *history*. No other genre can express that message as well as narrative."[1] Narratives are a statement about the nature of reality. As Fee and Stuart put it, "Their purpose is to show God at work in His creation and among His people. The narratives glorify Him, help us to understand and appreciate Him, and give us a picture of His providence

1. Sidney Greidanus, *The Modern Preacher and the Ancient Text: Intepreting and Preaching Biblical Literature* (Grand Rapids: Eerdmans, 1988), 188.

and protection. At the same time they also provide illustrations of many other lessons important to our lives."[2]

STORIES ARE IN

Not only does the Bible use stories extensively, but postmoderns tend to love them, which has led preachers to reengage with narrative in a remarkable way over the last thirty years.[3] It has, in many regards, been a positive development because, for too long, many of us preached the whole Bible as if it were all a Pauline epistle. The New Testament letters, Paul's theology, and didactic sermons with deductive structures were the "right" way to preach and perhaps the only way many of us knew. Greater sensitivity to genre and an increased range of sermon structure options have been healthy for expository preaching.

It is unhealthy, however, when inductive sermons on narrative passages are seen as the silver bullet that alone will reach postmoderns. If narrative is all we preach and inductive sermons are our only tool for getting the job done, we will likely leave unsaid much that needs to be said. Besides, too much of the impetus behind the push for narrative preaching has come from the theological left for evangelicals not to be a little wary of overdoing it.[4] David Larsen puts the pros and cons well:

> The homiletics of the left has gone for narrative to the virtual exclusion of all other literary genres. The result has been narrative theology,

2. Gordon D. Fee and Douglas Stuart, *How to Read the Bible for All Its Worth: A Guide to Understanding the Bible* (Grand Rapids: Zondervan, 2003), 74.

3. The development of the new homiletic, with its emphasis on inductive and narrative preaching, began with Craddock's seminal work, *As One Without Authority* (1971), and was followed by key contributions by Eugene Lowry (*The Homiletical Plot*, 1975), David Buttrick (*Homiletic*, 1987), Richard Eslinger (*Pitfalls in Preaching*, 1996), and Lucy Atkinson Rose (*Sharing the Word*, 1997).

4. For the roots of the new homiletic and a basic evangelical assessment of it, see Scott M. Gibson, "Critique of the New Homiletic: Examining the link between the new homiletic and the new hermeneutic," in Haddon W. Robinson and Craig Brian Larson, eds., *The Art and Craft of Biblical Preaching: A Comprehensive Resource for Today's Communicators* (Grand Rapids: Zondervan, 2005), 476–81. See also L. Roger Owens, "Jesus Christ Is His Own Rhetoric! Reflections on the Relationship Between Theology and Rhetoric in Preaching," *Currents in Theology and Mission* 32, no. 3 (2005): 187–94.

narrative ethics, narrative spirituality, and so on. The present fixation on narrative (which is ultimately faddish, in my judgment) nevertheless does point out the invaluable treasure we possess in biblical narrative, recognizing that almost half of our Bible is narrative. . . . The biblical use of narrative is deliberate and is an open door to increased and more effective utilization of this intriguing biblical genre.

At the same time we must beware of a serious pitfall. With all of its communicative attractiveness, narrative has a serious limitation not always observed. Doctrine cannot be built on narrative since by its incidental nature, it is one happening and therefore incapable of generalization. Liberals sought to build soteriology on the parable of the prodigal son (Luke 15). Their construct required no cross or atonement. The parable does not contain any expiation.[5]

Narrative can easily be preached in a way that leaves both doctrine and life up in the air. Narrative sermons are often used to pose questions rather than to answer them, to stir reflection on where we fit in the story, to leave us with ambiguities and uncertainties that resonate with the unfathomables of our lives. That can be appealing but it can also be dangerous.[6] Narratives need interpretation and it is the preacher's job to interpret the story. That need not mean imposing foreign points, structures, and doctrines over the top of the narrative, but it does necessitate unfolding the story in a way that highlights God-intended truths and necessary responses. By the end, not everything should be up for grabs.

Michael Quicke comments in a balanced way when he observes that

both the old homiletic and the new homiletic have been in danger of mistreating story. On the one hand, the old homiletic, with its points and outlines, can atomize story, reducing something living to

5. David L. Larsen, "Preaching the Old Testament Today," in Scott M. Gibson, ed., *Preaching the Old Testament* (Grand Rapids: Baker, 2006), 178.

6. Cornelius Plantinga comments on the extreme end of this tendency with reference to Lucy Atkinson Rose: "According to her theory, sermons ought to resemble conversations as much as possible, and especially open-ended ones. . . . If I understand her, Rose rejects any use of assertions, claims, declarations, or statement—that is, the kind of thing that could be true or false." See Cornelius Plantinga, "Dancing on the Edge of Mystery: The New Homiletics Celebrates Pilgrimage, Not Propositions," *Journal of the Evangelical Homiletics Society* 2, no. 5 (2005): 76.

alliterative headings that appeal to left-brained people. But on the other hand, those applying the new homiletic can be so obsessed with story form that they lose sight of what the gospel means. Boykin Sanders warns that preoccupation with either biblical exegesis or narrative theology means "the major focus becomes how preaching is done rather than what is preached . . . the gospel."[7]

Our challenge in preaching narrative, therefore, is twofold. First, we need to handle it in a genre-sensitive way, not treating the story as a disposable husk to be peeled off as quickly as possible so as to get to the core truths that the passage is really about. We need to genuinely engage with the story and let our hearers do so as well.[8] But second, we need to interpret the story, saying what it means. We need to put a spotlight on the doctrines it incarnates and enunciate the responses it calls for. Narrative, like all genres, can teach and rebuke, train and correct, test and convict, encourage and exhort. We need to look at narratives in terms of the living application preaching process we have considered in order to see how God would have us respond to each story. They are not there just because we like stories. They are in the Book because they make us wise for salvation and are profitable for teaching, rebuking, correcting, and training in righteousness.

THE NARRATIVE CHALLENGE

Working out the particular profitableness of each story, however, can be almost distressingly challenging. Applying narrative is one of the hardest tasks the preacher faces. Is there, then, any help from the living application preaching process? And how does narrative give rise to holistic, not bolt-on, application?

Because narratives are descriptive rather than prescriptive, they don't tend to tell us what to do in response. Now that we have broadened

7. Michael J. Quicke, *360-Degree Preaching: Hearing, Speaking, and Living the Word* (Grand Rapids: Baker; Carlisle, UK: Paternoster, 2003), 112.

8. This may be done with either an inductive or a deductive structure. See Laurence A. Turner, "Preaching Narrative: Plot," in Grenville J. R. Kent, Paul J. Kissling, and Laurence A. Turner, eds., '*He Began with Moses . . .': Preaching the Old Testament Today* (Nottingham: IVP, 2010), 20–22.

our view of application, that is not a problem in and of itself. We realize that application isn't just about telling people what to do. Between description and prescription, we may find several shades of usefulness in a story. It may be instructive without being prescriptive. It might be suggestive, illustrative, illuminating, convicting, or damning. It might warn or encourage. It might leave us with things we need to think about (concerning God, ourselves, human nature, the world, sin, the enemy, life, or death). It might impress truth more deeply on us because we have seen it in action and it has become concrete rather than abstract. It might bring deep conviction of sin or of a needed change because we have found ourselves looking in the mirror and not liking what we see. It might leave us feeling deeply moved, having seen afresh God's grace, wrath, or power. In other words, the story may not be addressed to our will but to our mind, conscience, or passions.

In making choices about how each narrative applies today, we must, of course, avoid leapfrogging from "there and then" to "here and now," ignoring the two, three, four, or more thousands of years that stand between the story and us. In chapter 2 we noted that timeless truths are not static truths. Truths of timeless importance and relevance revealed in earlier stages of the biblical narrative come to us with greater force and power because of subsequent redemptive history. We must always apply these truths to ourselves in the light of the finished work of Jesus, our current place in salvation history, and the future that is yet to be fully revealed.

The default setting of many Christians when they read Old Testament narratives is to identify with the central character of the story and make immediate connections between that person and themselves. They want to learn directly from Abraham, Moses, Samuel, David, or Jonah. They do the same with Jesus too, prompting the question, "What would Jesus do?" This intuitive approach is not all bad. Jesus is an example to us and there is much we can learn from Old Testament characters. Hebrews 11 teaches us to draw encouragement from the faith of a remarkably motley bunch of saints. James points us to Elijah, a man "just like us," who was effective in prayer. Jesus tells us to remember Lot's wife. Paul speaks of the Israelites as "types" of us whose experiences are a warning to us (1 Cor. 10:6, 11).

However, while there is much to be learned from the people in the story, and sometimes we rightly identify with the main character, that should not be our default setting. There are times when we should most certainly not be learning from the main characters of the stories or identifying ourselves with them. For example, we are not Old Testament-type prophets, priests, or kings. So instead of aligning ourselves with David when he stands up to Goliath, we'd do better to align with the people of Israel who are cowering on the sidelines, hoping someone will take on this big beast but certainly not offering to do so themselves.

How, then, do we draw correct lines from *then* to *now*? Whom should we identify with in a narrative? How do we know whether or not a narrative intends us to draw lessons from the people in the story? To answer such questions, we need to have an interpretive framework that allows us to place the story in a wider context that embraces us as well. If, while exploring a little town in England on Google Maps, I zoom out, I can see where that town is in relation to the rest of the country, and then in relation to Europe, and eventually in relation to Australia. While with "street view" I can see cars and houses, zoomed out I realize it's a very long way from where I live.

FRAMEWORKS

The best way to zoom out in Bible reading is to read the narrative theocentrically rather than anthropocentrically. That is to say, we focus on God rather than the human characters in the story. Our default setting is not to look for examples to follow but to look for God's action in the narrative. He is the hero of every story.[9] He is the one making the play even when he is seemingly absent or invisible (as he is in the book of Esther). He is the one unfolding a larger story, of which any given story is but one scene in one act. Dale Ralph Davis practices theocentric interpretation with aplomb and summarizes what he calls "the premier

9. Fee and Stuart, *How to Read the Bible for All Its Worth*, 98, 106.

presupposition that should undergird all our biblical interpretation: *God has given us his word as a revelation of himself; if then I use his word rightly, I will long to see him, and he will be the focus of my study.*[10]

Davis urges us to keep our eye on God all the way. Look at what he is doing and you will discover his typical ways of working—vintage Yahweh! There is an immediate applicability to that. The "lesson" is drawn not from the character directly to us, but from the character's experience of God to our experience of God.[11]

In Judges 13 we read the story of Manoah and his wife. It's the prelude to the bizarre antics of their son Samson recorded in the next three chapters. In chapter 13 we spend time with a little old man and a little old woman in the nowhere town of Zorah. What's the chapter about? It's about God. God is beginning to prepare salvation for his people. He is beginning to raise up their next judge, the savior who will begin to deliver Israel from the oppression of their Philistine rulers. But God's salvation is unsought, unexpected, and unhurried. It is unsought because his people have not cried out to him despite living under Philistine rule as a result of their own sinfulness. The cycle constantly repeated in Judges (disobedience, discipline, distress, deliverance) is interrupted here. There is no mention of distress. They appear to live contentedly under Philistine rule and do not seek rescue (cf. 15:11). But God is the God of unsought salvations and he is beginning to intervene, even though his people are oblivious to it. He is also the God of unexpected salvations. He comes to the little old man and his wife, barren, unknown, and unimpressive, and promises them a son who will be a savior. Does that sound familiar? This is indeed vintage Yahweh. But, third, this is to be an unhurried salvation. There will be a pregnancy, then a childhood, then a youth, and some time, probably about twenty

10. Dale Ralph Davis, *The Word Became Fresh: How to Preach from Old Testament Narrative Texts* (Fearn: Christian Focus, 2006), 122 (his italics).

11. Bryan Chapell's approach fine-tunes this, prompting us to look for the fallen condition of the original recipients that necessitated that revelation of God and to connect that to our own fallen condition and therefore our need of the same divine revelation. Bryan Chapell, *Christ-Centered Preaching: Redeeming the Expository Sermon* (Grand Rapids: Baker, 1994), 40–44, 263–66.

years down the track, we will arrive at the start of the next chapter. God is in no rush in his works of redemption. He will save, but his people will wait some years yet.

These three themes are entirely God-centered and replete with applicatory potential. All this can be drilled down into our lives in a most helpful way. But while theocentric application is a vast improvement on anthropocentric interpretation, by itself it still carries dangers. God does not always act in the same ways. Sometimes God's ways are unique and time-specific. He spoke to prophets, but he might not speak to us; he opened the Red Sea, but he may not give us a miraculous escape from our enemies; he enabled David to defeat Goliath, but that does not mean he always gives the little guy power over the big one. We need other frameworks in place if we are to safely draw the right applications from a theocentric interpretation.

Thankfully, theocentric interpretation has two beautiful hand-maidens: redemptive-historical interpretation and christocentric interpretation.[12] Redemptive-historical interpretation means that our focus on God is always in terms of the wider story of what God is doing. We zoom out further. God is not just up to something in a particular text and with particular people. He is always engaged in something larger. He is unfolding a grand plan of redemption that stretches from Genesis 3 to Revelation 22. The gospel promise is advancing throughout the ages, spreading from one man to the ends of the earth. The Old Testament contains many signs and types of what is to come, and the New brings an age of fulfillment. We live in the "already" of fulfillment but also in the "not yet" of further promises. Fulfillment has come and is coming.

Every text in the Bible fits somewhere into the overall plan of redemption. Of course, if we focus too much on the wider scope of redemptive-history we can end up preaching a framework that eventually sounds boring and repetitive. That can easily happen as preachers who are committed to redemptive-historical preaching predictably place

12. A Christ-centered, redemptive-historical approach to preaching is masterfully presented in Dennis E. Johnson, *Him We Proclaim: Preaching Christ from All the Scriptures* (Phillipsburg, NJ: P&R, 2007).

every event within the metanarrative of Scripture and then draw the same bottom line from story after story. As we preach what God is doing in the big picture, we must do so paying close attention to his particular work with particular people.[13]

Christocentric interpretation means that our focus also goes to where redemptive history ultimately points: the finished work of Jesus Christ.[14] That is not to say that every text specifically preaches Christ. When Jesus said that the Old Testament preached himself, he did not indicate that every verse, every paragraph, or every story was specifically about him.[15] We need not dream up fanciful ways of making the text about Jesus, come what may. But every text is a part of the overall picture, which is ultimately a picture of redemption in Christ.

Christ is the climax of the whole story and God's dealings with us are always in and through him.[16] While we don't have to try to find Jesus in every text, we do need to preach the (theocentric) truths of the text in the light of Jesus. Every truth must come to us via the gospel. If the text shows us our sin, that drives us to Christ. If it shows us something of God's character, we will come to know it for ourselves in Christ, in whom all the fullness of the deity lives in bodily form. If the text calls us to faith, it calls us to faith in Christ specifically, not just in God generally. If it calls us to adore God, we can come and adore him only through Christ, who is seated with him on the throne. No hermeneutical gymnastics are required. It's just that the Old Testament truths come

13. See the objections to redemptive-historical preaching summarized in ibid., 51–54.

14. Sidney Greidanus states that preaching christocentrically means "preaching sermons which authentically integrate the message of the text with the climax of God's revelation in the person, work, and/or teaching of Jesus Christ as revealed in the New Testament." Sidney Greidanus, *Preaching Christ from Genesis: Foundations for Expository Sermons* (Grand Rapids: Eerdmans, 2007), 1. Chapell argues, "A sermon remains expository and Christ-centered not because it leapfrogs to Golgotha, but because it locates the intent of the passage within the scope of God's redemptive work." Chapell, *Christ-Centered Preaching*, 296. Jensen helpfully says, "Preaching the gospel . . . is not about overlaying every passage with your favorite gospel outline, but rather seeing how the gospel illuminates each passage that we preach and how the passage itself illuminates the gospel." Phillip D. Jensen and Paul Grimmond, *The Archer and the Arrow: Preaching the Very Words of God* (Kingsford, New South Wales: Matthias Media, 2010), 33–34.

15. The key texts are Luke 4:18–21; 24:25–27, 44–47; John 5:39; 8:56.

16. See Heb. 1:1; Col. 2:2–3; 1 Cor. 1:30–31; 2 Cor. 1:20.

to us in, through, and for Christ, who is the climax of all God's actions and the one for whose glory we live.

When studying the Old Testament, we need to employ these three different levels of zoom. First, we examine what God is doing in the text, with those people, at that time. We use "street view" with a theocentric focus. We want to get to know these people and God's dealings with them as well as we can. Second, we zoom out and look at where the story fits into God's age-long plan of redemption. Third, we proclaim the story's truths about God to people today in the light of the climax of God's plan, the fullness of the gospel of Jesus Christ.[17] Or, to put it another way, we first *look down*, taking a God's-eye view of the narrative, as we ask, "What is God doing here?" Then we *look back and forth*, along the timeline of redemptive history, asking, "Where does this fit into the history of salvation?" And finally we *look forward*, to God's ultimate work in Christ, to which all the Old Testament narratives are heading. We ask, "How does this passage bear testimony to the gospel?"[18]

Only after we have explored the text along these lines are we ready to *look now* at what God is saying to us today.

THE BIG PICTURE

To aid the application of narratives within a theocentric, redemptive-historical, christocentric framework, it is useful to plot the large contours of the biblical story. Four great themes reverberate throughout the entire biblical narrative. Knowing and working with these themes enables big-picture preaching that is well earthed both in the ancient text and in people's lives today.

Conflict

Since the fall, which of course takes place very early in the biblical narrative, the gospel story (or redemptive history) centers on a funda-

17. This is similar to the three levels approach in Fee and Stuart, *How to Read the Bible for All Its Worth*, 91–92.

18. See Graeme Goldsworthy, *Preaching the Whole Bible as Christian Scripture: The Application of Biblical Theology to Expository Preaching* (Grand Rapids: Eerdmans, 2000), 21.

mental conflict between what God has promised to do and the circumstances in which he has promised to do it. The story of Abraham, the father of the faith, is paradigmatic. He is given great gospel promises: he will become a great nation, blessing will come through him to the ends of the earth, and those who bless him will be blessed while those who curse him will be cursed (Gen. 12:2–3). These promises will be fulfilled in a land God will give him and through a son with whom God will bless him.

All sounds great, except that Abraham is a seventy-five-year-old idol-worshiper in Haran, his wife is almost as old and is barren to boot, and the land he is promised is occupied by the aggressive and wicked Canaanites. The promises were not made in a vacuum; they were made in the context of circumstances that seemed to negate them at every point. An enormous gap existed between the promise and reality.[19]

That, of course, was no accident. God repeatedly chooses to work in such circumstances so that when the promises are fulfilled, it is clear that the fulfillment is by his power and grace alone. We find the gap throughout the Bible's stories. Barrenness is a classic, not only for Sarah, but then for Rebekah and Rachel, and later for Hannah, Manoah's wife, and Elizabeth. God's people are promised the land of the Canaanites, but famine comes to the Promised Land and they have to relocate to Egypt. Jacob's sons are meant to be leaders of God's new nation, but, in reality, they look like anything but leaders as they bicker, deceive, betray each other, and stray morally. Israel is promised that the Lord will provide, but he provides in a wilderness where they wander for forty years under his disciplinary hand. Joshua is told to be strong and courageous, but the people of the land are huge, the cities are fortified, and the military strategy (marching around a city and shouting) is, to be honest, utterly bizarre. Gideon is promised victory but given a mere three hundred soldiers.

At every point the gap exists. God continually holds out his promise, enlarging and expanding the expectation of blessing to the ends of

19. See Iain M. Duguid, *Living in the Gap Between Promise and Reality: The Gospel According to Abraham* (Phillipsburg, NJ: P&R, 1999).

the earth, but almost always in tension with visible reality. As we flick pages into the New Testament, things don't change. The King of Glory is born in a manger; the disciples are ordinary, unschooled men; the church, of which so much is promised, is comprised not for the most part of scholars and noblemen but of the "foolish things of the world." We have entered the last days, even the last hour, but another two thousand years have passed and still the King has not returned. Our own experience in gospel ministry is as Paul described it: "We have this treasure in jars of clay to show that this all-surpassing power is from God and not from us" (2 Cor. 4:7).

Preaching what God is doing in the text will, then, more often than not lead us to deal with the conflict between promise and reality, between what God is meant to be doing and what is actually happening on the ground, between the hope and the facts. As we preach the promises, we preach the tensions in which those promises exist. That means we do not sell people a lie. We show them what God is about. But we make them well aware that his work is unfolding in a world where it looks impossible. We therefore fully expect that to be the case in our own lives as well. As we connect the text to our world, the first point of connection may well be the conflict between promise and reality. Holistic application is, as we have seen, concerned with life as it really is. This theme reminds us that life, as it really is, often seems to contradict what God has pledged to do in Christ.

Struggle

The conflict between promise and reality inevitably produces struggle in our lives. It certainly did for Abraham and his successors. The record in Genesis shows how hard the early saints found it to cling to the promise, trusting that God would somehow work it out despite their circumstances. Abraham doubted, lied, and repeatedly took things into his own hands. He figured God needed some help. In fact, Genesis as a whole is full of lying, deceitfulness, envy, and rivalry. Later in Israel's history, God's people are constantly trying to find easier ways to worship (a golden calf, perhaps, or altars in Bethel and Dan), easier ways to get rich (let's just tithe the lame animals), and easier ways to enjoy life (how about some Canaanite women?).

Of course, the gap between promise and reality is bridged only by faith. We must cling to the promises of God and the God of the promises, no matter what. But that is hard. So, as we preach the promises, we preach from the lives of the Old Testament "saints" the reality of struggle: the struggle to believe, to obey, to love, to trust, to be pure, to be holy. There is abundant evidence in the biblical record that it is not easy. Constantly there is temptation to idolatry, to self-help, to pride, to ignoring the promise and settling for a comfortable life instead, and a host of other promise-denying ways of responding to God. Not to preach the struggles of the biblical saints is to gut the story of its tensions. Every good story revolves around tension, and we will see what God is really doing only as we also observe how hard people find it to take. That's why eventually God's people handed their Messiah over to the Romans to be killed.

It just so happens, however, that the struggles actually encourage people. A weeping Hannah, a suffering Job, a fearful Gideon, or a faltering Peter do not set examples of what to do as much as they show us realities we will also have to wrestle with as we proceed along the journey of faith. Our application cannot be a naive link from them to us—pray and you'll have a baby, don't listen to what others say but wait for God to speak to you, put out the fleece and God will show you what to do. Rather, our application is at the level of the experience of struggle. We live in the gap between promise and reality—and it's hard. It has never been otherwise.

This reflects the fact that the Old Testament contains "types" not only of Christ but also of us. In 1 Corinthians 10:1–14 Paul speaks of the Israelites as "examples" to us, or more literally "types" of us (vv. 6, 11). Their experiences warn us against falling into similar temptations to theirs.[20] We may, therefore, rightly see in the lives of God's old

20. Paul uses *tupos*, "type" (and the adverb *tupikōs*), rendered elsewhere as "pattern," "model," and "form" as well as "example." Carrick notes that Paul draws "a straight line from the experience of the Israelites in the wilderness to the experience of the Corinthians—a straight line

covenant people realities that teach/rebuke, train/correct, test/convict, and encourage/exhort us as new covenant people. Even those who hold some theocratic office and function as types of Christ are also, at another level, types of us in the struggle to live in the gap between promise and reality. Moses is a type of Christ but also, in his excuse-making or grumbling, a type of us who struggle to take God at his word. David, as king of Israel, is a type of Christ, but in his sin with Bathsheba he is a type of us as he fails to have his heart set on God alone. The judges are not just (bizarre) types of Christ, showing the unexpected ways in which God saves, but also types of us in their sin, fearfulness, rashness, and compromise.

These things are all written for our benefit. Of course we must preach them carefully, noting discontinuities, since redemptive history has moved on and we stand on the other side of the cross. But at the level of struggle we rightly relate to God's pre-cross people.

Discipline

Much of the gospel story, in both Old and New Testaments, is the story of God dealing with the hearts of his people as they struggle to live by faith. Within the larger narrative of God's redemptive purposes, there are numerous smaller stories of God changing, refining, and disciplining his people. He teaches faith and obedience, he rebukes and encourages, he is patient, sometimes indulging even their sinfulness because of their hard hearts (cf. Matt. 19:8, in which Jesus says Moses permitted divorce because of their hard hearts), he is slow to wrath and abounding in lovingkindness, yet he also punishes iniquity and ordains consequences for sin.

Redemptive history is covenantal history. It is the story of God's covenantal dealings with his covenant people. We dare not ride so high above the details of the narrative that we do not observe God's typical ways of refining his chosen ones. One classic is to make people wait (think of Abraham's wait for an heir, or Israel's four-hundred-year wait

from the past to the present. He has turned indicatives into imperatives." John Carrick, *The Imperative of Preaching: A Theology of Sacred Rhetoric* (Carlisle: Banner of Truth, 2002), 122.

for the Promised Land). Another is to give future leaders lengthy times out of the public eye so as to prepare them for public ministry (think of Joseph, Moses, David, and Elijah). Repeatedly he refines through suffering (Jacob as well as Job, and Israel as a whole in the wilderness and in exile). He also makes people experience their own sin in order to face up to it (as was the case for Jacob, the deceiver who was deceived).

As we preach the promises, we should preach God's classic ways of bringing his people to faith in the promises. This does not mean that every description is a prescription. Because God did it then, it does not mean he will necessarily do it now. But he may. These stories are instructive and suggestive. They invite reflection. They call for a growing understanding of how God works, both kindly and sternly, to bring his chosen ones to glory.

Triumph

Thankfully, after conflict, struggle, and discipline comes triumph. The triumph is always the victory of God's grace appropriated by faith. God, who pursues his people with relentless grace, eventually has his way in their lives. We see people changed, forgiven, renewed. Abraham, Jacob, and Joseph's brothers all end up vastly improved—not perfect, but significantly changed. We are also given pictures of true godliness (such as Ruth, Abigail, and Job). We see people overcome fear and be used mightily of God (like Gideon) as well as people who are forgiven their sin, despite bearing its consequences, and continue to be used of the Lord (such as David and Peter).

What is most striking, however, is that at the end of the day the biblical record applauds faith alone. How come Lot can be called "a righteous man" (2 Peter 2:7)? His life seems to be a mess from beginning to end. But the bottom line is that he believed God when his wife and sons didn't. How come Samson, the rollicking hooligan of a judge, makes it into the faith Hall of Fame? Because, when push came to shove (and shove is exactly what it did come to), he knew who God was, he knew who the enemy was, and he called on God, in faith, to enable him "one more time" to defeat the foe.

Faith is what matters—faith that rises above doubts and fears, laying hold of the God of the promises and of his ultimate provision for us, Jesus Christ, the righteous one. As we preach the conflict, the struggle, and the discipline, we do so urging people to a life of faith in Christ, evidenced by obedience to him. And we point further forward to the day when our faith will be sight. Come quickly, Lord Jesus!

THE LIVING APPLICATION PREACHING PROCESS

These four themes reflect a God-centered, redemptive-historical proclamation that deals with the particularities of each text while driving our hearers toward the ultimate goal, namely, faith in Jesus Christ as the only way of appropriating what God has promised us in the gospel. We need to sound these themes frequently: the *conflict* between God's promises and the situations we find ourselves in, the difficult *struggle* to live by faith and not sight, the grace of God to work with us and *discipline* us toward obedience, and the *triumph* of faith in those who look to Christ.

These overarching themes do not produce sameness, because each occurs with endless variety. The conflict comes in many different settings, the particular struggles vary greatly, the means of discipline change, and, while faith is always the final call, the life of faith is an adventure that is multidimensional. We are calling people not to a decision for Jesus each time, but to a life of discipleship, trusting and following Christ, and, by faith, engaging in the plan of redemption that God has been unfolding throughout the ages.

This larger framework for preaching the stories of the Bible interfaces well with the living application preaching process we have considered for developing the applicatory potential of a text. In the first part of the process (studying the living Word), we are interested in asking what the God-intended purpose of the text is. Is its purpose to teach truth or to rebuke error, to train in godliness or to correct wrong behavior, to test our hearts and convict us of sin or to encourage and exhort us? Each is a possibility in narrative. The *conflict* will often teach us truths about God's large plans and purposes. While we struggle on the ground, God is doing something larger that we may not see and can't understand. The stories put flesh and blood on the truth that his ways and thoughts are higher than ours (Isa. 55:9). The *struggle* in the text may well encourage us but it will also often convict and test us. To what extent, for example, have we also sought to take God's plans into our own hands, trying to give him a hand in the fulfillment of his promise because we did not trust his methods or timing? The *discipline* of the text will not only teach us God's typical ways of working with his recalcitrant people, but will also often rebuke, correct, and convict us of changes we need to make if God is to be sovereign in our lives. The *triumph* of the text will exhort and encourage us to faith in Christ and obedience to him, by which alone we can lay hold of the promises of the gospel.

The second part of the living application preaching process encourages us to draw from our reservoir. Our life experience and kingdom perspective will sharpen our insights into the situations we speak to today. Interfacing the message of the text with our own experience, observation, and knowledge will help us ground the truths of the text in realities today. The conflict, struggle, discipline, and triumph of the biblical story need to be connected to the conflicts, struggles, disciplines, and triumphs we experience. We must avoid, however, simplistic equations. If the struggle in the story is barrenness, the parallel struggle today is not couples in the church struggling with infertility (though there may be some secondary implications for them in terms of God's sovereignty in opening and closing the womb), but the church and Christian people who feel that fulfilling the calling God has given them is simply impossible. We look at what God asks of us and at our own circumstances and the two simply don't add up. We might look at the size of the gospel task, and the seeming weakness of preaching and verbal witness, and feel we need to help God come up with something more strategic. We might see spiritual deadness in the church and the Bible's pictures of the vitality of the church and begin to take it into our own hands to generate some life.

The third part of the living application preaching process sees us examining the lives of our hearers and thinking hard about how to penetrate deeply into people's hearts. How can the message of the text be worked into their minds, consciences, wills, and passions? Is the text oriented toward teaching, convicting, motivating, or moving people? Narrative can do all four. Biblical stories often teach truths about God and his ways that we need to grasp (highlighted by *conflict* and *discipline*). They often convict us of ungodly responses to his works and ways (revealed in *struggle* and *discipline*). They frequently motivate us to live lives of faith and obedience (as we observe *discipline* and *triumph*). But supremely they call us to align ourselves passionately with the purposes of God in this world even though we may fail to understand them and find them hard to live with. We will align with them because we know that his purposes will not fail. All his promises are "Yes" and "Amen" in Christ, and, when he does bring about the full realization of them, we will enter into eternal joy and the endless pleasures of God. All four themes must ultimately be driven home to the affections so that we move people to love Christ, and all that is wrapped up in him, more than they love themselves or anything this world offers.

The living application preaching process also trains us to think about the soul condition of our hearers, prompting us to take note of the different people and audiences to whom the story may apply. This part of the process always calls for tailored application. Not everyone is feeling the conflict right at the moment; they are not all struggling desperately, or sinning grievously, or experiencing the Lord's discipline, or triumphing by faith. We are unwise to make blanket equations between the condition of Israel and the condition of our people, or between a particular character in the story and every person in the church. It is here that a God-centered, Christ-focused reading of the text is far more helpful than a leapfrogging approach. As we sketch the conflict, the struggle, the discipline, and the triumph, we can ask people where they are, what their experience is, where they fit. We can sketch varying scenarios and different responses to the truth. We can call unbelievers to faith for the first time, and believers to renewed trust and obedience. We call the discouraged to see that victory is all by faith in an all-sufficient

Savior, while at the same time calling others to be responsive to the Lord's discipline.

WHAT DOES IT LOOK LIKE IN PRACTICE?

Our discussion of God-centered, redemptive-historical, christocentric application shaped around four great narrative themes (conflict, struggle, discipline, and triumph) and interfaced with three phases of the living application preaching process (the living Word, the life of the preacher, and the lives of the hearers) may all sound rather complex and abstract. To make these ideas more concrete, we will conclude this chapter by thinking in more detail about the Samson narrative. Earlier, I outlined a theocentric perspective on Judges 13, where Mr. and Mrs. Manoah find themselves caught up in God's unsought, unexpected, unhurried salvation plans. The rollicking account of Samson in the next three chapters poses in the mind of the preacher the robust question, What on earth am I meant to do with all this?[21]

Conflict is written all over the narrative. God intends to save. These are his covenant people, Israel, the chosen nation, who have not been long in the Promised Land. But they are being oppressed by Philistines. Samson is to be their judge who will bring about their deliverance. Yet the Israelites don't even seem to want salvation. They are living contentedly under Philistine rule (cf. 15:11). They have forsaken their calling as God's holy people, have been handed over to their enemies, and fail to recognize Samson as their savior. Of course, Samson is not what you would probably be looking for in a savior. He compromises his allegiance to God, evidencing a tendency to fall for the wrong kind of women and allowing them to manipulate him into giving away key secrets. Yet God's power rests on him, and his astounding strength is not from pumping iron but from the Spirit of God. At least, that is the case until God abandons him to his own weaknesses (16:20), which leads

---

21. Two commentaries I have found particularly helpful in thinking about the application of this narrative have been Dale Ralph Davis, *Judges: Such a Great Salvation*, Focus on the Bible (Fearn: Christian Focus, 2000); and Michael Wilcock, *The Message of Judges: Grace Abounding*, The Bible Speaks Today (Downers Grove: IVP, 1993).

in turn to the Philistines celebrating the glorious victory they believe Dagon has given them.

The conflict between God's purposes and the situation on the ground couldn't be greater. But is there *struggle*? Significantly, there is far less struggle than there should be on the part of Israel. They are so low spiritually that they don't cry out to God for salvation as they have every other time the disobedience-discipline-distress-deliverance cycle has gone around. Now they settle for Philistine rule, seemingly not feeling any need for God to intervene. Samson is different, not in having higher moral standards but at least in recognizing who the enemy really is. He has been raised up by God to fight the enemy singlehandedly. He is all too like Israel, but he is the one man around who recognizes that there is a fight on. And this, for most of the story, is the main focus of the narrator. Samson's dodgy liaisons and aggressive behavior are not reprimanded by the storyteller. Instead, we are told repeatedly that "this was of the LORD" and that "the Spirit of God came on him" (see 13:25; 14:4, 19; 15:14, 19). God wanted a struggle. He set up tensions between Samson and the Philistines so that someone would actually take them on.

The third theme, *discipline*, also features prominently in the story. It is the Lord's discipline that has brought Israel into their current situation. God has handed them over to their enemies because of their disobedience. Unfortunately, Israel doesn't seem to be getting the message of their "time out." They are like a little boy sent to his room because he's been naughty and who there finds all sorts of toys to play with. Time out is quite fun. But while Israel almost seems to be a lost cause, God holds up to them Samson as a mirror image of themselves so that they might see what is actually going on. They as a nation, like him, had been brought into being by God's pure grace against all the odds (beginning with an old man and his barren wife), they too had been called to be set apart for him as a holy nation, they too had seen God's power time and again, they too had fallen for foreign women and been led to compromise their commitment to God, they too had come into conflict with the nations around them and been subjected to foreign rule. Samson's life was a mirror in which they needed to see themselves and God's dealings with them for what they really were. They needed to be brought to their senses, to their knees, and back to their God.

Dark and stormy as the story is, however, it is finally a story of *triumph*. Through Samson God achieves his purposes. It is a tragic triumph but a triumph nonetheless. Samson, believing in the power of God as Israel should have, calls on him one more time. God comes in grace and power to an undeserving individual for the sake of his own name, his own purposes, and his own people. He cannot forsake them. Grace and mercy triumph. But the triumph is limited. At the end of the story, there is no indication that there was peace in the land. What was needed was a more ultimate judge/king than Samson.

The four themes are clearly present and are pregnant with applications. The following seven lines of application seem to be particularly appropriate and helpful.

First, as we saw from Judges 13, God is the God of unsought, unexpected, unhurried salvations. That can be seen in many places in the Bible, but nowhere more clearly than in the greatest act of salvation in Jesus Christ. The gospel comes to sinners who have never sought God. It comes in the person of One who was a most unlikely kind of Messiah. And it came many centuries after the initial promise was made. We need to develop an eye for God's continued unsought, unexpected, and unhurried ways of working in our lives as the gospel advances. What a mercy that he acts that way. What an encouragement, for example, to people who feel insignificant and to churches that lack resources. What hope it brings to those who have friends not crying out to God, or to people who feel they have waited forever for God to answer prayer.

Second, God wants us to see that it is a travesty when we live contentedly under enemy rule. In Samson, he held up a mirror to Israel, showing them their unique blessings that had been squandered. He showed them that they were meant to cast themselves on God's grace for deliverance, they were meant to fight the enemy and not quietly acquiesce to their rule, they were meant to be holy to the Lord. We are meant to do the same. We are never in a worse place spiritually than when we passively acquiesce to the values of the world around us, thinking that all is fine when all is not.

A third line of application grows out of God's demonstration of his ability to empower the man of his choosing to defeat the enemy. He did so through just one man—Samson. And for us he has also done so more fully, through one man—Jesus Christ our Lord. The Spirit of the Lord was on Christ, enabling him to resist the Devil and defeat the power of the grave. We are now called to fight, too, but only in the light of Christ's victory and the indwelling of his Spirit. We are to be engaged in the battle, knowing it is already won. But fight we must. We are not called to be passive, to fiddle our days away, or to presume upon God's grace. God is at work in this world through the power of the gospel, and we need to be on board with what he is doing.

Fourth, God uses all sorts of people. Barren Mrs. Manoah and flirtatious Samson are fascinating cases in point. Not that Samson's actions should incline us to presume upon God's grace, but what a comfort to know that God can use even our sins to advance his purposes. He is able to strike a straight blow with a crooked stick. He did so supremely when wicked men put his own Son to death on a cross. Through the greatest evil, God achieved the greatest good. What confidence that should give us that God is well able to make his purposes thrive in this world. They will not be thwarted.

A fifth theme is that sin has terrible consequences. As Israel looked in the mirror of Samson's life, they could see some awful realities. The man with Spirit-empowered biceps ended up the laughingstock of the Philistines, blindly grinding grain in one of their prisons and hearing in his ears a celebration of Dagon's power. Because sin works out well sometimes, it doesn't mean it always will. Because God uses even our compromises, it doesn't mean he will not allow us to reap the consequences of our folly. And when one of God's people falls, the greatest tragedy is that God's name is muddied.

The sixth line of application is that God is well able to defend the glory of his own name, bringing triumph from tragedy. The great

212

reversal with which the story ends is typical of the great reversals in which God specializes. None is more significant than the reversal wrought on the cross. Samson, it turns out, does point us very clearly to Christ. The one mocked becomes the conqueror, strength is displayed in weakness, victory comes through tragedy, triumph comes through death. God, in the story of Samson, paves the way for the final deliverer—the most unorthodox of them all. He is the Savior we need.

Finally, there is living application in God's call to us to live by faith in his power and grace. He does hear the cries of his people. His mercy is astounding. Significantly, the last word on Samson in the Bible is not found in Judges but in Hebrews 11. Samson is included in the great lineup of those "who through faith conquered kingdoms, administered justice and gained what was promised" (Heb. 11:32–33). No matter what our failings, or how low we fall, God has ordained that people triumph by grace through faith alone.

Each of these lines of application needs to be thrust into people's hearts and lives using the arrows we considered in chapter six. From the living Word, the applications include teaching and rebuking, training and correcting, testing and convicting, encouraging and exhorting. The handling of these themes will be enriched from our own experience of life and our observation of the ways of God and of people, that is, from our life reservoir. The truths can then be pressed against the lives of our hearers. Some applications will strike at the mind, some at the conscience, some at the will, some at the passions, as we speak to the faculties of the human heart. Some will be pitched at believers in varying spiritual conditions, others at those who are as yet outside the people of God, as we consider the different conditions of our hearers' souls. And the result, by God's grace, will be some intriguing, engaging, challenging messages about the God of Samson who is still at work in the world today and who works in our lives by the power of the gospel.

Preaching from the Old Testament narrative can be filled with varied, penetrating, living application.

DISCUSSION QUESTIONS

1. Do you love or loathe preaching from the narrative books of the Bible? Why?

2. Why are preachers so easily drawn to moralizing Old Testament narratives by drawing lessons and examples from the central human character?

3. Why does redemptive-historical preaching easily produce predictability and blandness in application? How can this be avoided?

4. What does it mean to preach Christ from an Old Testament narrative text? Should every sermon be Christ-centered?

5. Choose an Old Testament story (maybe one you have preached on recently) and identify ways in which the story echoes the themes of *conflict* (between promise and reality), *struggle* (in the lives of God's people), *discipline* (as God deals with his people), and *triumph* (of faith in God and his promises).

6. From this analysis, tease out some of the main applications that could be made from this story.

|9|

PREACHING THE "IVES"

I BELONGED TO one of the generations of school students "down under" who never really learned much English grammar. Hopefully things were better in other parts of the world, but in Australia and New Zealand, the teaching of grammar was out of vogue in the latter part of the twentieth century. Language was something to enjoy and to experiment with, not something to be restricted by pedantic rules. So I, and many others, developed an intuitive approach to grammar. We learned to tell whether it sounded good—whoops—right (or is it well, or correct?). I often can't tell why a certain word sounds right; I just have an ear for it. But then my ear for it all depends on what I've been exposed to. Having been surrounded by the poor grammar of semi-illiterate classmates, my intuitions are not always accurate. Consequently, many university students have poor writing and speaking skills, and students arriving at a theological college to learn Greek or Hebrew discover that the first thing they have to learn is some English grammar. That scarcely makes for a riveting introduction to theological study; it is a rare student who gets excited about grammar.

If your excitement levels are still rather low when it comes to grammar and your grammatical knowledge is rudimentary at best, there are nonetheless three very basic grammatical forms that make a world of difference when it comes to application in preaching. Indicatives, imperatives, and subjunctives—the three "ives"—litter the pages of the New Testament and are loaded with applicatory possibilities and pitfalls.

The three "ives" sound like a bit of a mouthful, but each can be quite readily identified. *Indicatives* are verbs that assert something or present a certainty.[1] They are most commonly used to state facts and make assertions, as Paul does, for instance, in 1 Timothy 1:15, when he says, "Christ Jesus came into the world to save sinners." Narrative, of course, depends on indicatives to tell a story ("A farmer went out to sow his seed," Mark 4:3) and, since the gospel is fundamentally a story, it is full of the most significant indicatives, as we will see.

Imperatives are most commonly commands.[2] They tell people what to do or not to do. Jesus commanded his disciples to "Follow me!" (Mark 2:14). Paul commanded Timothy to flee ungodliness and "pursue righteousness, godliness, faith, love, endurance and gentleness" (1 Tim 6:11). Such exhortations are found throughout the Scriptures and have a distinct place in the Christian life and in preaching.

Subjunctives, and in particular hortatory subjunctives, are commands that include both the speaker and the listeners. These are usually indicated in English translations by "let us."[3] So, for example, in 1 Thessalonians 5:8 Paul exhorts both himself and his hearers, saying, "Since we belong to the day, let us be self-controlled." This particular approach to exhortation is deserving of the preacher's attention.

Of course there is much else in Greek grammar that is loaded, too, but when we develop living application, the three "ives" are of particular significance.

Too often the "ives" are abused. In the first place, it seems preachers often do not know how to apply indicatives. As a result of our tendency to reduce application to telling people what to do, indicatives just don't

1. See Daniel B. Wallace, *Greek Grammar Beyond the Basics: An Exegetical Syntax of the New Testament* (Grand Rapids: Zondervan, 1996), 448.

2. Wallace defines the imperative mood as the mood of intention and identifies command as the most common use. Ibid., 485.

3. According to Wallace, "The subjunctive is commonly used to exhort or command oneself and one's associates. This use of the subjunctive is used 'to urge someone to unite with the speaker in a course of action upon which he has already decided.'" Ibid., 464.

cut it. They are seen as theological but not practical (a false dichotomy if ever there were one). Second, then, imperatives become the preacher's pet. They have real applicatory freight, allowing us to lay down duty and obligation. The problem is, imperatives are easily separated from the indicatives on which they build, and, without the connection, we preach legalism and moralism, not grace. Third, subjunctives tend to be overlooked. They are simply not on the preacher's radar, despite bringing a unique dimension to application.

So what is the applicatory potential of the "ives"? I want to suggest that indicatives invite us to enjoy God and what he has done, imperatives call for obedience that is motivated and empowered by the gospel, and subjunctives teach us to work together with our people to do what Christ has called us to. Each one is both theological and practical.

INDICATIVES: ENJOYING GOD AND WHAT HE HAS DONE

Gresham Machen declared that "Christianity begins with a triumphant indicative."[4] That, for him, was the most foundational difference between biblical Christianity and liberalism. Liberalism, he maintained, was preoccupied with the imperative mood—with telling people what to do. Christianity has its primary focus on what God has done.

So what has God done? He has created the world. He has chosen for himself a people. He called Abraham, gave him an heir, formed a nation, brought them out of Egypt, divided the Red Sea, gave them the Law, provided for them in the desert, brought them into the land he had promised them, and raised up for them judges who saved them from their own sinful folly. He provided them with kings to rule in his name, handed them over to their enemies when they rebelled against him, sent them prophets to call them back to himself, sent them into captivity and brought them back to their own land, and sent to them his own Son to be their Savior and Shepherd—the one whom he offered up for the sins of the world, raised from the dead, exalted to his own right hand, and appointed as judge of all men, and

---

4. J. Gresham Machen, *Christianity and Liberalism* (1923; repr., Grand Rapids: Eerdmans, 1977), 47.

through whom he has poured out his Spirit on the church as the first installment of eternity.

The whole biblical story is the story of what God has done. The fundamental mood of the Bible is the indicative mood. The indicative states, declares, announces, asserts, explains, and proclaims.[5] It deals with facts and with actions. It sets forth what is. In this regard it is significant, as we saw in the last chapter, that the predominant genre of Scripture is narrative. The Bible is not chiefly a set of rules with stories to illustrate them, but a story about God's actions in history, with instructions on how to live the story out.[6] Lloyd-Jones put it this way: "The Bible is the record of the activity of God. God is the actor. God is the center. Everything is of God and comes from God, and turns to God. It is God who speaks. It is God who acts. It is God who intervenes. It is God who originates, who plans everything everywhere."[7]

Preach God

The first implication for the preacher, then, is that preaching must invariably begin with what God has done. All that we call for and all that we want people to aspire to must be rooted in what God has already done. Sermons ought to be full of the acts of God. All good application depends on that. It is the foundation for praise and worship. It is the only way in which we will inculcate a right sense of sin, of the human predicament, and of future judgment. It is the only basis for understanding the glorious grace of the gospel. It is the foremost means of giving people hope beyond themselves. The preacher's task, first and foremost, is to lift people's eyes to something higher than themselves, their job, their house, their family, or their next holiday. These are the

---

5. Wallace says, "The indicative mood is, in general, the mood of assertion, or *presentation of certainty*." It is most commonly used "to *present* an assertion as a non-contingent (or unqualified) statement." Wallace, *Greek Grammar Beyond the Basics*, 448–49 (italics in original).

6. This idea is from an address by Timothy Keller, "Being the Church in our Culture," *Resurgence*, accessed December 8, 2010, available online at http://theresurgence .com/2006/07/05/being-the-church-in-our-culture-video.

7. Quoted in Iain H. Murray, *Lloyd-Jones: Messenger of Grace* (Edinburgh: Banner of Truth, 2008), 8.

things people are often thinking about when they walk into church but, by the time they leave, we hope their gaze will be somewhere else. John Piper astutely wrote,

> People are starving for the greatness of God. But most of them would not give this diagnosis of their troubled lives. The majesty of God is an unknown cure. There are far more popular prescriptions on the market, but the benefit of any other remedy is brief and shallow. Preaching that does not have the aroma of God's greatness may entertain for a season, but it will not touch the hidden cry of the soul: "Show me thy glory!"[8]

Think, for example, of a woman who comes along to church regularly. She's in a difficult marriage with a husband who seldom worships with her, is often angry, and is just plain hard to live with. She herself is not exactly the woman of most men's dreams. She's inclined to depression, rather disorganized, and frequently unmotivated. She desperately wants her husband to understand her, to talk and to listen to her. But it's easier to talk to the vacuum cleaner than to him. So she comes along to church each Sunday with a bundle of deeply felt needs: the need to be listened to, to be happy, to improve her marriage, to be more disciplined in life. She's naturally drawn to a preaching ministry that has sermons on such topics as overcoming depression, keys to a happier marriage, and steps to better communication.

But what if she stepped into a church where she heard about a God who loved people eternally and unconditionally, a God who is sovereign and works in all situations, a God who is pleased to work his sovereign power in weakness? What if she heard of a Savior who intercedes and a Spirit who regenerates, renews, and revives? What if she learned of a God who restores the years the locusts have eaten away, who keeps his covenant, who invites persistent prayer, and who promises to draw near to those who draw near to him? Would not these themes do her more good than ten steps to a successful marriage—things that put all the

8. John Piper, *The Supremacy of God in Preaching* (Grand Rapids: Baker, 1990), 9.

onus back on her and her dysfunctional marriage? She doesn't chiefly need imperatives. She needs divine indicatives. Instead of leaving church looking at herself, her husband, and her marriage, she would leave looking at God, and Christ, and the promises of his Word.

Cotton Mather, an American Puritan, said, "The great design and intention of the office of a Christian preacher [is] to restore the throne and dominion of God in the souls of men."[9] In the words of Isaiah, the great note we must sound in our gospel preaching is, "Your God reigns" (Isa. 52:7).

We may well start a sermon with people's felt needs but our real goal is to move their focus as we go. The fact is, much of life is petty, painful, and pedantic. There's plenty of work that is not particularly inspiring, mundane chores that grate (who thrives on putting out trash, changing diapers, or getting up to babies crying in the night?), and trivialities that consume too much time (commuting, watching soap operas, jostling with crowds in the shopping center). All that this world offers wears thin after a while: new possessions only give a short-term buzz, partying hard doesn't leave you feeling great the next day, a sex-driven life fails to satisfy the yearning for love and security, and even the best marriage cannot satisfy our deepest longings. Preachers, therefore, have the privilege of lifting people to a higher plane.

When we are strongly God-centered in our preaching, we do people a twofold favor. First, we help them to know God and come into relationship with him, which is more important than anything else in this world. John Piper has reminded us that "God is the Gospel."[10] Everything in the gospel leads to him. Forgiveness clears the way to God, justification makes us right with God, adoption makes us children of God, sanctification transforms us into the likeness of God, and glorification ushers us into the presence of God. Only when we are God-centered in our preaching do we do people the great favor of helping them see and know God.

9. Ibid., 22.

10. See John Piper, *God Is the Gospel: Meditations on God's Love as the Gift of Himself* (Leicester: IVP, 2005).

Second, when we are God-centered we help them see themselves in right perspective. Our natural fallen tendency is to think that what *we* do is of chief importance. We think that our actions are determinative of our future, that what people think of us is of enormous significance, and that our efforts can make us better people. The gospel declares the contrary. It takes our eyes off us and puts them on God.

If we are to lift people's eyes to God, we must frequently take up the highest and mightiest of the Bible's doctrines. Great preaching depends on great truths. We need to preach on the attributes and works of God, the person and work of Christ, and the work of the Holy Spirit. A diet that regularly serves up messages on creation, election, and providence; heaven and God's excellence, hell and God's wrath; the love, mercy, and justice of God; Christ's atoning work, kingly rule, priestly intercession, and prophetic ministry; justification by faith alone and union with Christ; the Spirit's power, conviction of sin, regeneration, sanctification, and revival—such a diet will draw people away from themselves and up to God.

Applying Indicatives

The applicatory payload of indicatives is chiefly this: God is to be treasured and enjoyed. We are to enjoy the fact that he acts, he reigns, he knows what he is doing, he is in control, his plans and purposes are ultimately good, and, by his astounding grace, we are his. We are to treasure a relationship with him. In preaching indicatives, we will want to constantly stir confidence in God and adoration of him. We will drive at worship and trust.

This necessitates three things. First, we need to show the wonder of his works. Our posture is to be like that of someone standing at the bottom of an enormous waterfall, looking up at torrents of water cascading hundreds of meters down over rock and pounding into the deep pool below. The response is an inevitable "Wow! Isn't that amazing? Look at that!" There is, however, one critical requirement for any preacher who says to his people, "Isn't that amazing?" The amazing thing must have been presented in a way that has truly shown its wonder. If we

221

have taken our people on a boring journey through dense theological territory, and then, when they are almost asleep and wondering if the lecture will ever finish, we say, "Isn't that amazing?," they are not likely to agree with us. We will have taught them that God is boring. That is perhaps the greatest travesty in preaching.

It is the preacher's calling to present truths about God clearly and compellingly. All the arrows we considered in chapter six should be used. We need to use illustrations and testimonies. We need to search for fresh ways of putting things. We should anticipate the questions people have. We must speak with genuine passion, showing that this comes from the heart, not just the head.

The second thing we must do in applying indicatives is to tease out the implications of God's works for our lives now. Implications are one of the most helpful aspects of application. The basic formula is, "If this is true, it implies that . . ." The implications are not necessarily stated in the text, nor do they need to be imperatives—something we have to do. The implication may be another indicative—something we need to know and take to heart.

The great truth of God's sovereignty, for example, has vast implications. Paul unpacks some in the latter half of Romans 8. In verses 28–30 he describes the sovereign purposes of God in the lives of those he has chosen, such as that all things work together for their ultimate good. The question in verse 31, then, begins to probe these implications. "What, then, shall we say in response to this?" He tells us not things we must do but things we must know. If God is for us, as he is in our salvation, no one can ultimately be against us. If God gave us his Son, as he did, he will most certainly give us everything else we need as well. If God, in his redemption plan, has justified us, nothing can bring about our final condemnation. If God is in control of all things, nothing can separate us from him. These are glorious implications of God's sovereignty in salvation, and they drive us to confidence and adoration.

We could push the implications further into life scenarios. If nothing can separate us from God's love, then we need not fear when people unfairly undermine us. It hurts, but it doesn't change anything of ultimate

222

importance. If our salvation is secure in Christ, then we don't have to despair of ourselves or fear separation from God when we fall back into old sins. If all things will finally work out well, as God has promised, then though we long for our children to be saved, our life is not over if one of them strays. God has even that in his hands and will bring about what is ultimately best.

The third thing we should do with indicatives is to move to what Wayne McDill calls "can" applications. Instead of turning indicatives into a response of "we need to," "we ought to," "we must," and "we should" (imperatives), McDill argues that "the best term for maintaining indicatives while challenging your audience is *can*."[11] Instead of saying you *ought to* love your neighbor, or honor your parents, or tell the truth, the preacher may say, you *can* do these things. The law becomes a promise, based on the work of Christ in us. The word *can* more readily raises the question, "How?," and the answer can be rooted in the sufficiency of the gospel.[12] The bottom line of the indicative is that you can trust God, and you can change, and you can be useful to the Lord, and you can grow in grace because God has provided everything necessary for you. As Peter so confidently states, "His divine power has given us everything we need for life and godliness through our knowledge of him" (2 Peter 1:3).

One final thing needs to be noted about preaching indicatives. As they call believers to glorify God and enjoy him forever, they also call unbelievers to reckon with who God is. The indicatives may imply that since it is true that if God is for you nothing can be against you, so it is also true that if God is against you, nothing can be for you. The reverse side of an indicative is not always valid, but it should be considered as a possible implication.[13] God has acted and those who ignore or reject his actions incur his wrath. There are immense implications for unbelievers.

11. Wayne McDill, *12 Essential Skills for Great Preaching* (Nashville: Broadman & Holman, 2006), 196.

12. Ibid., 197.

13. For comment on the validity or otherwise of negative inferences, see D. A. Carson, *Exegetical Fallacies* (Grand Rapids: Baker; Carlisle, UK: Paternoster, 1996), 101–3.

Indicatives can lead to application that is more life giving than we ever imagined. They don't lead us to tell people what to do, but instead they prompt us to help people enjoy God for who he is and what he has done. If our preaching of biblical indicatives leads people to look away from themselves and rejoice in God, we have done the most significant applicatory work of all.

IMPERATIVES: CALLING FOR GOSPEL-EMPOWERED OBEDIENCE

Imperatives flow out of indicatives. What the gospel calls us to do is always rooted in what God has first done for us. This is the fundamental structure of biblical revelation, and it is essential to always operate in terms of the indicative-imperative construct of the gospel.[14] It is significant that, in Romans, not a single second-person-plural imperative is found prior to 6:11. Up until that point the focus is on what is, not on what we must do. From 12:1 onward there are thirty-three second-person-plural imperatives. Similarly, in Ephesians, there is only one imperative in the first three chapters but twenty-nine in the last three. That is the broad structure of Paul's ministry: doctrine first, then life. It is also the pattern of the law given at Sinai. God declares, "I am the LORD your God, who brought you out of Egypt, out of the land of slavery" (Deut. 5:6). On that basis he then issues the ten commands: "You shall have no other gods before me" (v. 7).

There are two important implications for preaching in this indicative-imperative pattern of Scripture. First, the indicative must always precede the imperative; second, while the gospel begins with a triumphant indicative, it does not end there.[15] Both implications need to be teased out.

Gospel Resources and Motivations

The indicative must always precede the imperative. When we preach through a New Testament epistle, we tend to carve it into sec-

14. See John Carrick, *The Imperative of Preaching: A Theology of Sacred Rhetoric* (Carlisle: Banner of Truth, 2002), 5.
15. See ibid., 83.

tions, preaching it over several weeks and thereby separating what God initially joined together. Ephesians, for example, was not written with the expectation that the challenges of Ephesians 4–6 would be dealt with several weeks or months after the truths of chapters 1–3. Therefore, when we preach imperatives from the latter chapters, we must consciously reconnect them with the doctrine that precedes them. If we fail to do so, we cast people on their own resources to try to keep the commands. We imply that they must help themselves, improve themselves, pull themselves up, try harder, do better. Such commands will either deflate them as they find they are utterly unable to do so, or inflate their egos as they feel that they are doing well in their obedience. Either way, the gospel has been lost.[16]

In preaching imperatives, we must always point to the gospel's resources and motivations for obedience. The gospel alone can empower obedience and provide the right incentive to obey. It is not that we are saved by grace and then sanctified by our own effort, but we are saved by grace and sanctified by grace as Christ takes up residence within us through his Spirit, working in us to will and to act according to God's good purpose.

If we fail to anchor imperatives in indicatives, we will find ourselves appealing to people to change and act for pragmatic and moralistic reasons, not gospel reasons. Tim Keller has identified these as the twin dangers between which we must guide our preaching.[17] Pragmatism sees us calling for a particular action because it works, not because it is right. In so doing, we appeal to people's self-serving spirit. We encourage them to give, or to be pure, or to be honest because that will bring them the best results in life. What we are really doing

---

16. Graeme Goldsworthy says, "To say what we should be or do and not link it with a clear exposition of what God has done about our failure to be or do perfectly as he wills is to reject the grace of God and to lead people to lust after self-help and self-improvement in a way that, to call a spade a spade, is godless." Graeme Goldsworthy, *Preaching the Whole Bible as Christian Scripture: The Application of Biblical Theology to Expository Preaching* (Grand Rapids: Eerdmans, 2000), 119.

17. Timothy Keller, "Preaching Morality in an Amoral Age," in Haddon W. Robinson and Craig Brian Larson, eds., *The Art and Craft of Biblical Preaching: A Comprehensive Resource for Today's Communicators* (Grand Rapids: Zondervan, 2005), 166–70.

is feeding their selfishness. The gospel, which exposes our selfishness and demands that Christ be Lord in our life, is short-circuited. The real issue is not whether a certain action makes your life better, but whether a certain action honors Christ. "If we argue too pragmatically, we unwittingly confirm the basic postmodern person's view that truth is whatever works; they won't see how radically you are challenging their thinking and life approach."[18] The gospel requires us to expose selfish pragmatism, not feed it.

Moralism, on the other hand, puts grace and works the wrong way around. In all other religions, the answer to the question "Why be moral?" is "In order to find God." Christianity, however, says, "Because God has found you."[19] If we lay on people biblical demands for moral living without pressing on them the steadfast love and grace of God, we gut the gospel of its good news, driving people to the helplessness of self-help or to the arrogance of self-achievement.

The gospel obedience that imperatives call for needs to be built on a fivefold recognition that we should drum into people's hearts.

First, we must recognize that Christ has fulfilled the law for us. In his active and passive obedience, he has met the law's demands in our place and borne its curse for us. We are now freed from the condemnation of the law. Therefore, obedience does not bring about a right relationship with God, and neither does disobedience bring about our spiritual demise. Rather, obedience is a response to what God has done for us in Christ, and disobedience simply drives us back to our Savior on whom all our hope is built.

Second, we must recognize that, in Christ, we are given a new ability to obey. We have been given not only a new standing with God but a new heart that is responsive to him. We are new creations, enabled to keep God's law in a way we never previously could. We are no longer in bondage to sin. Sin is no longer inevitable in our

18. Ibid., 169.
19. Ibid.

226

lives. The Spirit lives in us to empower and enable us to increasingly conform to God's will. We do not yet obey fully, but we can obey increasingly.

Third, we must recognize that our new freedom in Christ is expressed by glad obedience to his commands. Our new heart wants to respond to the Lord's love and the law defines for us how to do so. It teaches us how to love God and our neighbor. It is our rule of life, guiding and leading us in a life of commitment to the Lord. The imperatives of the New Testament show us how to live lives pleasing to God in which our freedom from sin and condemnation is used not to indulge the sinful nature but to live according to the Spirit. Jesus himself taught us that if we love him we will obey his commands.

Fourth, we must recognize that sanctification comes from communion with Christ. Growth in holiness comes not by trying harder within oneself, but by seeking an ever closer communion with God, an ever increasing indwelling of Christ, and an ever greater fullness of the Spirit. It is as we remain in Christ, and he in us, that we are sanctified by him. John Piper puts it this way:

> We are transformed into Christ's image—that's what sanctification is—by steadfast seeing and savoring of the glory of Christ. . . . The work of the Holy Spirit in changing us is not to work directly on our bad habits but to make us admire Jesus Christ so much that sinful habits feel foreign and distasteful. . . . Therefore, if we neglect the glory of God in Christ as the greatest gift of the gospel, we cripple the sanctifying work of the church.[20]

In preaching, we must stress that holiness comes not merely from trying hard to be holy but from being united to the holy one and being so full of him that we find he himself tears us both powerfully and winsomely from that which is unholy.

20. Piper, *God Is the Gospel*, 91–92.

227

Finally, we must recognize that when we break God's law, we spoil, but do not lose, our relationship with the Father. Sin mars the relationship but it does not put us out of the family. We therefore need to confess our sins daily, repent, and seek forgiveness. We need to experience daily conversion as we turn from sin and trust in Christ. We are able to do so because of the fullness of God's grace. His mercies are new every morning; his grace is sufficient for us; the blood of Christ covers all our sin.

These convictions must govern the way we preach the Bible's imperatives. All that we call for in terms of godly living must be rooted in these truths. That's why Paul urges sexual purity (1 Cor. 6) on the basis of gospel realities: You were washed, you were sanctified, you were justified. Your body was meant for the Lord, it will one day be raised by him, it is a member of Christ, and it is a temple of the Holy Spirit. Since you are not your own but have been bought at a price, don't engage in sexual impurity. In a similar way, he urges unity among believers (Phil. 2) on the basis of gospel truths: You have been united with Christ, comforted by his love, and drawn into fellowship with the Spirit and have experienced his tenderness and compassion and seen the attitude of Christ who gave himself as a servant to us. So don't put yourself forward ahead of others, but look to their interests first. You have sufficient security and strength in the gospel to do so.

This grounding of Christian ethics in the gospel can be seen throughout the New Testament and it needs to be explicit in our preaching. For every command issued, preachers should ask themselves, "Have I given gospel reasons for why this is important and have I shown the gospel resources that enable obedience?"[21] We will develop helpful living application only when the gospel itself drives our exhortations.

The Gospel Demands Response

The second implication of the indicative-imperative pattern of Scripture is that while the gospel begins with a triumphant indicative,

---

21. A very helpful description of a gospel-based approach to sanctification can be found in Tim Chester, *You Can Change: God's Transforming Power for Our Sinful Behaviour and Negative Emotions* (Nottingham: IVP, 2008).

it does not end there. The declaration of what God has done always demands response. In the first instance, it demands repentance and faith. The first imperative of the gospel is "Repent and believe." That is the repeated call of apostolic preaching. Subsequent to conversion, the gospel imperative is, in short, "Be holy as I am holy." The repeated call of the epistles is to God-enabled sanctification as we put off the old self and put on the new. In view of God's mercy (the indicative), we are called to offer our bodies as living sacrifices, holy and pleasing to God (Rom. 12:1–2).

That means that preachers should exhort boldly and frequently.[22] They must urge unbelievers to turn from sin and trust in Jesus Christ. They should press onto believers their responsibility to submit to Christ in every department of life. Paul wrote to the Thessalonians of how he had "dealt with each of you as a father deals with his own children, encouraging, comforting and urging you to live lives worthy of God, who calls you into his kingdom and glory" (1 Thess. 2:11–12).

Preachers will find value in a string of brief commands and exhortations that press home a necessary response. Think, for example, of the number of brief commands given in Romans 12:9–21 as Paul urges sincere love as an essential response to God's mercies.

Love must be sincere. Hate what is evil; cling to what is good. Be devoted to one another in brotherly love. Honor one another above yourselves. Never be lacking in zeal, but keep your spiritual fervor, serving the Lord. Be joyful in hope, patient in affliction, faithful in prayer. Share with God's people who are in need. Practice hospitality.

Bless those who persecute you; bless and do not curse. Rejoice with those who rejoice; mourn with those who mourn. Live in harmony with one another. Do not be proud, but be willing to associate with people of low position. Do not be conceited.

Do not repay anyone evil for evil. Be careful to do what is right in the eyes of everybody. If it is possible, as far as it depends on you, live

22. Carrick addresses the problem of some biblical theology preachers who major on indicatives but largely refuse to apply with imperatives. See Carrick, *The Imperative of Preaching*, 108–46.

at peace with everyone. Do not take revenge, my friends, but leave room for God's wrath, for it is written: "It is mine to avenge; I will repay," says the Lord. On the contrary:

> "If your enemy is hungry, feed him;
> if he is thirsty, give him something to drink.
> In doing this, you will heap burning coals on his head."

Do not be overcome by evil, but overcome evil with good.

In these verses there are only four indicatives, all of which occur in the quotations in verses 19–20. The bulk of the passage uses imperatives (x9) along with participles (x19) and infinitives (x2) with imperatival force. The contemporary preacher can usefully imitate this approach. A while back, I preached from Isaiah 52:7 at the ordination of a new minister. Part of my exhortation to the young pastor was more or less as follows:

> So preach Christ! Preach the fullness of his work. Expose him. Show that salvation is all of him. Don't place heavy loads on people, but show Jesus, who bore the load. Don't preach moralism, legalism, traditionalism. Preach the good news of Jesus—that we are saved and sanctified by grace. Make sure your preaching is full of Christ and what he has done and the grace, hope, freedom, joy, and power found only in him. Give your people confidence in Jesus Christ. Let them walk away feeling, "I can do all things through Christ who strengthens me." Make sure they leave calling on the name of the Lord, leaning on him, trusting in him, looking to him.

The paragraph consists almost entirely of brief imperatives, one on top of the other.

In developing living application we will probably find that we gravitate to imperatives in the text. They provide the most obvious lines of application. That is fine; we must preach imperatives. But we must think carefully about how to do so. Imperatives are commands to live the gospel. They are exhortations to put the gospel into action. They must always be rooted in the gospel itself, and response to them must be enabled by the gospel. Applied that way, they will be life giving; applied any other way, and they will lead to deadening moralism and legalism.

SUBJUNCTIVES: RESPOND TO CHRIST TOGETHER

While indicatives and imperatives provide the grammatical sub-structure of the gospel, subjunctives also have a place not only in Greek grammar but in applicatory preaching. The subjunctive has various uses, but it is, as we have seen, the hortatory subjunctive, with its distinctive "let us," that is of particular relevance to the preacher. In this form, the subjunctive is used by the author in the first person plural to urge his readers to join with him in living a certain way.

The epistle to the Hebrews, arguably the most sermonic of the epistles,[23] makes use of the hortatory subjunctive, first person plural, in the following verses. (I have highlighted the subjunctives by using italics in the following biblical quotations.)

Therefore, since the promise of entering his rest still stands, *let us be careful* that none of you be found to have fallen short of it. (4:1)

Let us therefore *make every effort* to enter that rest. (4:11)

Therefore, since we have a great high priest who has gone through the heavens, Jesus the Son of God, *let us hold firmly* to the faith we profess. (4:14)

Let us then *approach* the throne of grace with confidence. (4:16)

23. The case for this and its implications for preaching are discussed usefully in Dennis E. Johnson, *Him We Proclaim: Preaching Christ from All the Scriptures* (Phillipsburg, NJ: P&R, 2007), 171–97. For a consideration of aspects of the sermonic style of Hebrews that are suggestive for preachers today, see Murray A. Capill, "Hebrews as a Sermon: Learning from its Preaching Style," *Vox Reformata* 73 (2008): 40–53.

Let us draw near to God with a sincere heart. . . . *Let us hold* unswervingly to the hope we profess. . . . And *let us consider* how we may spur one another on toward love and good deeds. (10:22–24)

Therefore, since we are surrounded by such a great cloud of witnesses, *let us throw off* everything that hinders and the sin that so easily entangles, and *let us run* with perseverance the race marked out for us. (12:1)

Therefore, since we are receiving a kingdom that cannot be shaken, *let us be thankful*, and so worship God acceptably with reverence and awe. (12:28)

Let us, then, *go* to him outside the camp, bearing the disgrace he bore. (13:13)

Through Jesus, therefore, *let us* continually *offer* to God a sacrifice of praise—the fruit of lips that confess his name. (13:15)

It is significant that the subjunctive is frequently used here in conjunction with "therefore,"[24] indicating the strongest link between prior indicatives and the requisite response. As with imperatives, it is essential to connect the action that is called for in hortatory subjunctives to the gospel indicatives that drive the action. In fact, the hortatory subjunctive really just operates as a first-person imperative.[25] Its distinction is that it allows the preacher to stand with, rather than over, his hearers. It conveys a sense that "we are in this together."[26]

Someone once asked Donald Sunukjian how he saw himself as a preacher. He replied, "I see myself standing with you, under the

24. Usually *oun*, but also *toigapoun* and *dio*.

25. According to Wallace, "Since there is no first person imperative, the hortatory subjunctive is used to do roughly the same task. Thus this use of the subjunctive is an exhortation in the *first person plural*." Wallace, *Greek Grammar Beyond the Basics*, 464.

26. Porter denies that the first-person-plural subjunctive necessarily includes the speaker in the action, but he does not substantiate this argument. Wallace clearly includes the speaker in the action. See Stanley E. Porter, *Idioms of the Greek New Testament* (Sheffield: Sheffield Academic Press, 1994), 58; Wallace, *Greek Grammar Beyond the Basics*, 464.

Word of God, saying, 'Look at what God is saying to us.' "[27] That is a very different posture from that described by Jay Adams. He argues that one of the key differences between the lecturer and the preacher is that the latter uses the second person plural whereas the lecturer is "deathly afraid of saying 'you.' "[28] Adams rightly opposes those whose preaching style is mostly in the third person, but does that mean we must always use the second person? It would seem, as I have suggested earlier, that a balance between first and second person plural application is thoroughly biblical. Including ourselves in the applications prevents us from appearing detached from the congregation or more perfect than we are. It builds rapport with people, indicating that we are in this together. There is a very different message between saying to one of my children, "I want you to go to the supermarket and buy some milk," and saying, "Let's go to the supermarket and buy some milk."

The indicative says we *can*; the imperative says we *must*; the subjunctive says, *let's!* While the force is no less than the imperative, the flavor is different. Listen to this mode of application in the following appeals:

> Friends, we've seen that God has blessed us richly in Christ. And we've seen that his work is carried on not just in large churches, but in small ones like ours. So let's press on with hope. Let's pour our energy into the work God has given us to do in the community. Let's work together and pray together. Let's spare nothing, because Christ spared nothing in giving himself for us. Let's pick each other up when we fall and carry each other when we're weary. And let's expect that God himself will enable and use us in the work of the gospel.

Mixing up some hortatory subjunctives with indicatives and imperatives will enable us to encourage and exhort in varied and

27. Donald R. Sunukjian, *Invitation to Biblical Preaching: Proclaiming Truth with Clarity and Relevance* (Grand Rapids: Kregel, 2007), 9.

28. Jay Adams, *Preaching with Purpose: A Comprehensive Textbook on Biblical Preaching* (Phillipsburg, NJ: P&R, 1982), 54.

colorful ways.[29] It is, however, difficult to end a sermon in the subjunctive, just as it is usually awkward to end on a question. Even if the last spoken paragraph is filled with the hortatory subjunctive, it will usually be best to land on an indicative. So the previous example may then conclude: "Friends, let's do this, because God is with us and because he will build his church and because the gospel is the greatest cause in the world."

GRAMMAR AND LIVING APPLICATION

The three "ives" help us as we work with the living application preaching process. The indicative majors on the teaching function of the living Word and speaks chiefly to the faculties of the mind and the passions. The imperative is suited to the training/correcting and encouraging/exhorting purposes of the Word and speaks to the faculty of the will. The hortatory subjunctive exhorts while stirring the passions and pressing the conscience.

It would be useful for preachers to review a few recent sermons and examine how they have applied indicatives and imperatives, and what use they have made of subjunctives. I'll conclude this chapter in subjunctive mode: Let's make sure that we help our people enjoy God. Let's do so by focusing on him and on what we can do because of what he has done. Let's also make sure that we call people to respond to the gospel with obedient Christian living. But when we do so, let's ensure that we ground all our appeals in the gospel, pointing them to the resources and incentives we have in Christ. And let's not only stand over them, telling them what to do, but also with them, aspiring, alongside them, to do what together we've been called to do in Christ. Using each of these three distinct moods will aid us in crafting living application that is varied, helpful, and penetrating.

---

29. This is different from another use of the subjunctive in preaching as described by Wayne McDill. He gives the following examples: "If you and I would earnestly pray, we would see miracles." "If we were a more caring congregation, we would reach out to this neighborhood." "O that the power of God might fall!" McDill regards these as presenting a skeptical idealism that fails to come to terms with reality. See McDill, *12 Essential Skills for Great Preaching*, 195.

DISCUSSION QUESTIONS

1. Why are indicatives generally harder to preach than imperatives?
2. What are the practical applicatory benefits of being more strongly focused on what God has done than on what we must do?
3. What is the connection between preaching indicatives and preaching to the passions (or affections)?
4. How can you ensure that your preaching of biblical imperatives is strongly grounded in the gospel itself?
5. In application, when do you tend to say "we/us" and when do you say "you"? What are the respective advantages of using the first and second person?

| 10 |

PREPARING
HOLISTICALLY

ANECDOTAL EVIDENCE suggests that expository preachers typically spend anywhere from five to twenty hours preparing a sermon. I encourage preaching students to work toward allocating about twelve hours' preparation time to each message. Much more and they will struggle to do justice to all the demands of ministry, especially given that many of them will be expected to prepare two sermons a week; much less and they will shortchange both their exegetical and homiletical work. But what is the balance of time between exegesis and homiletics, between studying the text and considering how to shape from it a message for today? How should the hours of sermon preparation time be used?

The inclination for many expository preachers is to spend the vast majority of their time on exegesis and a lesser, but significant, slice of time writing notes or a manuscript. What usually gets squeezed out is time for developing living application and for choosing the best arrows in the quiver for firing the message home. Too frequently the result, as we saw earlier, is lecturing rather than preaching, with bolt-on applications delivered blandly instead of holistic applications delivered penetratingly.

It may seem, then, that a generous dose of time between exegesis and actual sermon writing, dedicated to thinking about application and impact, is the remedy. In some ways it is, but even that may be inadequate. A holistic approach to application demands that we are thinking application from beginning to end. We need to have an applicatory mindset as we exegete, as we gather sermon material, as we choose our sermon form, as we prepare notes, as we speak, and as we follow up afterwards. Application is the main game and it needs to be in view throughout. At least that is the goal, though achieving it means negotiating some significant hazards and challenges along the way.

APPLICATORY EXEGESIS

The first hazard is that in approaching the text with an applicatory quest in mind, we may begin to impose on the text what is not there. Our desire to be applicatory may lessen our commitment to listening to the text and letting it speak for itself. We bring to it an agenda. This is an equal and opposite error to approaching the text with no applicatory focus at all. If we forget that God's living Word is designed to teach/rebuke, train/correct, test/convict, and encourage/exhort, we may well end up with a purely academic approach to the text that misses its God-intended purpose.

Between the two extremes lies applicatory exegesis. As well as asking the regular exegetical questions of the text (Who wrote it? To whom? When? Why? What is the immediate and wider literary context? What is the significance of the word usage, grammar, form, and genre? What did it mean for the original readers?), we must also ask applicatory questions of the text. The living application preaching process has suggested questions to ask: questions about the text's purposes, about the ways in which it interfaces with life today, about the faculties of the heart to which it speaks, and about the kind of people to whom it applies. The text is not understood until we have answers to these questions. Stopping short of this means that we fall short of grasping the meaning of the text because, while we may understand what God *said*, we do not understand what God is *saying*; while we are aware of what God *did*, we are unaware of what he is *doing* now through the text. God's Word speaks and acts not only in the past but also in the present. To rightly understand the text is to rightly understand its impact *here and now* as well as *there and then*.[1]

This kind of processing is not found in most commentaries, so we cannot readily look up the answers to these questions.[2] This is the exegesis of prolonged thought and reflection, of wrestling with the Word and of wresting from it the message for today that God would have us bring to our people. It is the exegesis of prayer and meditation as well as word studies and textual analysis. Prayer is a powerful aid, not just as we seek insight but as we actually pray the passage into our own life. Many a time I have led family devotions on a passage of Scripture and have had neither time nor clarity of mind to make any particularly useful applications of the Bible reading. But then as I have led my family in prayer, a few brief petitions arising from the reading have begun to crystallize the way we ought to be responding to the text. If you can pray a passage, chances are you can apply it.

Peripatetic exegesis can also help. I am not the only preacher who finds it helpful to take a long walk to turn the passage over in my head and preach it to myself. Staying behind the desk easily locks us in to an academic mode of application that is less conducive to the creative thinking required for applicatory exegesis. Beyond the value of a walk, there is the greater value of living with the text for some time, turning it over in our mind and chewing on it in the context of life. It is for this reason that beginning sermon preparation late in the week is seldom smart. It leaves too little time between encountering the text and ministering from it for exegetical applicatory cogitation to take place.

---

1. In this regard some cautious use of speech-act theory may be of value to Bible interpreters and preachers. Graeme Goldsworthy wisely proposes further examination of the contributions of speech-act theory, while noting some of its potential advantages in biblical interpretation. See Graeme Goldsworthy, *Gospel-Centred Hermeneutics: Biblical-Theological Foundations and Principles* (Nottingham: IVP, Apollos, 2006), 215–17.

2. Phillip Jensen's warning about commentaries is worth noting: "Commentaries can be useful tools, but they can be deadening for preachers. . . . Scholars who write commentaries are usually talking to each other, answering each other's questions. They are not the questions that the person in the pew has, and they're often not what the text is about either. Even the best biblical commentators still have to answer many questions entirely irrelevant to the people you are serving on a Sunday. Knowing the answers to these questions is still important, but you can't let it take up all your sermon preparation time, let alone your congregation's valuable time as they listen to you preach." Phillip D. Jensen and Paul Grimmond, *The Archer and the Arrow: Preaching the Very Words of God* (Kingsford, New South Wales: Matthias Media, 2010), 147.

LIFE APPLICATION GRIDS

We have seen that in the living application preaching process we begin with exegesis. Identifying the purposes of the Word must lead the way. When the sermon is formed, the main thing we will be doing is teaching, rebuking, correcting, training, testing, convicting, comforting, encouraging, and exhorting. These purposes of the Word, however, are sharpened as we examine them in the light of the later stages of the preaching process. We examine the biblical applications in the light of our own reservoir of experience and knowledge, the faculties of the human heart, and the varying conditions of people's souls. Each stage of the process brings increased sharpness to the applications we make.

As we work on a sermon, we will find it useful to jot down applicatory possibilities from the four sources of applicatory insights this model suggests, as shown below.

Diagram 13: Four Sources of Applicatory Material

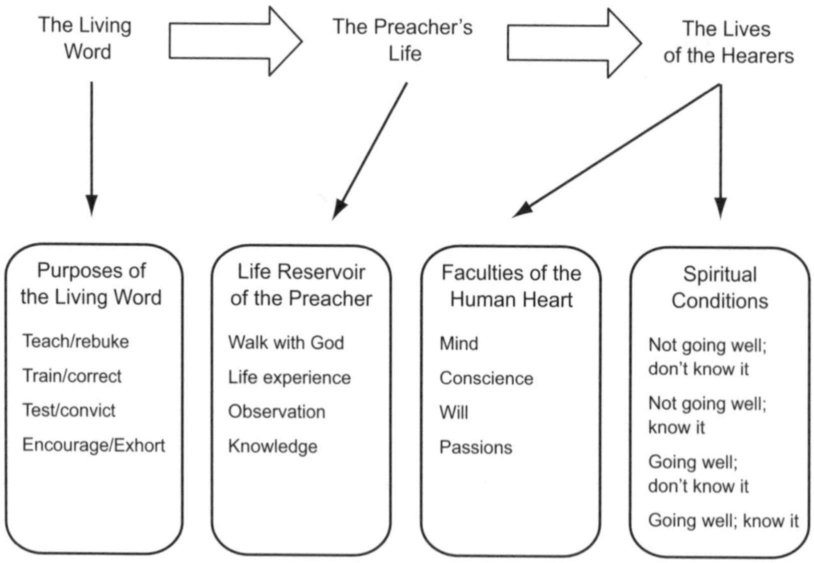

Purposes of the Living Word	Life Reservoir of the Preacher	Faculties of the Human Heart	Spiritual Conditions
Teach/rebuke	Walk with God	Mind	Not going well; don't know it
Train/correct	Life experience	Conscience	Not going well; know it
Test/convict	Observation	Will	Going well; don't know it
Encourage/Exhort	Knowledge	Passions	Going well; know it

These four sources can easily be used in chart form for developing sermon application. An example of a living application chart filled in for a sermon on 1 Thessalonians 2:13 is given below in diagram 14. Focusing on the Thessalonians' reception of God's Word led me to preach a message on the right hearing of God's Word. The first column identifies the main areas of teaching, training, testing, and exhortation that the text calls for. The subsequent columns identify key inputs from consideration of the reservoir, the heart, and the soul, each shaping and coloring the application.

This grid supplies a considerable range of life applications. While an experienced preacher is unlikely to fill in a grid like this for every sermon, it may be helpful to do so a number of times as one becomes accustomed to thinking in this way.

APPLICATORY HOMILETICS

After applicatory exegesis, the next task for the preacher is to determine the form the sermon will take. The preacher now moves into homiletical mode and it is, again, an applicatory task. Sermon form is a servant, not a master, a means to an end, not an end in itself. Recent attention by homileticians to form and structure, while helpful, has increased the danger of being inclined to work harder on how we say things than on what we say.[3] Yet while that is the wrong way around, how we say things does matter. A well-designed sermon aids clarity, coherence, interest, and impact. A rambling, predictable, or vague structure leaves hearers in a fog. Love for those to whom we speak necessitates effort in structuring a message well. But the reason for the effort is not so that we can present a well-structured literary work, but so that the message is effective. Structure is not the end game. Impact is.

For every message, then, we must ask ourselves, how can I best package this message in order to make the greatest impact on the lives of the people to whom I will be speaking? That is an applicatory question

---

3. John Sweetman interacts helpfully with the main sermon structure models that have been proposed over the last thirty years, proposing a foundational sermon structure that builds on the various options without leaving the preacher with an endless array of possibilities to sift for every sermon. See John Sweetman, "Towards a Foundational, Flexible, Sermon Structure," *Journal of the Evangelical Homiletics Society* 8, no. 2 (September 2008): 32–49.

Diagram 14: Application Chart for 1 Thessalonians 2:13

Purposes of the Word	From the Reservoir	For the Heart	Spiritual Conditions
Teach basic theology of the preached Word (including theology of the Word incarnate, written, and preached; work of the Spirit; activity of Word in human heart; the preacher's task)	Talk about my experience of listening to about four sermons a week; differences between preaching and listening	**Mind** needs to be persuaded of the theology of preaching so that there is a heart commitment to receiving God's Word aright	Three groups:
	Realities of our culture that militate against good listening: information overload (TV, Internet), age of technology and sensationalism (visual culture), time-consciousness	**Conscience** needs to be convicted of sinful patterns (e.g., listening for others and not self, focusing on preacher and not God, laziness in preparation, listening and response, hardness of heart, etc.)	1. Those who already **listen and respond well**—encourage them; in same place as Thessalonians; evidence of God at work in them
Rebuke false views of what preaching is (entertainment, lecture, old-fashioned)			2. Those who **listen but do not respond**—examine why (critical spirit, intellectualized process, hardness of heart, lack of faith and obedience, seed plucked away quickly . . .)
Train to listen actively and expectantly, to recognize and overcome common impediments, to respond with faith and obedience	Realities of life: children in the pews, late nights, boring preachers, difficult parts of Bible		
	Construct picture of poor listening from real life	**Will** needs to be motivated and helped to listen actively and respond spiritually	
Help people **test** their own way of listening to preaching and assess it	What helps: prepare (come well rested, expectant, having prayed); listen actively (take notes perhaps, sit where there are fewer distractions, interact with preacher in your head); respond (talk with people afterward about message; note things God wants you to do in response; revisit sermon next day; sometimes give feedback to preacher) . . .	**Passions** need to be stirred to love good preaching and expect change and blessing from it in own life and lives of others	3. Those who **do not listen well**—examine why (maybe distracted, uninterested, tired, ill-prepared, not yet able to understand, unregenerate . . .)
Encourage commitment to the preached Word and **urge** expectancy and response. Encourage those who listen well, as Paul did.			
	Outline helpful and unhelpful ways of responding to a preacher		
	Give examples of the great effect of preaching—revivals, conversions, own experience		

242

out of which a further set of applicatory questions flow: How should I begin so as to engage my hearers? How can I keep this message both anchored in the text and rooted in their lives from beginning to end? How should I move from "there and then" to "here and now"? At what point should I show my whole hand—early, to aid clarity of teaching (a deductive approach), or later, to retain a measure of intrigue (an inductive approach)? When should I fire my arrows—the stories, testimonies, illustrations, arguments, real-life scenarios, and pithy one-liners I have thought of? Do I have enough arrows? How will I end so as to ensure a final impact?

As we respond to these questions, there are three matters of paramount importance: engagement, proportion, and progression. Engagement concerns the need to build rapport with our hearers from the first sentence onward. This is usually done by beginning in the *here and now*. We begin with issues today and move from them back to the text for answers or perspectives. We will usually fire off a few arrows in the introduction. Then we will transition to the text, promising perspective or help from it. The engagement must be such that people will want to follow us to the text and then not be disappointed by the end. Michael Fabarez helpfully observes, "An introduction will not arrest your congregation if it doesn't address the question, 'What difference does all this make?' It must immediately show the relevance of the text to be preached. Therefore, the introduction is the place where your applicational thrust begins."[4]

Having engaged hearers at the beginning, we need to keep them involved throughout. We cannot afford to travel any great distance without reference to their lives or our world. Bolt-on application usually waits till the end to tack on some practical thoughts, by which time many listeners have tuned out. We need to find a form that will take them with us on the journey throughout. We will usually need to use both running and gathered applications.

That introduces the second crucial issue: proportion. The question is, what will be the ratio of "there and then" to "here and now"? If 90

4. Michael Fabarez, *Preaching That Changes Lives* (Nashville: Nelson, 2002), 102.

percent of the message is "there and then," it doesn't matter how striking the applications are, they will have little impact on people. The proportion is too small. Application gets lost in the woods. It needs a certain amount of airtime to make an impact. Expository preachers struggle with this because they have usually spent much time in careful exegesis and have made many fascinating discoveries along the way that they are dying to share with their congregation. But the congregation is not half as enthusiastic about those exegetical details as the preacher may think! They want to see the end product, not all the steps of planning along the way. While it is helpful to show some of our workings, we can never afford to show them all. People want to see the house that has been built, along with some comment about its highlights, but they don't want a blow-by-blow account of where the timber was purchased, what kind of nails were used, who did the electrical work, how the tiles were made, which tradesmen were delayed, and so on. Robinson's guideline is correct: "Give as much biblical information as the people need to understand the passage, and no more. Then move on to your application."[5]

In deductive sermons, my rule of thumb has been to have an introduction that is mostly "here and now" (without too much exegetical detail), at least one third of each main point connected to "here and now," and the conclusion mostly "here and now." Proportionally that gives a message of which at least half the airtime is connected specifically to our world, and it is not just the second half but is interwoven throughout. Of course, it is only a rule of thumb. It may be that we need to preload with more teaching in the first half and unpack it with more application later. But if that is the case, it is necessary to work hard at connectedness in the less applicatory sections. Illustrations of truth, pithy sentences with fresh words, interacting with people's objections or questions, and tremendous clarity of expression become all the more important so as to retain our hearers' attention while we spend time back "there and then."

5. Haddon W. Robinson, *Making a Difference in Preaching: Haddon Robinson on Biblical Preaching* (Grand Rapids: Baker, 1999), 87.

In deductive sermons, clearly worded main points are an invaluable tool for applicatory thrust. Fabarez suggests main points that are worded simply, in the second person, employing imperatives where possible, and all connected to the main preaching point.[6] While these guidelines will not always work, they are suggestive of what preachers ought to aim at. Main points are a giveaway as to whether the sermon will be connected to people or be merely scholastic. If the main points don't preach, then chances are the sermon will never fly.

An inductive structure calls for different proportions. The introduction should again be significantly in the "here and now," most likely raising a central question or problem that the sermon will address. The sections of the sermon progressively address that question. By keeping the question in view constantly, and by building the problem or deepening the dilemma as we go, we can retain the interest of our hearers. The latter stages of the message are likely to be extensively in the "here and now" as solutions are unpacked and specific applications are made. The end result should be a message that feels connected to us throughout.

Both inductive and deductive structures call for a third consideration: progression. Applications ought to increase in breadth, depth, intensity, and passion as the sermon progresses. They should be cumulative, taking people further and further in their grasp of what the text means for life. They should often be expansive, beginning with the text but then surging out into areas of life that people were not expecting. There is, in fact, a point in the sermon at which we should be no longer dealing with the details of the text but unfolding its implications and applications for life. That point may actually come quite early in the message. It is often possible to deal with explanation of the text in the first quarter of the sermon, allowing ample time to develop expansive application. The text is not used as a springboard for us to leap into whatever we want to say, but is like a stone thrown into a pool with ripples extending from the initial point of impact. The outcome we look for is well described by Haddon Robinson.

6. Fabarez, *Preaching That Changes Lives*, 61–67.

When I'm listening to a good sermon, there comes a point when I lose track of all the people around me. As the preacher speaks, I experience God talking to me about me. The time for explanation has passed; the time for application has come.

At that point, it's appropriate for the preacher to leave behind "we" in favor of "you." No longer is the preacher representing the people to God; he is representing God to the people. "We've seen the biblical principle; we've seen two or three ways others have applied it. Now, what does this say to you?"[7]

Once a form that promotes applicatory engagement, proportion, and progression has been determined, it becomes a mold into which we pour all the rich ingredients we have gathered from the text and our reservoir. At this point, however, we must not let the mold stifle freedom or creativity. Nineteenth-century pastor and Princeton professor James W. Alexander, in his *Thoughts on Preaching*, suggests the following formula.

1. Write rapid sketch, the faster the better.
2. In the first draught omit all partition, and do not force your mind to method.
3. Let thought generate thought.
4. Do not dwell on particulars; leave all amplification for the pulpit.
5. Keep the mind in a glow.
6. Come to it with a full mind.
7. Forget all care of language.
8. Forget all previous cramming, research, quotation, and study.
9. In delivery, learn to know when to dwell on a point; let the enlargement be, not where you *determined* in your closet it should be; but where you feel the spring flowing as you speak *let it* gush. Let contemplation have place *while you speak*.[8]

7. Robinson, *Making a Difference in Preaching*, 94.

8. James W. Alexander, *Thoughts on Preaching: Being Contributions to Homiletics* (1864; repr., Edinburgh: Banner of Truth, 1988), 18. His italics.

This is a fascinating formula, subjecting all care with words and form to the substance of the message that flows from careful study, a full reservoir, and a warm heart. It is good to have a plan for a sermon, but that plan may well change as we come to write and then speak. It is best to write as if preaching and best to preach as if talking animatedly to friends about something supremely important, as opposed to reading to them a carefully worded essay.

APPLICATORY DELIVERY

The reason for this is that impact is massively determined by the way we speak. I like to remind myself of what I am doing when I preach. I am not delivering a sermon (a very static concept) but proclaiming a message (a dynamic task). I have a message from God for the people he has given to me to speak to today. I have a word for them, from him, that has come from his Word. I have something of importance to say that I believe will make a difference to how people think, act, and feel. I have been commissioned to say this. I have a God-given right to proclaim it, and I will be held accountable for faithfulness in doing so.

Clearly, a monotone delivery will not be adequate. Neither will disengaged reading of a manuscript. Preaching must come *from* the heart as well as *to* the heart. So revisiting the faculties of the heart allows us to map effective communication.

First, we must preach with a clear mind. If we are not crystal clear in what we are saying, we are unlikely to take people with us or do them much good. It has been well said that when there's mist in the pulpit there's fog in the pews. We need to have complete clarity with respect to what we want to say. We need to be familiar enough with our material that we can put it in many different ways. We should be clear enough on the main ideas that, even if our notes were accidentally left behind on Sunday morning, we could still easily bring the message because it is in our heart and mind, not just on paper.

Second, we must preach with a clear conscience. Sin in our own life rips the heart out of application. It makes us either blunt our applications so as not to damn ourselves, or strike hard against particular sins as a kind of vicarious dealing with them in our own life. Preaching with a clear conscience means that we must face squarely our own heart issues before we address them in others. It may even be that for a time we are ill-qualified to speak to a certain issue. If the worshiper must leave his gift at the altar and first go to be reconciled to his brother, the preacher might also need to leave his sermon in the pulpit and first go and deal with some issue it has raised for him.

A clear conscience also involves integrity in our dealings with others, especially with those to whom we preach. When Paul claimed in the presence of the elders of Ephesus, or the congregations in Corinth and Thessalonica, that he had a clear conscience before God and man, his claim included such things as not having used them for his own advantage, not having ministered for dishonest gain, not having sought their praise, and not having dealt with them harshly or in a duplicitous manner. But herein lies a dilemma for the preacher. We all sin. Paul did too. The Word strikes at our hearts and convicts us as we prepare through the week, and it may be that we have no opportunity or ability to deal with it before Sunday. Or perhaps all is well until half an hour before we are to leave for church, and then one of our children misbehaves and we lose our cool, drive to church ill-tempered, and have to somehow settle ourselves to lead people in worship. We cannot bail every time we've messed up, nor can we use the pulpit as a confessional. So how do we preach with a clear conscience in such situations?

We can do so if we are genuinely and humbly confessing our sin before God and seeking his mercy. We preach not only as heralds but as sinners needing grace. If we are broken before God as we come to preach, we are not in a bad place. We can also preach with a clear conscience in such situations if there is integrity in our life as a whole. If we are dealing with sin in an ongoing way and gaining victory over it, if we do not usually snap when our children misbehave (and if we make amends when we do), if from time to time we acknowledge from the pulpit that we struggle with this or that issue, and if we have not sought in our public ministry to make ourselves out to be better than we are, then there is integrity in our living even though there is no perfection. Such authenticity is a necessary prerequisite for boldness in preaching. Finally, we can preach in such a situation if we follow up our preaching with the action we need to take. Maybe we haven't had time to deal with something before we preach, but we will have opportunity afterwards. Integrity means we continue to work at our own sanctification and don't just urge holiness on others.

That takes us, then, to the third faculty of the heart. We must preach with a will that is responsive to God's Word. If we want others to be doers of the Word, we must be also. The test of our applications must be the test of reality. Do we do it? Could we do it? Would we do it? If our advice to people is the counsel of perfection, it is a poor application. All application must be tempered by reality, and our own lives are a great measure of that. This measure must sometimes be theoretical because we will need to propose some applications that apply to others but not to us. What I propose to singles, I may not be able to test in my own life as a married man; what I recommend to tradesmen is mere theory to me as a lecturer. But within the limits of our own life situation, we must prove ourselves to be doers of the Word as we live the applications we bring to others.

Finally, we must preach with passion. Passion need not mean volume. You don't have to shout to be passionate, neither do you have to be always on the edge of tears. The way we express passion is shaped by our personality. But there must be an evident resonance between our passions and the passions of the text. We cannot speak of hell lightly, or of Christ disrespectfully, or of joy gloomily, or of love aggressively. We cannot afford to speak of the most important matters in the world (life and death, heaven and hell, salvation and damnation) in a detached, academic way. Our preaching needs to be infused with genuine emotion: enthusiasm, joy, earnestness, excitement, gravity, and gladness. These emotions must not be merely for pulpit display—they must be real and should be evidenced just as much *after* we have preached as *when* we are preaching. In our interactions with people afterward, there should be a consistency of demeanor.

249

APPLICATORY EXPECTATIONS

A vexed issue for preachers is how to evaluate one's own preaching ministry. Am I preaching well? Is my preaching hitting the mark? Expository preachers will often answer these questions in terms of biblical faithfulness. A biblically faithful sermon is a good sermon and a biblically faithful ministry is a sound ministry. Results, the argument goes, are out of our hands. It's God's Word and he can use it as he pleases. We know it will not return to him void but will accomplish its purposes. So, for our part, we just need to be faithful.

The potent question that needs to be asked of this argument, however, is, faithful in what? Faithful in explaining the original meaning of the text, or faithful in discharging the duties of a preacher? If it is the former, an exegetically sound sermon is indeed a good sermon. But if, as we saw in the introduction, a sermon is God speaking through the preacher to people today, then faithfulness must be not only to the text but to the preacher's calling to proclaim the truths of the text today. Preachers must be faithful in teaching and rebuking, training and correcting, testing and convicting, encouraging and exhorting. They must faithfully interface biblical truth with the realities of life, as understood from a rich and full reservoir. They must faithfully press God's Word against heart, mind, conscience, and passions. They must faithfully speak to the saved and the unsaved in their varying heart conditions. They must faithfully fire arrows deep into people's hearts, engaging every homiletical skill with which God has endowed them.

Because God owns the faithful preaching of his Word, we may be quite sure that this kind of faithfulness will produce fruit. The fruit, however, will be of varying kinds: to one the preached Word is the smell of death, to another the fragrance of life. As the apostles discovered, some will embrace the message warmly, others will want to inquire further, and yet others will reject it. There will be those who love the preacher and the preaching and those who hate both. But, positive or negative, faithful preaching will produce a response. It is divinely designed to do so.

The difficulty, however, is in reading the response. Spiritual fruit is not always immediately visible and God's work is inward before it is outward. We must resist the temptation to use scientific measures to quantify response. Just as counting the numbers of those going forward at an evangelistic campaign is no accurate measure of evangelistic faithfulness or effectiveness, so numbers at church, or the amount of verbal response after a sermon, or the presence of some complainers or flatterers, is no accurate gauge of the effectiveness of a preaching ministry. We also know that there are spiritual seasons in our personal lives, in churches, and even in entire nations. There may be seasons of revival and of spiritual declension. In one season, the fruit is much more positive, abundant, and visible than in another.

It is not easy for preachers to navigate these waters. We easily gravitate to those who say what we want to hear, or we rest back on exegetical faithfulness as being enough for us. But another route is required. Spiritual fruit can be measured only by spiritual means, and the means God has given us is to engage in spiritual conversation with people. In the regular course of pastoral care, pastors and other church leaders ought to have opportunity to engage hearers of the Word in conversations that allow some assessment of the impact the preaching is making on their lives. It will then be helpful for preachers if, from time to time, the leaders reflect together on this, evaluating the influence of the preaching ministry on the health of the church.

Any such evaluation must be undertaken with some understanding of what applicatory, expository preaching ought to be achieving in the life of a church. The foundational question is, what *impact* is the preaching ministry having? Out of that, many possible questions flow, such as:

- Is there evidence that the preaching ministry is encouraging people to take God's Word seriously?
- Are people able to testify to the preaching ministry fostering in them a growing commitment to Christ, love for the gospel, and confidence in God?

251

- In what ways have people been helped and empowered by the preaching to live for God 24/7, at home, at work, and wherever they go?
- What convictions and passions are growing in the life of the church as a result of the preaching ministry?
- Do people have confidence to bring others along to hear God's Word?
- Have people been saved under the preaching of the gospel?
- Is the preaching ministry fueling a church community committed to God, to one another, and to the community in which it is placed?

Such questions fall into the category of qualitative rather than quantitative research. It will take time and determination to glean genuine feedback that is not superficial. But assessment of this nature is important because it takes the focus off any one sermon and puts it on the ministry as a whole, it moves from a concern for biblical faithfulness alone to a concern for biblical faithfulness that impacts lives, and it looks not for numbers but for testimonies to change, challenge, encouragement, and gospel empowerment.

The feedback may not be comfortable for preachers. But why spend a lifetime shooting at a mark and never realizing that you were always missing? Why invest in a calling of helping others without ever having the courage to find out if you are actually helping? The preacher committed to preaching for life application wants applicatory outcomes and is prepared to endure the pain of asking others to help assess whether, by God's grace, those outcomes are being attained.[9]

SIX LEVELS OF APPLICATION

There is one final tool that can help preachers assess their own applicatory effectiveness. Along the way, we have noted several different levels of application, from the more obvious level of exhorting the will to the more complex work of stirring godly passions. We can summarize

9. For comment on the importance of sermon review, see T. David Gordon, *Why Johnny Can't Preach: The Media Have Shaped the Messengers* (Phillipsburg, NJ: P&R, 2009), 97–99.

what we have seen in a total of six different levels of application. By asking ourselves which of these levels we regularly use in our preaching, we can measure our applicatory depth and variety.

Level one application tells people *what to do* (and what not to do). We may urge people, for example, to pray and to do so regularly and perseveringly. We might warn against a prayerless Christian life. Such applications are pitched mainly at the will.

Level two application is about *how to do it* (and how not to). We can help people learn how to pray regularly, giving them suggestions concerning times, places, praying out loud, using a prayer list, recording answers, and so on. We can also talk about how not to pray. Jesus did that in the Sermon on the Mount, telling his disciples not to pray like pagans or like the Pharisees. This is, again, will-oriented application.

Level three application concerns *what it looks like* (and what it shouldn't look like). Now we might use one of our arrows and give pictures of effective prayer. James gave the picture of Elijah. We may tell stories of effective prayer warriors and also depict ungodly approaches to prayer. As we help people see what it looks like in practice, we speak to the mind and the passions. Stories often help stir response.

Level four application presents *why you should* (and why you shouldn't). To the practical advice given about prayer, we could add motivations and incentives. We may lay out several reasons for the hard work of prayer. Jesus did this when he spoke of our heavenly Father giving us only what is good. We may also expose false motivations. At this level we are urging rational response as we speak to the will via the mind.

Level five application addresses *where you are* (and where you should or shouldn't be). Now we might use tests that help people measure their prayer life. This should not be done by way of predictable questions (e.g., how is your prayer life going?) but by helping people measure themselves in a real way. We might suggest some marks of a strong prayer life. Or we might present several things that are no real sign of a heart for prayer. This is application aimed at the conscience.

Level six application speaks about *what drives it* (and what shouldn't drive it). It is one thing to pray out of duty but another altogether to pray out of delight in God and love for him, with hope and eager expectation of his being able to do immeasurably more than we ask or imagine. Conversely, our prayers ought not to be driven by fear (We'll be in trouble if we don't) or pride (I'm so good at praying!). Such applications address our heart passions and, potentially, our heart idols as well.

The six levels together make for tremendously compelling application. If we speak of what to do, how to do it, what it looks like, why you should, where you are, and what drives it, we speak to the whole heart in both practical and penetrating ways. The first three levels are the most practical; the latter three are the most penetrating. Of course, ordinarily, we will not use all six together. We will pick and choose what is most pertinent to the message we are bringing. But the test for preachers is this: what levels of application do you regularly use? Many preachers operate only in levels one to three; some never get beyond the first level. Yet it is levels four to six that will add greatly to applicatory impact. So ask yourself this: over my last few sermons, which levels of application have I used?

The point of this exercise reflects the point of this book as a whole: living application is practical, penetrating, and varied. The message as a whole should be preached to the person as a whole for life as a whole. We cannot merely append a few applicatory thoughts to an otherwise theoretical message and expect lives to change. We must work with the text diligently, drawing from it the God-intended applications latent within it and then driving them home to people's lives winsomely and forcefully.

APPLICATORY OVERLOAD

The range of applications that are possible from the living application preaching process necessitates that preachers clarify how any given application rates in the overall scheme of things. There is a difference between a text's primary application, its secondary applications, and other implications arising from it. If every application is delivered with the same level of urgency and importance, we may undermine the impact of the most important application.

According to Fabarez, "When mere implications of a preaching text are consistently and authoritatively presented as necessary applications, the preacher soon gains a reputation for crying wolf."[10] He goes on to suggest four kinds of application: applications that are certain (to be preached with greatest force and authority), probable (in which a logical case can be mounted for responding a certain way), possible (in which avenues of application are suggested), and improbable but possibly helpful (in which a specific application is suggested not as a direct consequence of the text but as a possible way of implementing the application of the text).[11] David Cook, former principal of Sydney Missionary and Bible College, teaches the importance of identifying the necessary, possible, and impossible applications of a text. The necessary application is the response the text certainly calls for; the possible applications are ways the text may be applied; the impossible application is how you must not respond to it. Haddon Robinson speaks of distinguishing between various types of implications from the text. "Implications may be necessary, probable, possible, improbable, or impossible."[12]

However we choose to rank applications, the fact is that they must be ranked. Not everything we say is equally imperative. Of the many applicatory comments made in a sermon, some are primary and deserve the most airtime and the greatest intensity, while others are made more in passing or by way of suggestion. We increase buy-in and impact by differentiating the status of applicatory comment.

The very fact that we are now addressing the possibility of applicatory overload indicates that we have come a long way from the dearth of application and the use of weary bolt-ons addressed at the start. Preachers need not be scratching around for a few applicatory comments to append to their dry lecture on the text. God's Word is replete with living applications, and he has charged preachers to proclaim his Word today.

10. Fabarez, *Preaching That Changes Lives*, 137.
11. Ibid., 138.
12. Haddon Robinson, "The Heresy of Application," in Haddon W. Robinson and Craig Brian Larson, eds., *The Art and Craft of Biblical Preaching: A Comprehensive Resource for Today's Communicators* (Grand Rapids: Zondervan, 2005), 306–11.

DISCUSSION QUESTIONS

1. How long do you spend preparing a sermon and how do you use that time? Has this book encouraged you to make any changes to your sermon preparation approach?
2. How will a strong focus on application shape the way you go about your exegetical work?
3. How will a strong focus on application affect the sermon forms and structures that you adopt?
4. What proportion of your sermons is typically given to application?
5. How do you prepare your own heart (mind, conscience, will, and passions) for preaching?
6. What kind of feedback do you receive on your preaching and what mechanisms do you have in place to assess its impact in the life of your church?
7. Of the six levels of application, which levels do you commonly employ and which levels do you need to consciously work on?

CONCLUDING
THOUGHTS

AS I REFLECT ON the model of expository sermon application I have presented, my mind can't help skimming over dozens of conversations I've had with preachers, feedback I've heard from many congregations, and hundreds of sermons I've preached over the years. The repeated theme is that application in preaching matters enormously. Sure, many of us find it hard, but congregations crave it and God's Word is full of it. We must preach application-laden sermons.

The point of the living application preaching process is that application need not be hit and miss in expository preaching. When we allow the God-purposed truths of his living Word to speak into life as we know it, into the faculties of the human heart, and into the varying spiritual conditions of men, women, and children, our preaching will not be theoretical and abstract. When we then fire truth home with sharp arrows, our applications will not be bland or prosaic. And when we deliver applications at multiple levels, we will not fail to be penetrating and pertinent. We are, of course, utterly dependent on the Holy Spirit to enable these applications to make an eternal impact on people's hearts. Without his powerful work, our work will come to nothing. But we have work to do—great work in applying God's Word to life today.

Application doesn't need to be the forte of topical preachers while remaining the nightmare of expository preachers. It doesn't need to be confined to a few closing remarks. It doesn't need to be predictable and hackneyed, nor does it need to be moralistic and damning. There are endless ways of presenting life-giving applications from God's Word—

applications that are compelling and engaging, heart-oriented and grace-filled, practical and penetrating, varied in intensity and focus.

Of course, we will often come away, after our best efforts, feeling that we preached a dud. But, thankfully, God's Word does not return to him void, and he is able to use even the poorest of sermons to bring about gospel fruit. Such is his grace. But preachers must not presume on his grace. We need to work as hard at applying biblical truth to people's lives as we do at understanding and explaining what the text meant for the original hearers. We should undertake this work believing that God is pleased to own such preaching and is able to endow it with great power to accomplish his purposes.

APPENDIX

LIVING APPLICATION TOOLS

THE MAIN DIAGRAMS and questions that have been presented in this book for developing living application are reproduced below, on separate pages, so that preachers can copy and use them in their sermon preparation as they see fit. You'll find:

A. The Living Application Preaching Process diagram
B. Application Questions to Ask of the Text
C. Heart Questions Worth Asking
D. Spiritual Conditions Grid
E. A blank copy of the Application Chart
F. Six Levels of Living Application

A. THE LIVING APPLICATION PREACHING PROCESS

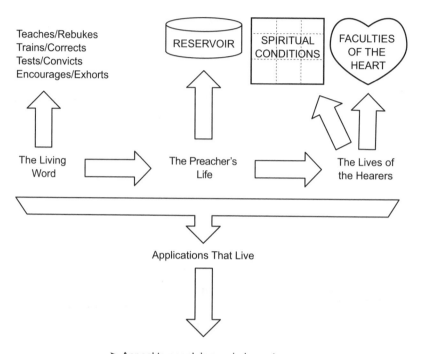

Teaches/Rebukes
Trains/Corrects
Tests/Convicts
Encourages/Exhorts

RESERVOIR

SPIRITUAL CONDITIONS

FACULTIES OF THE HEART

The Living Word

The Preacher's Life

The Lives of the Hearers

Applications That Live

➤ Appeal to people's own judgment
➤ Anticipate and answer objections
➤ Give reasons, motivations, incentives
➤ Be specific, pointed, and direct
➤ Use illustrations for clarity and impact
➤ Provide testimonies to the truth
➤ Show what it looks like in practice
➤ Use fresh, vivid words
➤ Speak personally and passionately

B. APPLICATION QUESTIONS TO ASK OF THE TEXT

Main question: What is this text doing?

1. Is it teaching?
   - What truths are taught?
   - What errors should be opposed?
   - What teaching should I give?

2. Is it training?
   - What behavior is called for?
   - What wrong ways of conduct need correcting?
   - What "how to" and "how not to" application is called for?

3. Is it testing?
   - Does the text suggest tests against which we should measure ourselves?
   - In what ways does the text convict us of sin?

4. Is it exhorting?
   - What exhortations are given?
   - How does it challenge us?
   - What encouragements are given?
   - How does this text spur us on?

C. HEART QUESTIONS WORTH ASKING

1. Mind (overlaps with teaching/rebuking)
   = What are the central truths of the text that people must know and believe?
   - How can I make those truths clear?
   - Why are they important?
   - What wrong views must I oppose?
   - How will these truths help a person?
   - How can I persuade them of this truth?
   - What might stop people from believing this?
   - Will they buy it? How can I help them accept it?

2. Conscience (overlaps with testing/convicting)
   = What in the text should convict and challenge us?
   - What truths do people need to become deeply convicted of?
   - What failures, sins, or omissions should people be convicted of?
   - In what ways should people be testing and examining themselves?
   - What would justify a clear conscience in regard to the text?
   - How might people have an oversensitive conscience on this matter? How do I give them peace?
   - How might people have a seared conscience on this matter? How do I bring conviction?

3. Will (overlaps with training/correcting)
   = What are the key actions and responses this text calls for?
   - What response do I want to see people make?
   - What practical difference should this make?
   - What should this look like in practice?
   - What am I going to ask the congregation to do?
   - What motivations and incentives can I give them?
   - What help can I give them?
   - Where will this show up in everyday life?

4. Passions

= What are the passions of the text and the passions it should produce?

- What are the deep desires of the heart this truth should stir?
- How ought this text to make people feel (and how can I help them feel that?)
- What impact should this truth have on them?
- In what ways should people be stirred, moved, inspired, humbled by this truth?
- What drives/ambitions should this cultivate or inhibit?

5. Heart idols

= What heart idols does this text confront and what true worship does it call for?

- What might people be clinging to instead of God?
- What wrong passions, desires, hopes, and dreams should be confronted?
- What effect will false worship have?
- What will true heart worship of God look like?

D. SPIRITUAL CONDITIONS GRID

	Not Going Well	Going Well
Don't Know it	Arrogant/Complacent → Challenge/Confront	Struggling/Discouraged → Comfort/Spur on
Know it	Backsliding/Seeking → Help/Advise	Positive/Grateful → Encourage/Teach

	Not Going Well	Going Well
Don't Know it		
Know it		

E. APPLICATION CHART

Purposes of the Word	From the Reservoir	For the Heart	Spiritual Conditions
Teach/rebuke Train/correct Test/convict Encourage/ Exhort	Walk with God Life experience Observation Knowledge	Mind Conscience Will Passions	Not going well; don't know it Not going well; know it Going well; don't know it Going well; know it

F. SIX LEVELS OF LIVING APPLICATION

Level 1: **What to do** (and what not to do)
    - for addressing the will

Level 2: **How to do it** (and how not to do it)
    - for addressing the will

Level 3: **What it looks like** (and what it shouldn't look like)
    - for addressing the mind and the passions

Level 4: **Why you should** (and why you shouldn't)
    - for addressing the will via the mind

Level 5: **Where you are** (and where you should or shouldn't be)
    - for addressing the conscience

Level 6: **What drives it** (and what shouldn't drive it)
    - for addressing the passions and heart idols

BIBLIOGRAPHY

Adam, Peter. *Hearing God's Words: Exploring Biblical Spirituality*. New Studies in Biblical Theology. Downers Grove: IVP, Apollos, 2004.

————. *Speaking God's Words: A Practical Theology of Preaching*. Leicester: IVP, 1996.

Adams, Jay. *Preaching to the Heart: A Heart-to-Heart Discussion with Preachers of the Word*. Phillipsburg, NJ: P&R, 1983.

————. *Preaching with Purpose: A Comprehensive Textbook on Biblical Preaching*. Phillipsburg, NJ: P&R, 1982.

————. *Truth Applied: Application in Preaching*. Grand Rapids: Ministry Resources Library, 1990.

Alexander, James W. *Thoughts on Preaching: Being Contributions to Homiletics*. 1864; repr., Edinburgh: Banner of Truth, 1988.

Arthurs, Jeffrey D. *Preaching with Variety: How to Re-Create the Dynamics of Biblical Genres*. Grand Rapids: Kregel, 2007.

Ash, Christopher. *The Priority of Preaching*. Fearn: Christian Focus, 2009.

Azurdia, Arturo G. *Spirit Empowered Preaching: The Vitality of the Holy Spirit in Preaching*. Fearn: Christian Focus, 1998.

Beeke, Joel R. "Calvin's Piety." *Mid-America Journal of Theology* 15 (2004): 33–65.

Bratt, James D., ed. *Abraham Kuyper: A Centennial Reader*. Grand Rapids: Eerdmans, 1998.

Bridges, Charles. *The Christian Ministry*. 1830; repr., London: Banner of Truth, 1967.

Brooks, Phillips. *Lectures on Preaching: Delivered before the Divinity School of Yale College in January and February 1877*. London: Allenson, 1895.

Capill, Murray A. "Hebrews as a Sermon: Learning from its Preaching Style." *Vox Reformata* 73 (2008): 40–53.

————. *Preaching with Spiritual Vigour: Including Lessons from the Life and Practice of Richard Baxter*. Fearn: Christian Focus, 2003.

Carrick, John. *The Imperative of Preaching: A Theology of Sacred Rhetoric*. Edinburgh: Banner of Truth, 2002.

Carson, D. A. *Exegetical Fallacies*. Grand Rapids: Baker; Carlisle, UK: Paternoster, 1996.

Chapell, Bryan. *Christ-Centered Preaching: Redeeming the Expository Sermon*. Grand Rapids: Baker, 1994.

————. *Using Illustrations to Preach with Power*. Wheaton: Crossway, 2001.

Chester, Tim. *You Can Change: God's Transforming Power for Our Sinful Behaviour and Negative Emotions*. Nottingham: IVP, 2008.

Dabney, Robert Lewis. *Sacred Rhetoric*. 1870; repr., Edinburgh: Banner of Truth, 1979.

Davis, Dale Ralph. *Judges: Such a Great Salvation*. Focus on the Bible. Fearn: Christian Focus, 2000.

————. *The Word Became Fresh: How to Preach from Old Testament Narrative Texts*. Fearn: Christian Focus, 2006.

"The Directory for the Publick Worship of God." In *The Confession of Faith*. Inverness: Free Presbyterian Publications, 1981.

Dodd, C. H. *The Apostolic Preaching and Its Developments*. London: Hodder & Stoughton, 1944.

Doriani, Daniel M. *Putting the Truth to Work: The Theory and Practice of Biblical Application*. Phillipsburg, NJ: P&R, 2001.

Duguid, Iain M. *Living in the Gap Between Promise and Reality: The Gospel According to Abraham*. Phillipsburg, NJ: P&R, 1999.

Dunn, James D. G. *Romans*. Word Biblical Commentary. Dallas: Word, 1988.

Duvall, J. Scott, and J. Daniel Hays. *Grasping God's Word: A Hands-on Approach to Reading, Interpreting, and Applying the Bible*. Grand Rapids: Zondervan, 2001.

Edwards, Jonathan. *The Works of Jonathan Edwards*. Edinburgh: Banner of Truth, 1974.

Eswine, Zack. *Preaching to a Post-Everything World: Crafting Biblical Sermons That Connect with Our Culture*. Grand Rapids: Baker, 2008.

Fabarez, Michael. *Preaching That Changes Lives*. Nashville: Nelson, 2002.

Fee, Gordon D., and Douglas Stuart. *How to Read the Bible for All Its Worth: A Guide to Understanding the Bible*. Grand Rapids: Zondervan, 2003.

Ferguson, Sinclair B. "Preaching to the Heart." In *Feed My Sheep: A Passionate Plea for Preaching*, edited by Don Kistler. Morgan: Soli Deo Gloria, 2002.

Flemming, Dean. "Contextualizing the Gospel in Athens: Paul's Areopagus Address as a Paradigm for Missionary Communication." *Missiology* 30, no. 2 (2002): 199–214.

Garretson, James M. *Princeton and Preaching: Archibald Alexander and the Christian Ministry*. Edinburgh: Banner of Truth, 2005.

Gibson, Scott M., ed. *Preaching the Old Testament*. Grand Rapids: Baker, 2006.

Goldsworthy, Graeme. *Gospel-Centred Hermeneutics: Biblical-Theological Foundations and Principles*. Nottingham: Apollos, IVP, 2006.

———. *Preaching the Whole Bible as Christian Scripture: The Application of Biblical Theology to Expository Preaching*. Grand Rapids: Eerdmans, 2000.

Gordon, T. David. *Why Johnny Can't Preach: The Media Have Shaped the Messengers*. Phillipsburg, NJ: P&R, 2009.

Greidanus, Sidney. *The Modern Preacher and the Ancient Text: Intepreting and Preaching Biblical Literature*. Grand Rapids: Eerdmans, 1988.

———. *Preaching Christ from Genesis: Foundations for Expository Sermons*. Grand Rapids: Eerdmans, 2007.

Hollinger, Dennis. "Preaching to the Head, Heart and Hands: A Holistic Paradigm for Proclaiming and Hearing the Word." *Journal of the Evangelical Homiletics Society* 7, no. 1 (2007): 18–24.

Jensen, Phillip D., and Paul Grimmond. *The Archer and the Arrow: Preaching the Very Words of God*. Kingsford, NSW: Matthias Media, 2010.

Johnson, Dennis E. *Him We Proclaim: Preaching Christ from All the Scriptures*. Phillipsburg, NJ: P&R, 2007.

Keller, Timothy. *Counterfeit Gods: When the Empty Promises of Love, Money and Power Let You Down*. London: Hodder & Stoughton, 2009.

———. "A Model for Preaching (Part One)." *Journal of Biblical Counseling* 12, no. 3 (1994): 36–42.

———. "A Model for Preaching (Part Two)." *Journal of Biblical Counseling* 13, no. 1 (1994): 39–48.

———. "A Model for Preaching (Part Three)." *Journal of Biblical Counseling* 13, no. 2 (1995): 51–60.

———. "Reformed Worship in the Global City." In *Worship by the Book*, edited by D. A. Carson. Grand Rapids: Zondervan, 2002.

Kent, Grenville J. R., Paul J. Kissling, and Laurence A. Turner, eds. *'He Began with Moses . . .'.* Nottingham: IVP, 2010.

Kuhatschek, Jack. *Taking the Guesswork out of Applying the Bible.* Downers Grove: IVP, 1990.

Lenski, R. C. H. *The Interpretation of St. Paul's Espistle to the Romans.* Columbus: Wartburg, 1945.

Lloyd-Jones, Martyn. *Life in the Spirit in Marriage, Home and Work: An Exposition of Ephesians 5:18 to 6:9.* Edinburgh: Banner of Truth, 1974.

———. *Romans: An Exposition of Chapter 6: The New Man.* Grand Rapids: Zondervan, 1973.

Machen, J. Gresham. *Christianity and Liberalism.* 1923; repr., Grand Rapids: Eerdmans, 1977.

McDill, Wayne. *12 Essential Skills for Great Preaching.* Nashville: Broadman & Holman, 2006.

Mohler, R. Albert, and Don Kistler. *Feed My Sheep: A Passionate Plea for Preaching.* Morgan: Soli Deo Gloria, 2002.

Murray, Iain H. *Lloyd-Jones: Messenger of Grace.* Edinburgh: Banner of Truth, 2008.

Murray, John. *The Epistle to the Romans: The English Text with Introduction, Exposition and Notes.* The New International Commentary on the New Testament. Grand Rapids: Eerdmans, 1968.

Olyott, Stuart. *Preaching—Pure and Simple.* Bridgend: Bryntirion, 2005.

Overdorf, Daniel. *Applying the Sermon: How to Balance Biblical Integrity and Cultural Relevance.* Grand Rapids: Kregel, 2009.

Owens, L. Roger. "Jesus Christ Is His Own Rhetoric! Reflections on the Relationship between Theology and Rhetoric in Preaching." *Currents in Theology and Mission* 32, no. 3 (2005): 187–94.

Perkins, William. *The Art of Prophesying and The Calling of the Ministry.* 1606; repr., Edinburgh: Banner of Truth, 1996.

Peterson, Eugene H. *The Contemplative Pastor: Returning to the Art of Spiritual Direction.* Grand Rapids: Eerdmans, 1989.

Piper, John. *God Is the Gospel: Meditations on God's Love as the Gift of Himself.* Leicester: IVP, 2005.

——————. *The Supremacy of God in Preaching*. Grand Rapids: Baker, 1990.

Plantinga, Cornelius. "Dancing on the Edge of Mystery: The New Homiletics Celebrates Pilgrimage, Not Propositions." *Journal of the Evangelical Homiletics Society* 2, no. 5 (2005): 64–82.

Porter, Stanley E. *Idioms of the Greek New Testament*. Sheffield: Sheffield Academic Press, 1994.

Quicke, Michael J. *360-Degree Preaching: Hearing, Speaking, and Living the Word*. Grand Rapids: Baker; Carlisle, UK: Paternoster, 2003.

Robinson, Haddon W. *Biblical Preaching: The Development and Delivery of Expository Messages*. Grand Rapids: Baker, 2001.

——————. *Making a Difference in Preaching: Haddon Robinson on Biblical Preaching*. Grand Rapids: Baker, 1999.

Robinson, Haddon W., and Craig Brian Larson, eds. *The Art and Craft of Biblical Preaching: A Comprehensive Resource for Today's Communicators*. Grand Rapids: Zondervan, 2005.

Ropelato, Jerry. "Internet Pornography Statistics." Internet Filter Review, http://internet-filter-review.toptenreviews.com/internet-pornography-statistics.html.

Runia, K. *The Sermon under Attack*. The Moore College Lectures. Exeter: Paternoster, 1983.

Schutt, Michael P. *Redeeming Law: Christian Calling and the Legal Profession*. Downers Grove: IVP, 2007.

Stalker, James. *The Preacher and His Models: The Yale Lectures on Preaching, 1891*. London: Hodder & Stoughton, 1891.

Stott, John R. W. *Between Two Worlds: The Art of Preaching in the Twentieth Century*. Grand Rapids: Eerdmans, 1982.

——————. *The Letters of John: An Introduction and Commentary*. Tyndale New Testament Commentaries. Leicester: IVP, 1988.

——————. *The Message of Acts: To the Ends of the Earth*. Leicester: IVP, 1990.

——————. *Romans: God's Good News for the World*. The Bible Speaks Today. Downers Grove: IVP, 1994.

Strobel, Lee. *Inside the Mind of Unchurched Harry & Mary: How to Reach Friends and Family Who Avoid God and the Church*. Grand Rapids: Zondervan, 1993.

Sunukjian, Donald R. *Invitation to Biblical Preaching: Proclaiming Truth with Clarity and Relevance*. Grand Rapids: Kregel, 2007.

Sweetman, John. "Towards a Foundational, Flexible, Sermon Structure." *Journal of the Evangelical Homiletics Society* 8, no. 2 (September 2008): 32–49.

Tripp, Paul David. *Instruments in the Redeemer's Hands: People in Need of Change Helping People in Need of Change.* Phillipsburg, NJ: P&R, 2002.

Veerman, David. *How to Apply the Bible.* Life Application Books. Wheaton: Tyndale, 1993.

Wallace, Daniel B. *Greek Grammar Beyond the Basics: An Exegetical Syntax of the New Testament.* Grand Rapids: Zondervan, 1996.

White, James F. *Introduction to Christian Worship.* Nashville: Abingdon, 2000.

Wilcock, Michael. *The Message of Judges: Grace Abounding.* The Bible Speaks Today. Downers Grove: IVP, 1993.

Wright, John W. *Telling God's Story: Narrative Preaching for Christian Formation.* Downers Grove: IVP, 2007.